Baseball in Catawba County

BASEBALL IN CATAWBA COUNTY

Tim Peeler and Brian McLawhorn

ARCADIA
PUBLISHING

ISBN 978-0-7385-1713-1

Published by Arcadia Publishing
Charleston, South Carolina

Printed in the United States of America

Library of Congress Catalog Card Number: 2004108894

For all general information contact Arcadia Publishing at:
Telephone 843-853-2070
Fax 843-853-0044
E-mail sales@arcadiapublishing.com
For customer service and orders:
Toll-Free 1-888-313-2665

Visit us on the Internet at www.arcadiapublishing.com

Contents

Preface 6

Introduction 7

1. Beginnings 9

2. Rebels

Early Years 15

Outlaws 23

Later Years 35

3. Twins 53

4. Bears 67

5. Spinners 85

6. Tweener Years 97

7. Crawdads 109

PREFACE

What is history but a fable agreed upon?
—Keith Flynn

Perhaps it is important to begin with a bit of a disclaimer. In assembling this volume, it was our foremost intention to highlight the baseball players and teams that have meant so much to the Catawba Valley area. Although an effort was made to follow chronological order, this book is by no means a definitive history of the local game.

Whenever possible, we relied upon private photo collections and personal recollections of events, teams, and players. We reviewed newspaper archives and the previous research of baseball historians such as Hank Utley and Chris Holaday for verification of facts and for statistical information. In all cases, we have made accuracy a priority.

We must offer grateful acknowledgment to the many wonderful people who contributed their photographs, knowledge, and memories, including Dicky and Elizabeth James; Ted, Myra, and Dave Hefner; Dick Stoll; Harold Lail; Junior and Ruby Young; Linda Morgan; Kim Gilliland; Gary Yount; Chris Cooke; Don Stafford; Charlie Bost; Shayle Edwards; Gene Miller; Betty Miller; Dyke Little; Sidney Halma; Bill Baird; Tom Watson; Evaleene Fowler; Chris Holaday; Gary Mitchem; Hank Utley; John Karrs; Kevin Karrs; Jim Burnette; David Haas; Jim McLean; Lee Burnette; Dennis Whitener; Bill Barkley; Bryan Harvey; J.L. Peeler; Charles Cline; Jackie Dellinger; Earl Holder; John Isaac; Naomi Taylor; Steve Peeler; Ben Goodman; Penny Peeler; Tom Shores; George Murphy; Jolene York; and Cindy Coulter. We thank David McLawhorn, Margaret Allen, and Thomas Peeler for outstanding technical assistance.

Finally, we heard many good arguments for the quality of play during a given time by a given team or the importance of a particular player, league, or story. We were impressed with them all. In this book we attempted to cover what we found to be both entertaining and historically significant without shortchanging any team or era of the game. We hope that you enjoy your stroll through these pages as much as we enjoyed the conversations with the remarkable people who helped shape this book and the history that it proclaims.

INTRODUCTION

Like the history of the county, the history of baseball in Catawba County is a multi-faceted story dominated by legendary characters and heroic performances. Games between town teams were played as early as the 1880s. Local newspaper accounts indicate that a Hickory team, playing as the Bantams in 1907, drew players from as far away as Florida and played in an independent league against teams such as the Durham Bulls. While baseball in the county had begun as the first collegiate sport on the local college campus in 1903, the game gained wide acceptance among the local population in 1933 when charismatic former Hickory High School sports star Norman "Pinkie" James organized the Hickory Rebels baseball team. This semi-professional team, which featured players James had brought in from his days at Duke University, played a challenging and entertaining level of baseball that drew thousands of fans. Equally important to their success was the introduction of night baseball thanks to the repositioned lights at Lenoir-Rhyne's College Field. During the summer of 1933, James's Rebels played day-night double-headers with teams representing other area towns. Many of the players on this early Rebels team would figure prominently in other versions of local ball clubs.

After the 1933 season, James was signed by the minor-league Charlotte Hornet team and for several years pursued a career that included stops in Birmingham and Atlanta. In the meantime, the Hickory semi-professional team continued to play in 1934 and 1935, eventually becoming the basis for the first professional team in the county. From 1936 through 1938, the Hickory Rebels participated in the independent Carolina League. Although the Carolina League operated outside the jurisdiction of organized professional baseball, it offered extremely competitive salaries. As a result, this version of the Rebels included former minor- and in some cases major-league players such as Pete Susko and Vince Barton. Stressed by financial troubles and threatened by the National Association of Professional Baseball Leagues, the league folded after the 1938 season.

In 1939, the Rebels joined the Class D Tar Heel League and participated for two seasons. After a year without a team in 1941, the Rebels participated for a year in the North Carolina State League. Following 1942, play was suspended because of World War II. The North Carolina State League resumed play in 1945, and Hickory fielded a team through 1951. In 1952, the Rebels switched to the Western Carolina League, which was also Class D. Unfortunately, game attendance dwindled during this season and the league folded. Hickory played one more complete season in the old Tar Heel League. The league ceased play, however, by late June. The Rebels gave it one last try in 1960 when they fielded a team in the Western Carolina League.

Starting in 1937, the towns of Newton and Conover also operated a Class D minor-league franchise. This version of the Twins folded early in the 1940 season and did not reappear until 1948. For several years, the club played outstanding ball before a large, loyal fan base. Newton-Conover continued play until 1951, when their teams suffered, like the Rebel teams, from a decline in attendance. The Twins' last effort occurred from 1960 to 1962 when they participated for three final seasons in the Western Carolina League.

Professional baseball was absent from Catawba County for the next 31 years until local entrepreneur Don Beaver led a group of investors who landed a franchise in the Class A South Atlantic League. Playing first as a Chicago White Sox farm club and later under the umbrella of the Pittsburgh Pirates, the Crawdads were wildly successful in terms of fan support. After 11 years, they remain a steady source of entertainment for an area that cherishes its rich baseball history.

However, the story of baseball in Catawba County is not limited to the professional game. Many of Catawba County's most compelling stories involve amateur teams. The 1948 Hickory American Legion team reached the national semi-finals of the tournament. Coming at what was perhaps the peak of area baseball interest, this was a huge media event. Another big story was the back-to-back-to-back high school State Champion teams at St. Stephens High School. Catawba County Sports Hall of Fame member Harry Frye coached the 1971–1973 Indians.

Finally, one cannot speak of Catawba County baseball history without mentioning the great contribution made by the many players who participated in semi-professional, sandlot, and textile leagues. This tradition, which reaches back to the late 19th century, captured the spirit and imaginations of local residents when America was still a baseball country. Small towns like Maiden, Brookford, and Longview were represented in games that at times matched and may have even outmatched the play of local minor-league teams. Of these teams, the one with the most storied history is the Hickory Spinners, who played in their own stadium in Longview until the mid-1950s.

In a city that Hickory Rebel Dick Stoll remembered as "a great baseball town," the game is alive and well. In the future, Catawba County will certainly add new names to legendary ones like Pinkie James, Don Stafford, Eddie Yount, Tracey Hitchner, and Troy Washam.

One

Beginnings

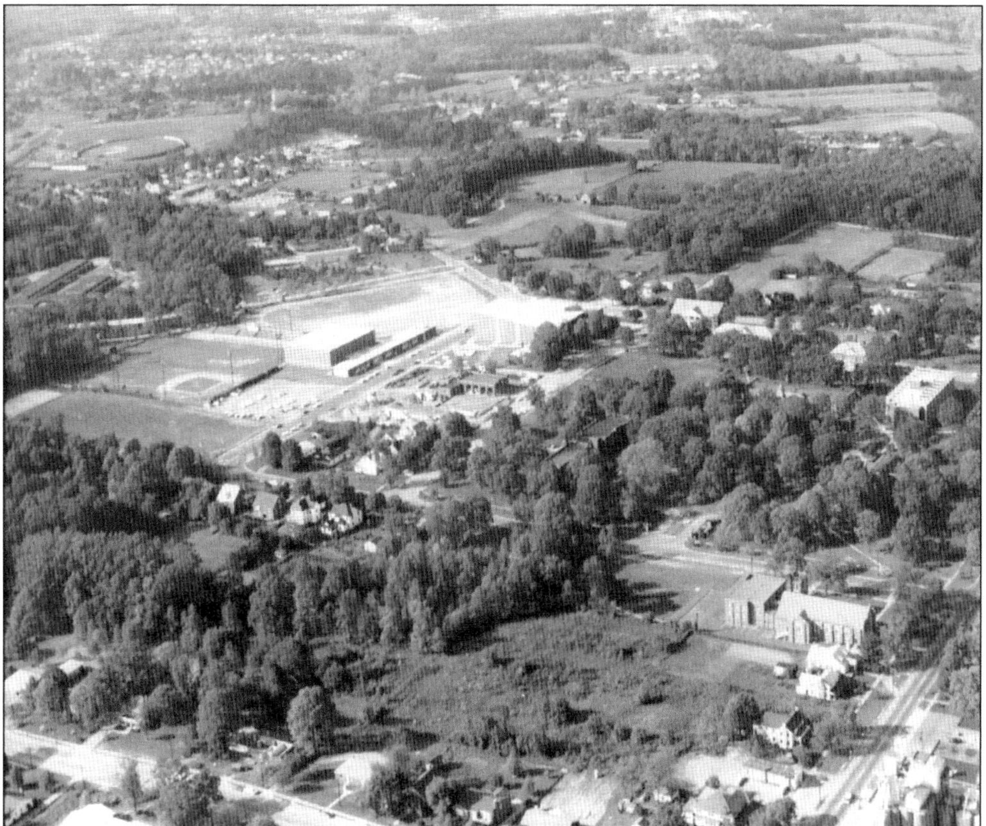

This aerial view of the Lenoir-Rhyne College campus, shot in the early 1960s, shows the college baseball field at left center next to Shuford Gymnasium. Most of the college and Hickory Rebel home baseball games were played here. At top left is the American Legion fair ground and field, now the location of Hickory High School. (Courtesy of Lenoir-Rhyne College.)

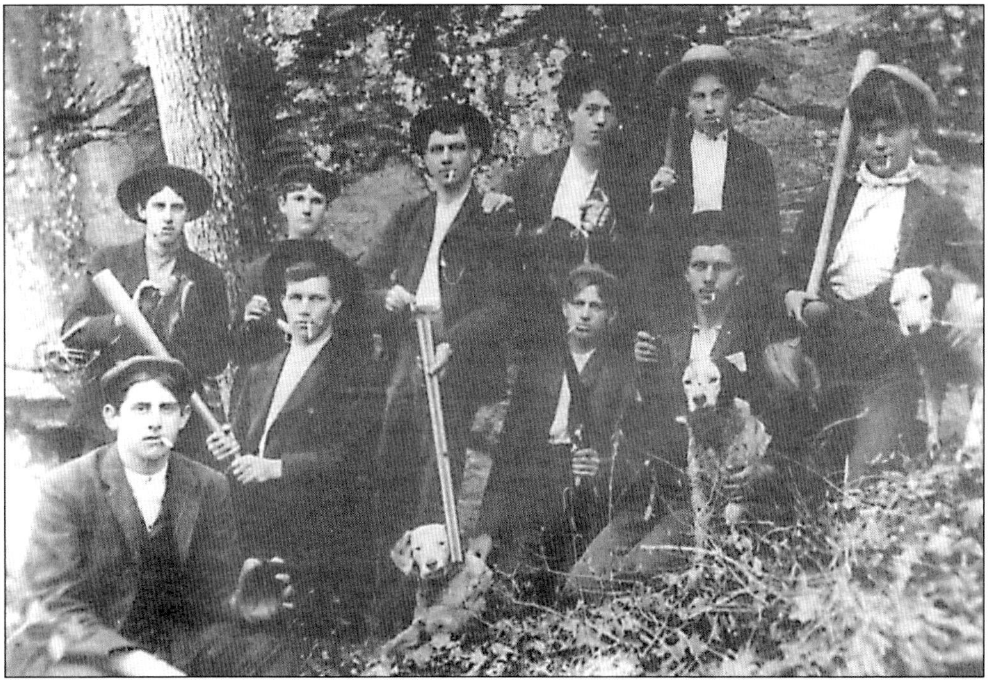

The 1912 Brookford Mill baseball team was equally prepared for a game or a hunt. Note the glove size and the homemade bats. Seen in the image above, from left to right, are (front row) Reed Isenhour, John Hollar, Wilburn Pope, and Cleave Hollar; (back row) Jim Whitener, Billy Bolick, Teal Pope, unidentified, Henry Whitener, and Will Pitts. (Courtesy of Dyke Little.)

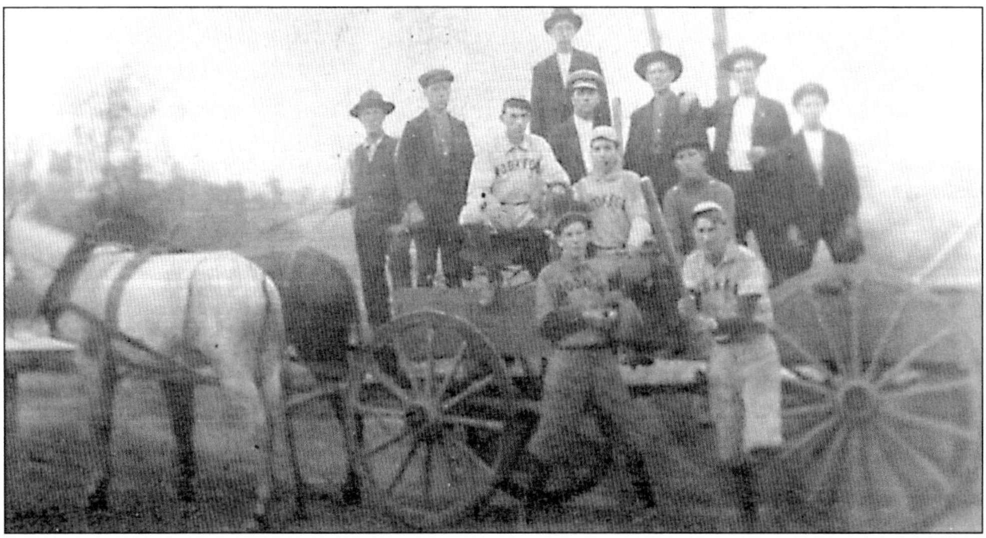

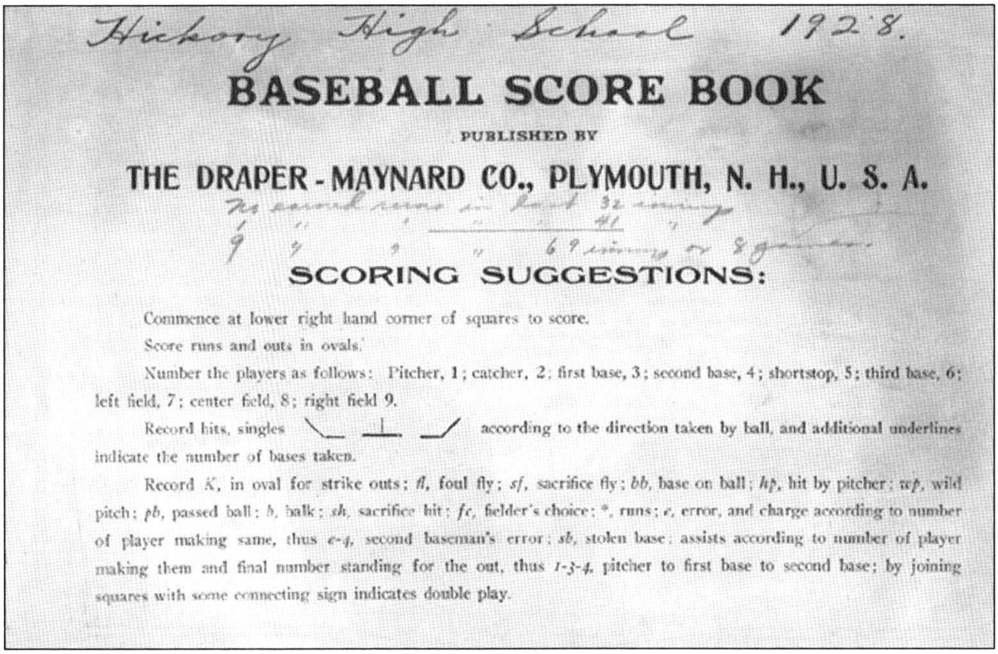

Hickory High School 1928.

BASEBALL SCORE BOOK

PUBLISHED BY

THE DRAPER-MAYNARD CO., PLYMOUTH, N. H., U. S. A.

SCORING SUGGESTIONS:

Commence at lower right hand corner of squares to score.

Score runs and outs in ovals.

Number the players as follows: Pitcher, 1; catcher, 2; first base, 3; second base, 4; shortstop, 5; third base, 6; left field, 7; center field, 8; right field 9.

Record hits, singles _ ⊥ _/ according to the direction taken by ball, and additional underlines indicate the number of bases taken.

Record *K*, in oval for strike outs; *fl*, foul fly; *sf*, sacrifice fly; *bb*, base on ball; *hp*, hit by pitcher; *wp*, wild pitch; *pb*, passed ball; *b*, balk; *sh*, sacrifice hit; *fc*, fielder's choice; *, runs; *e*, error, and charge according to number of player making same, thus *e-4*, second baseman's error; *sb*, stolen base; assists according to number of player making them and final number standing for the out, thus *1-3-4*, pitcher to first base to second base; by joining squares with some connecting sign indicates double play.

Featured above and below are pages from the 1928 Hickory High School Scorebook. (Courtesy of Dicky James.)

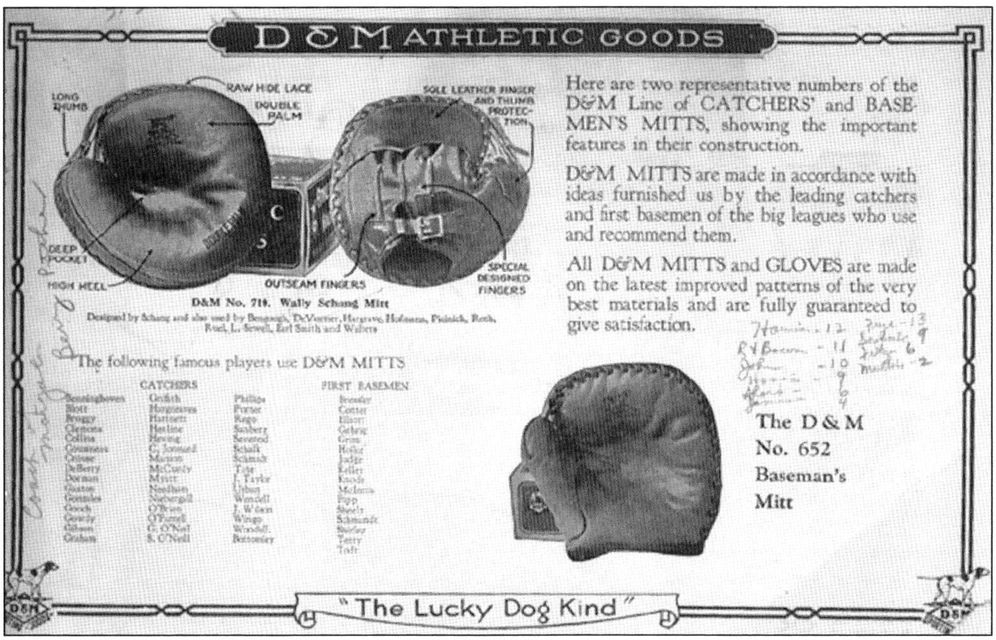

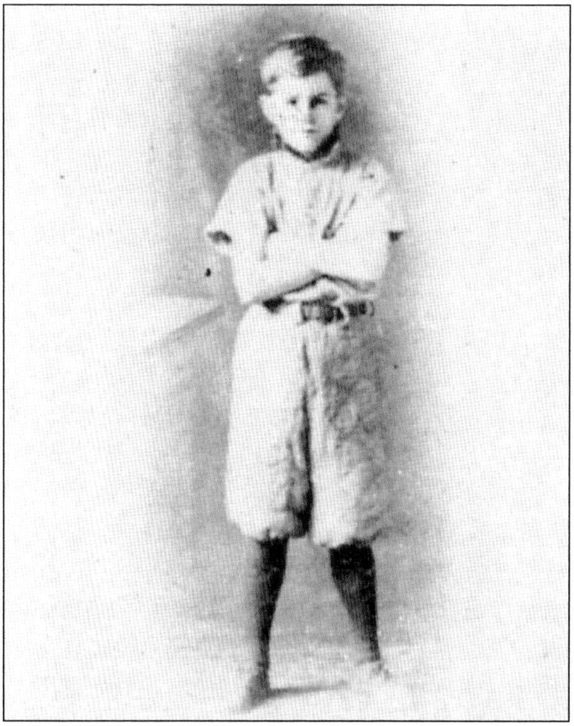

Pat Shores is pictured in his first baseball uniform in 1911 at the age of eight. (Courtesy of Lenoir-Rhyne College.)

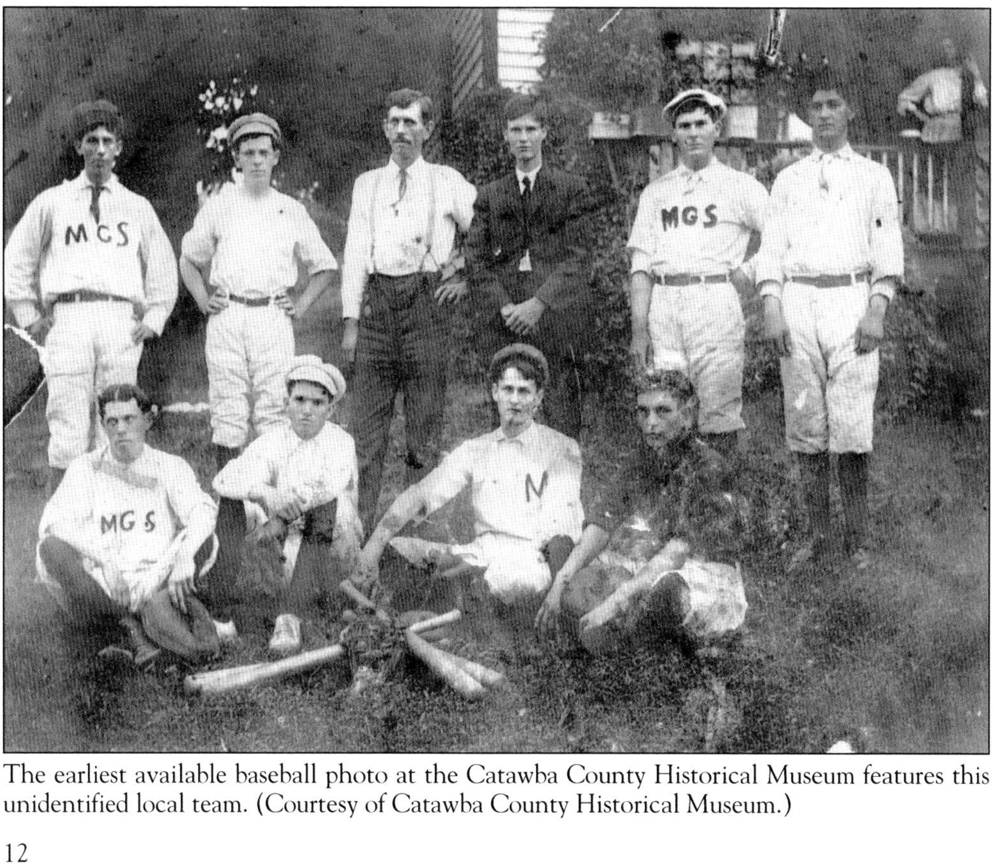

The earliest available baseball photo at the Catawba County Historical Museum features this unidentified local team. (Courtesy of Catawba County Historical Museum.)

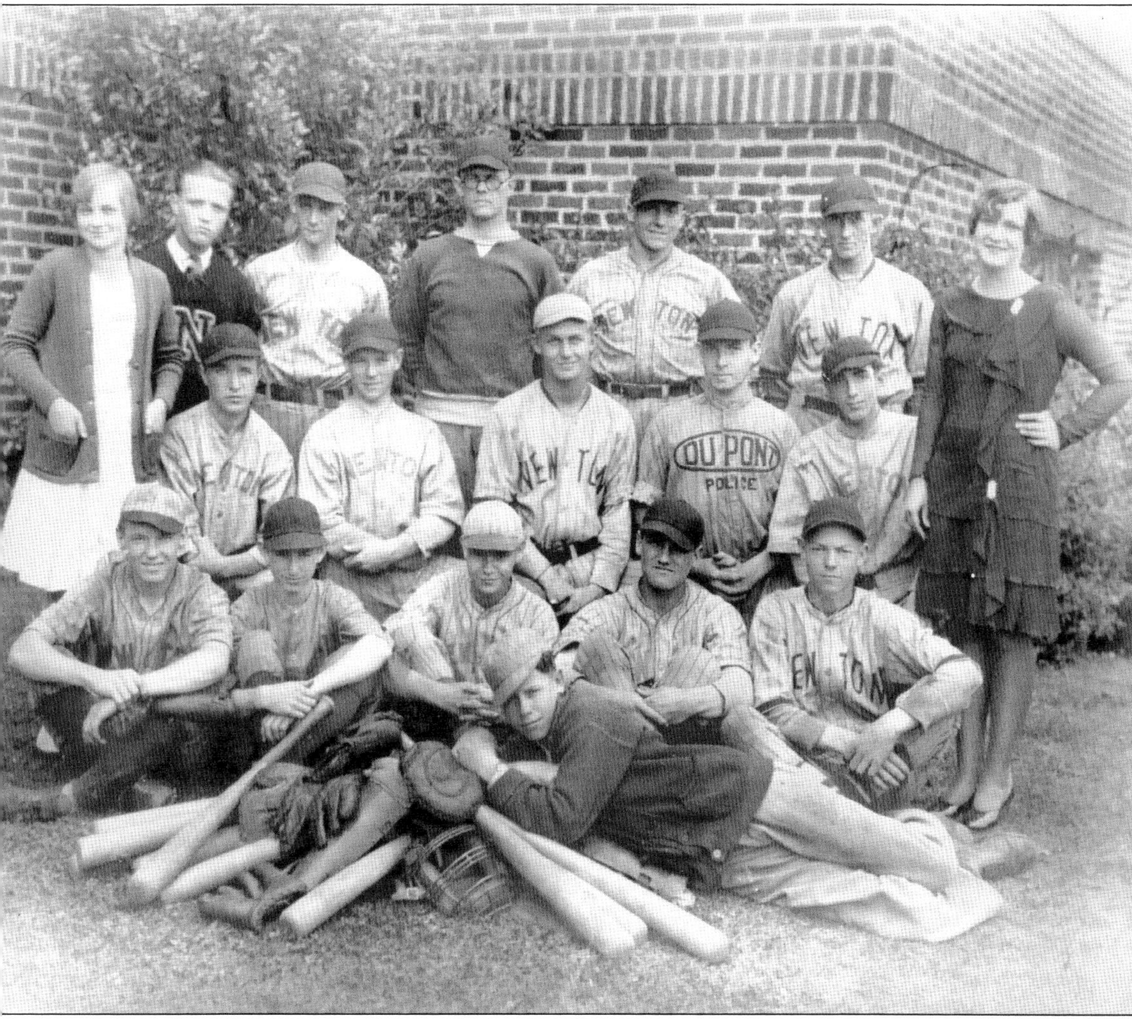

The museum's collection also includes these Newton High School baseball photos from the 1920s and 1930s. (Courtesy of Catawba County Historical Museum.)

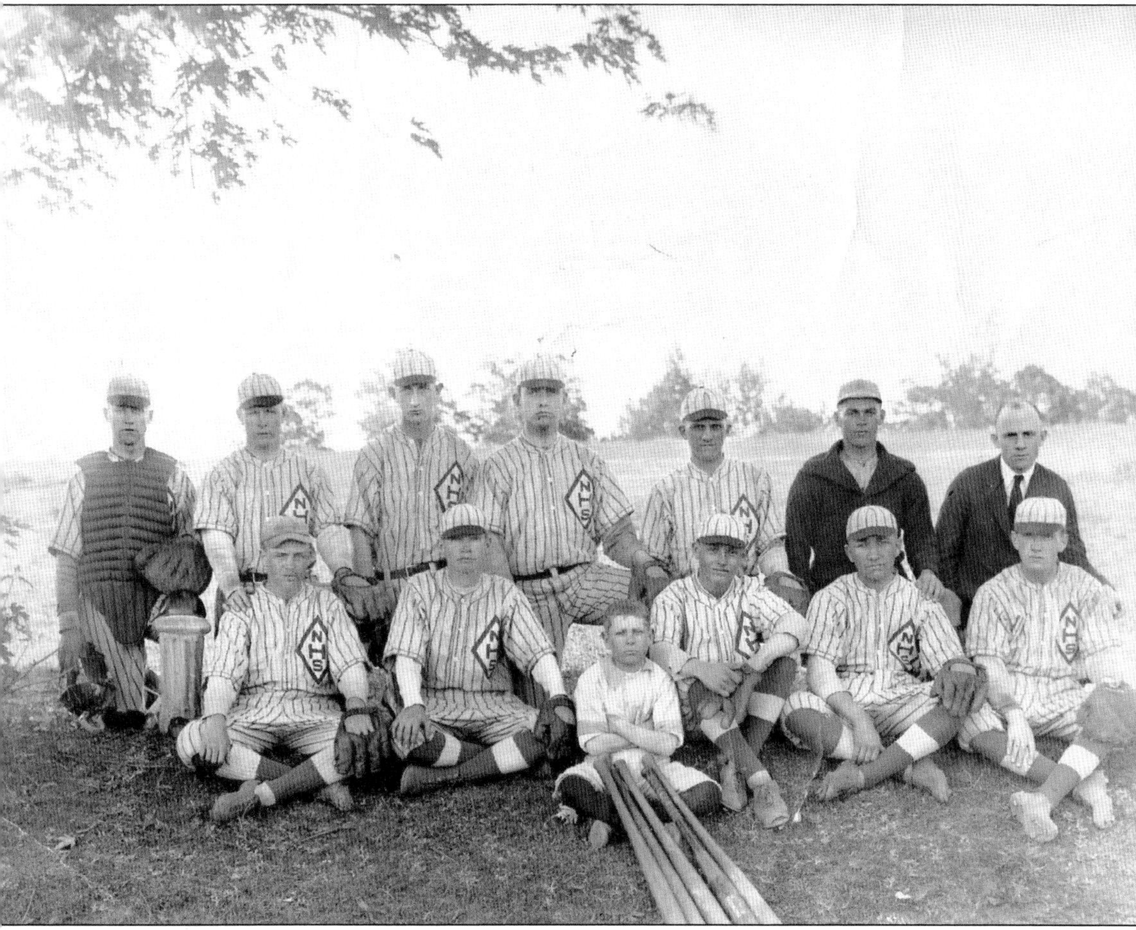

Newton High School athletic teams have maintained a reputation for winning and toughness. This Depression-era team featured the area's most stoic batboy. (Courtesy of Catawba County Historical Museum.)

Two

Rebels

Nettled because he wasn't allowed to play baseball while attending Duke University on a football scholarship, Norman "Pinkie" James re-organized the Hickory Rebels in 1933.
—R.M. "Pat" Shores

Early Years

While two teams had played under the Rebel name—one independent league team in 1927 and one "play-for-gate" team briefly in 1928—it is the 1933 Hickory Rebels, led by Norman "Pinkie" James, that is remembered as the most significant of the early teams. In the summer of 1933, James returned from Duke, where he played football, with baseball players Phil Weaver and Sammy Bell in tow. They stayed the summer at his grandmother's boarding house. James also recruited other players, including John Whitely and Johnny Mackorell from Davidson and a number of Lenoir-Rhyne College players, such as Jess Bumgarner, Nate Hovis, and Lloyd Little. Local players Jimmy Mullins, Charlie Frye, Murphy Bumgarner, and Bud Munday were also included. Old pro and high school coach Pat Shores played as well, posting a 10-5 pitching record. The team participated in the Carolina League, and the highlight of the season was the *Charlotte Observer* Carolina's Tourney. This summer also featured the introduction of night baseball to the area. James convinced the college to relocate the football lights in order to coordinate this endeavor. The first game on July 19, featuring the Rebels and the rival Newton Indians, attracted a large crowd. Unfortunately, they were disappointed after a few innings of play by a summer downpour that ended the game.

The Rebels played semi-professional ball for two more years. The 1934 team introduced Emory "Stumpy" Culbreth to the area as its manager. That year the team won its league and the *Observer* Tourney, posting a phenomenal .711 winning percentage. Their top performer was "Old Folks" Andy Ferguson, who led the pitchers and batted .437. Another outstanding player was Don Padgett, who had just completed his freshman year at Lenoir-Rhyne College and was only a few years away from a seven-year career with the St. Louis Cardinals and Philadelphia Phillies.

The 1935 Rebels completed another winning season, including the tournament. Two important additions to this team were Charles "Country Boy" Randleman and left-handed pitcher, switch hitter, and first baseman Hal D. "Rube" Wilson. Brookford product and Hickory High School star Neil Stepp starred for this team as well before embarking on a minor-league career.

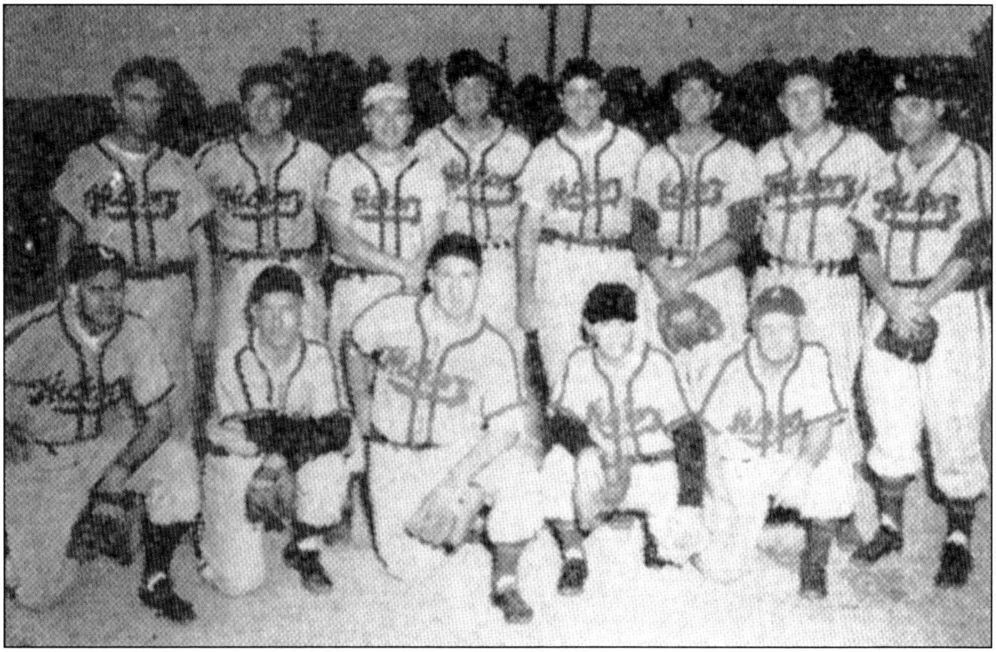

The following members of the 1933 Hickory Rebels pose from left to right for a photograph during the 20th reunion game: (front row) Jack Kiser, Sammy Bell, Jack Bell, Jimmy Mullins, and Nate Hovis; (back row) Fred Sherrill, Johnny Mackorell, Duke Stetler, Rube Wilson, Jess Bumgarner, ? Stuart, Manager Pinkie James, and Cloyd Hager. (Courtesy of Dicky James.)

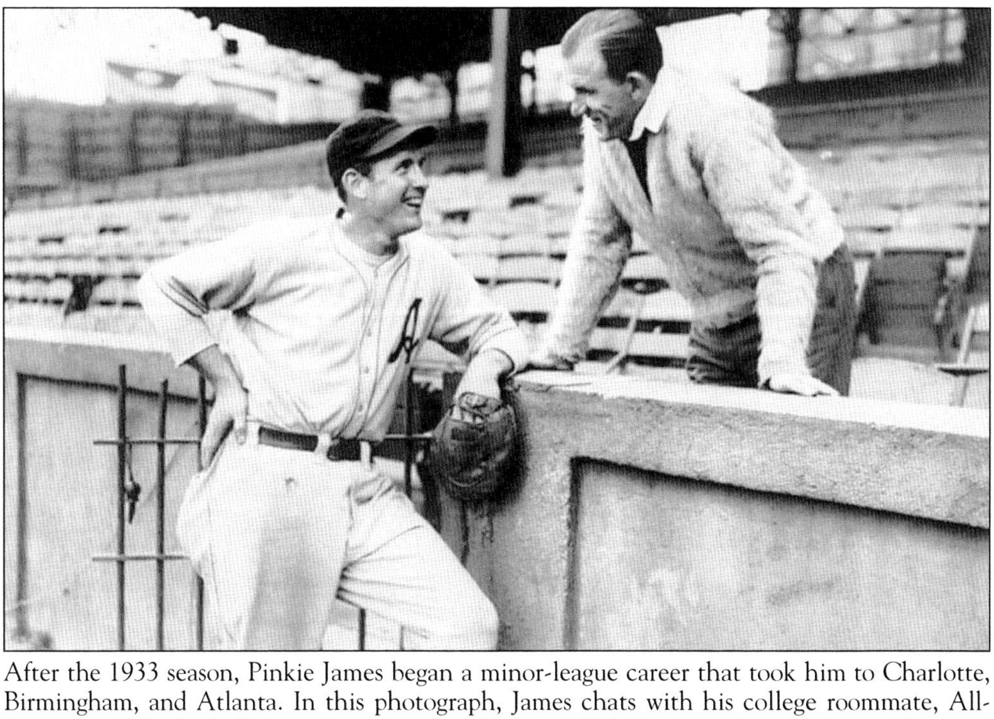

After the 1933 season, Pinkie James began a minor-league career that took him to Charlotte, Birmingham, and Atlanta. In this photograph, James chats with his college roommate, All-American Duke football player Sam Crawford, before a 1934 Cracker game in Atlanta. (Courtesy of Dicky James.)

This image features Norman "Pinkie" James's senior high school football photo. (Courtesy of Dicky James.)

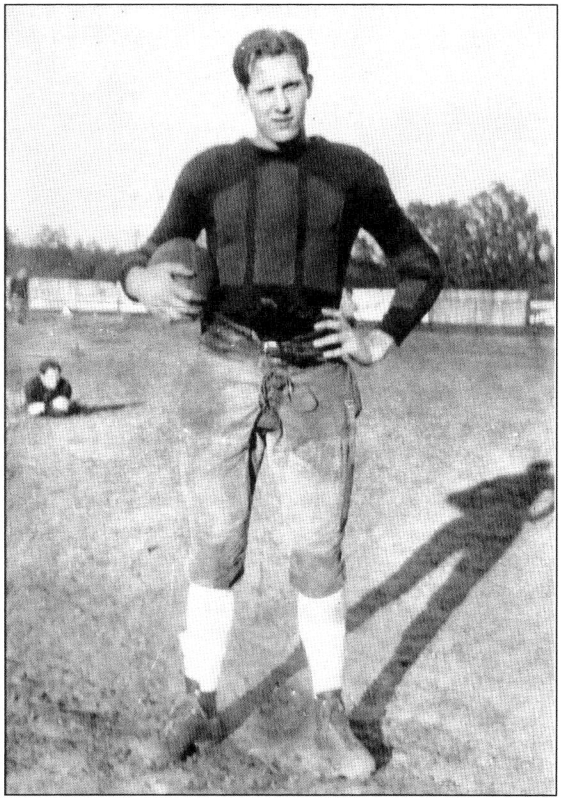

tapped for a brace in the fifth and a trey in the eighth.

Charlotte saved itself a shutout in the eighth when Earl Nelson singled to drive in Durham and Roy Mort doubled scoring Red Barnes and Nelson.

Barnes worked Johnny Allen and DeShong for three walks—all that were issued the locals.

YANKEES:	AB	R	H	PO	A	E
Combs, cf	5	2	3	2	0	0
Rolfe, ss	4	2	2	2	2	0
c—Crossetti, ss	1	1	0	3	2	0
Ruth, lf	4	0	1	0	0	1
a—Hoag	2	3	0	0	0	0
Gehrig, 1b	3	3	2	4	0	0
Saltzgaver, 1b	2	0	2	4	2	0
Chapman, cf	3	2	0	3	1	0
Lazzeri, 3b	3	2	3	1	0	0
Lary, 3b	2	0	0	1	1	0
Dickey, c	1	1	0	1	0	0
Heffner, 2b	3	0	1	2	3	0
Allen, p	2	0	1	1	1	0
b—Sewell	1	0	0	0	0	0
Deshong, p	1	0	0	1	0	0
Totals	40	14	15	37	12	1

HORNETS:	AB	R	H	P	A	E
Barnes, cf	2	1	1	3	0	1
Gillis, ss	5	0	0	3	4	1
Nelson, lf	5	1	3	0	1	1
Mort, 1b	4	0	1	11	0	0
Luckey, c	3	0	1	2	0	0
Bastruf, c	1	0	0	0	0	0
James, rf	4	0	3	1	0	0
Lipscomb, 2b	4	0	0	7	2	0
Mabry, 3b	2	0	0	0	2	0
d—Brown	2	0	0	0	0	0
Martin, p	0	0	0	0	0	0
Durham, p	4	1	2	1	5	0
Totals	36	3	10	27	14	3

a—Ran for Ruth in 5th.
b—Batted for Allen in 6th.
c—Batted for Rolfe in 6th.
d—Batted for Mabry in 7th.

YANKEES ....630 020 030—14
HORNETS ....000 000 300— 3

While a member of the Charlotte Hornets, James played in several exhibition games against prominent players. In this game, he got three hits against the big league pitchers while playing against the likes of Ruth and Gehrig. (Courtesy of Dicky James.)

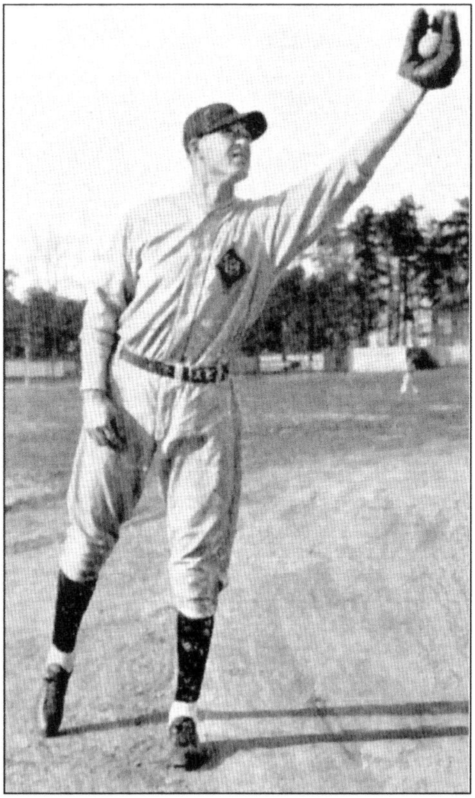

Pictured at left is Lenoir-Rhyne athlete Cloyd Hager, who played for the 1928 and 1934 Hickory Rebels and the 1933 Newton Indians. He was the business manager of the Rebels for many years. (Courtesy of Lenoir-Rhyne College.)

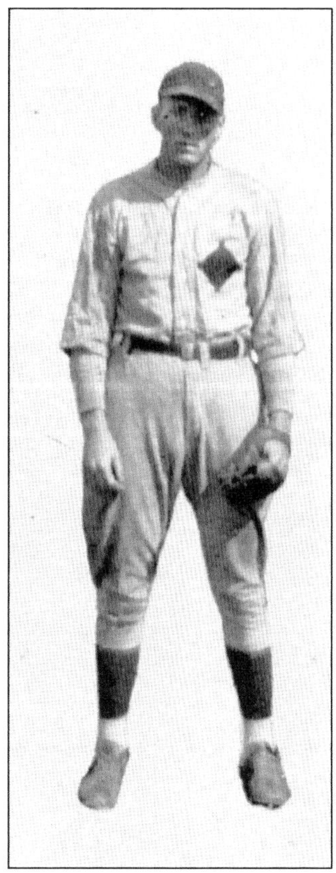

A great athlete at Lenoir-Rhyne College, Lloyd Little worked in the outfield for the 1933 Rebels before becoming a legendary basketball coach in his native Shelby. (Courtesy of Lenoir-Rhyne College.)

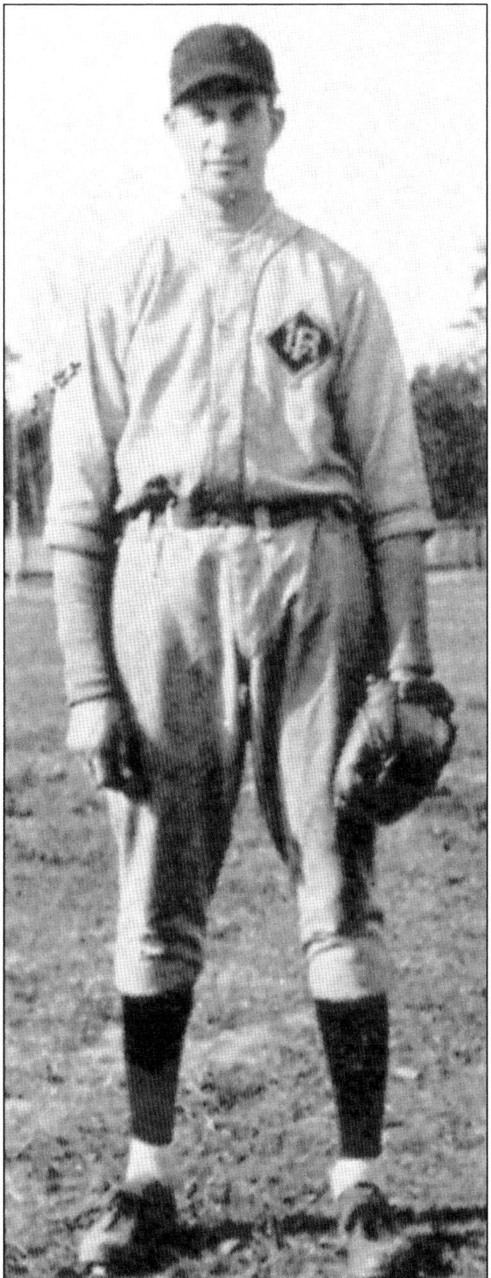
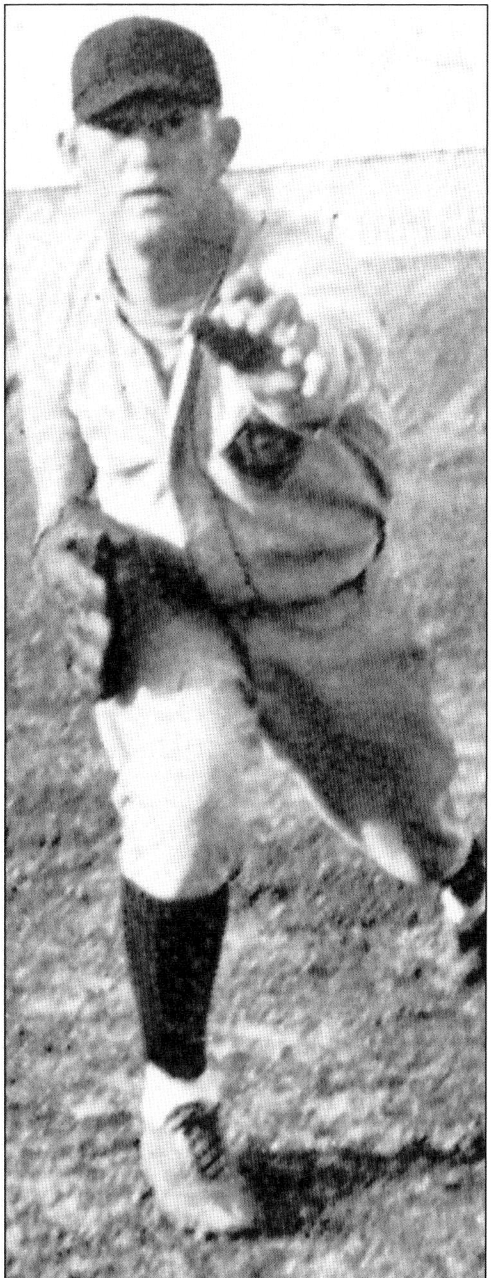

Jack Kiser and Shine Rumple, each a star in his own right at Lenoir-Rhyne College, played for the 1928 Hickory Rebels. Kiser returned to play for the 1933 team. (Courtesy of Lenoir-Rhyne College.)

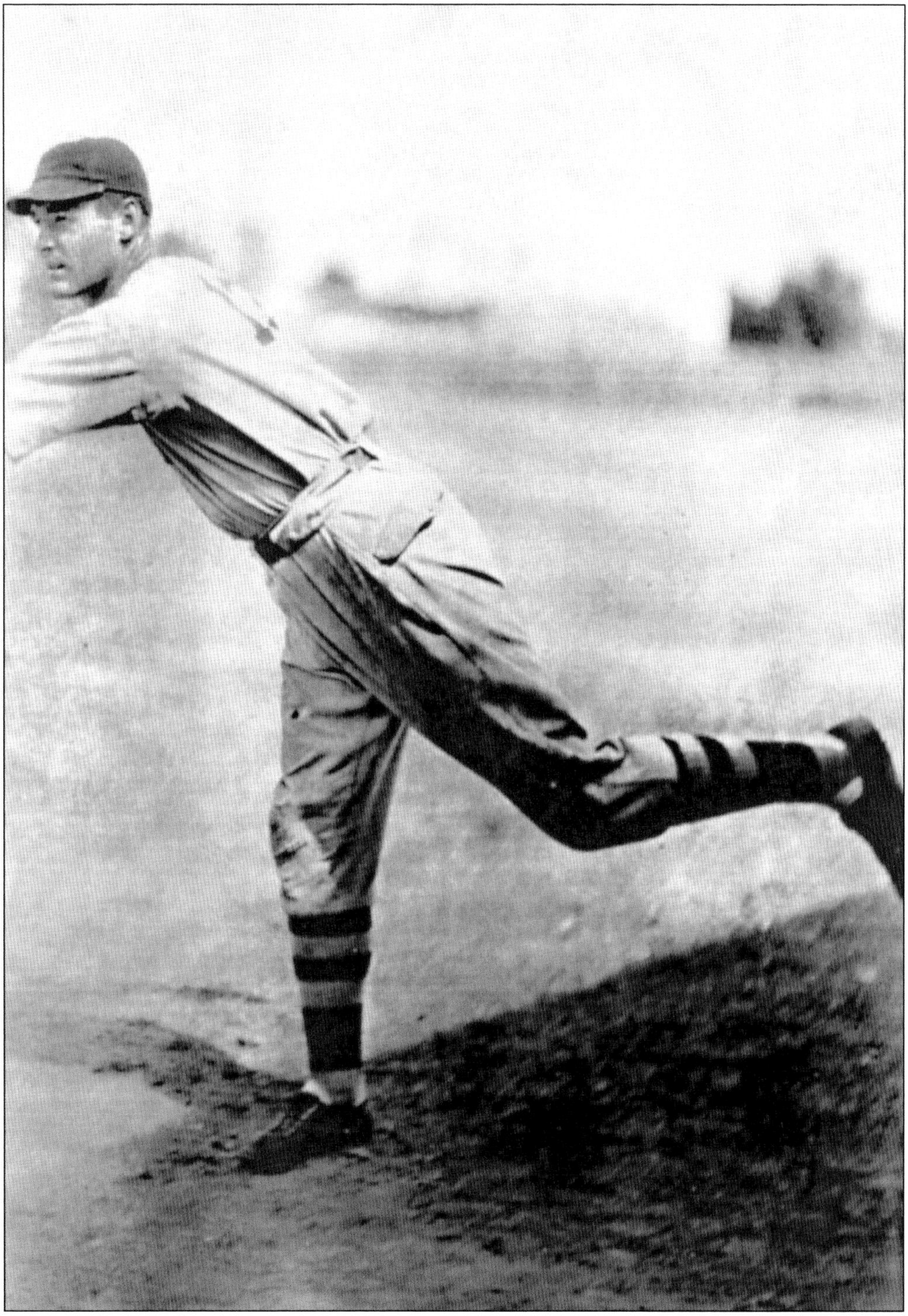

Hal D. "Rube" Wilson, a local fan favorite, pitched for the 1935 Rebels semi-professional squad and then for the outlaw teams. (Courtesy of Hank Utley.)

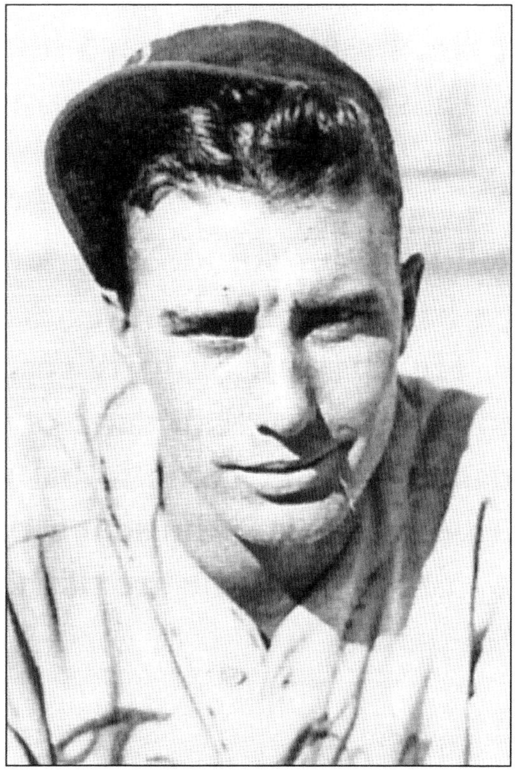

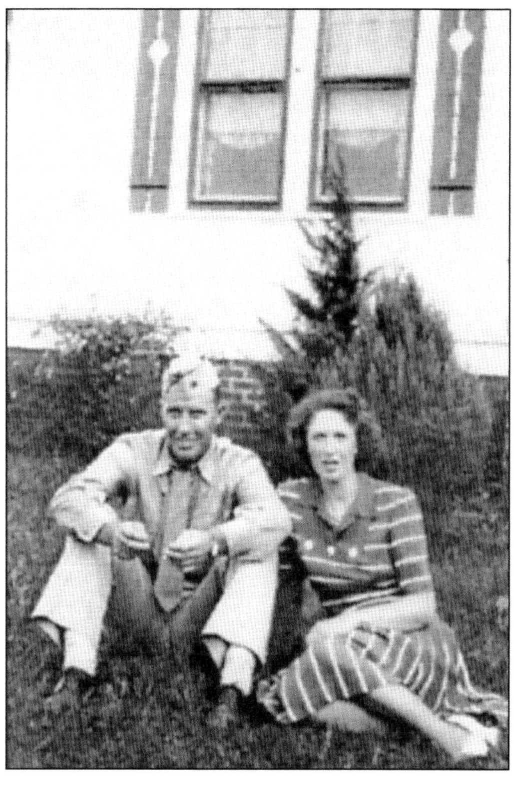

Neil Stepp, one of Brookford's best ballplayers, played for the 1935 Rebels before beginning his minor-league career. He is pictured here in his Tyler, Texas, uniform and with his wife before leaving for World War II. (Courtesy of Dyke Little.)

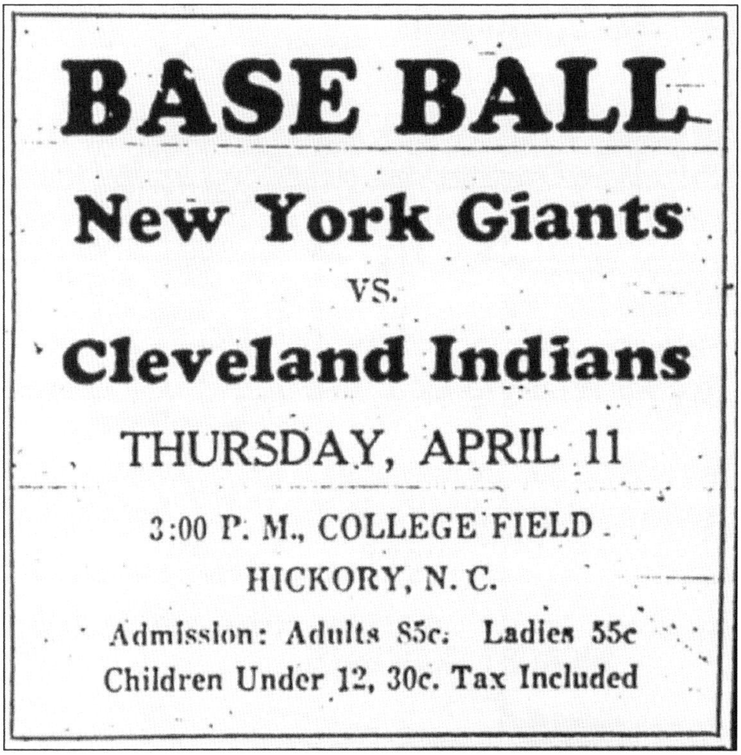
BASE BALL

New York Giants

VS.

Cleveland Indians

THURSDAY, APRIL 11

3:00 P. M., COLLEGE FIELD
HICKORY, N. C.

Admission: Adults 85c; Ladies 55c
Children Under 12, 30c. Tax Included

This is a *Hickory Daily Record* advertisement for the first major-league exhibition game in the area. (Courtesy of Don Stafford.)

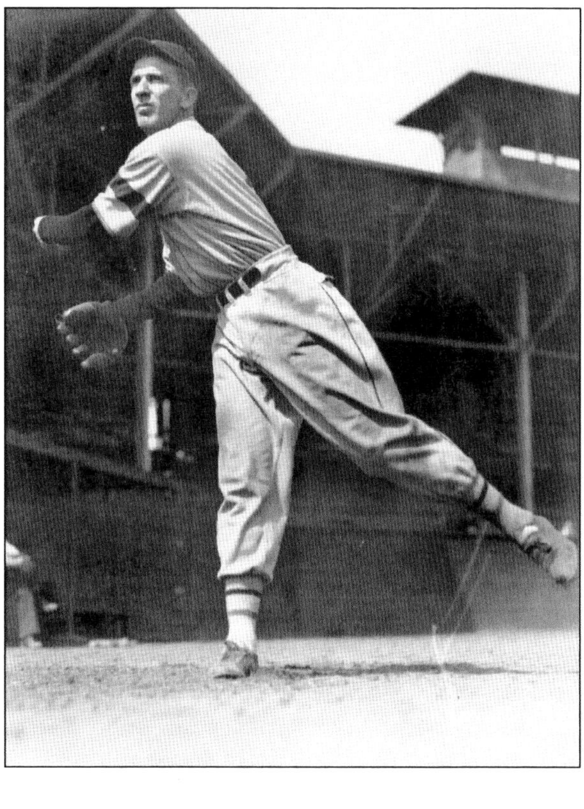

Carl Hubbell warms up before the 1935 exhibition game between the Cleveland Indians and New York Giants. After his Hall of Fame career, Hubbell worked for the New York Giants system. In 1946, at Sammy Bell's request, he and another Giants representative watched Hoyt Wilhelm pitch. Unimpressed by the knuckleballer, they met with Bell in Hill's Café in downtown Hickory. Before the meeting was over, Wilhelm had signed his first professional contract. (Courtesy of Catawba County Historical Museum.)

Outlaws

If rules were highways, these folks would travel the back roads.
—Hank Utley

The Carolina League was formed at a meeting on March 4, 1936, in Newton, North Carolina. A full-time independent professional league, it drew its teams from what remained of the semi-professional Carolina Textile League and the Class D minor-league Western Carolina League. The Hickory Rebels were joined in this organization by teams from Concord, Salisbury, Kannapolis, Shelby, Valdese, Conover, and Forest City. However, Conover dropped out before league play began, and a Charlotte team entered.

Leaders of industry in these towns saw baseball as a diversion and entertainment for their workers. With memories of the General Strike of 1934 still fresh, they were willing to gamble on a venture that would separate them from the Northern-controlled professional baseball organizations. Their goal was to prove that, working together, they could produce a higher quality game than their "outsider" competitors.

The new league expanded play from four games per week to six games per week. This, in addition to the geographic size, which had increased by two-thirds, had many fans concerned about the support for the league. Most of the teams did not have buses, so the players would ride with fans to away games. Fan travel was much more difficult when weekday road games took teams as far as from Charlotte and Concord to Forest City and Lenoir. The winding roads that led to these foothills towns were not quite as inviting as today's interstates.

The outlaw teams succeeded, however, because they were mill-supported and offered competitive Depression-era salaries as well as the added allure of off-season jobs for their players. This is not to say that each operation was not streamlined as much as possible. In fact, team rosters were limited to 15 players, including the manager. The Rebels manager, Stumpy Culbreth, was also one of the team's top performers on the field. A few other rules made for some "wild and wooly" activity among the participants. Teams could sign new players up to two weeks before the end of the season at Labor Day. As a result, there was a virtual revolving door on some club rosters. One observer noted that the Concord team played as many as 100 different players in one season. Another rule that opened the door for "legal strategy" was the one that stated, "Any official ball could be used in any game." This vague statement allowed teams with strong pitching to opt for the deadest balls they could find. Strong hitting teams sought out lively specimens for game play.

The Carolina League proved to have adequate fan support, and teams raised money both by subscription and at the gate. However, when players continued to break minor-league contracts, the league caught the attention of Judge W.G. Branham, the president of the National Association of Professional Baseball Leagues. He made threats and eventually began to blacklist players who participated in the league. As a result, the Carolina League was given an outlaw label, which it kept for its three rambunctious years of existence.

The Hickory Rebels participated in all three years with various levels of success, finishing fifth in 1936 (48-49), third in 1937 (54-45), and second (52-44) among the four teams that survived the 1938 campaign. Included here are photographs of important Rebel players as well as some of the legendary characters from other outlaw teams.

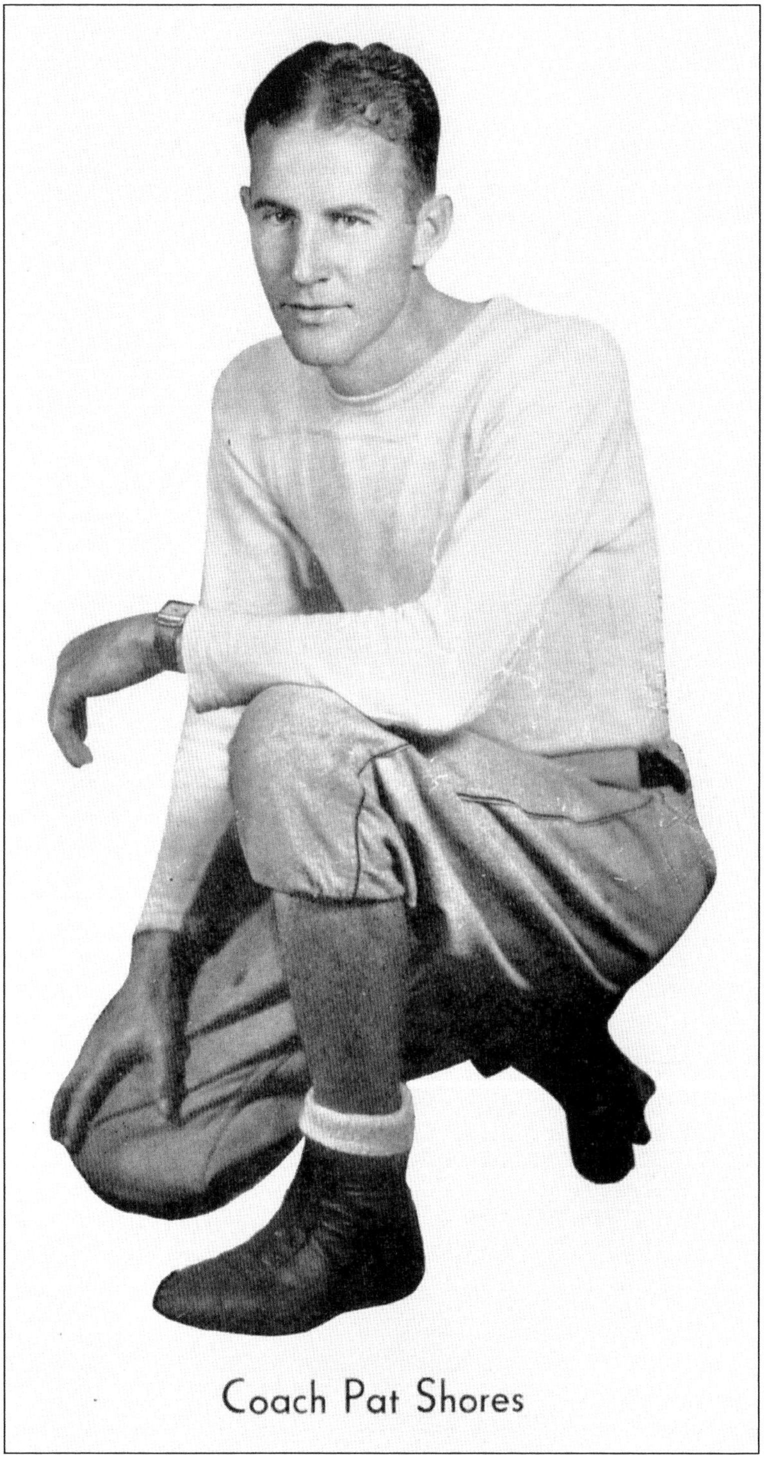

Pat Shores, who coached many great teams in multiple sports at Hickory High School and Lenoir-Rhyne College, served as the business manager for the outlaw Rebels teams. (Courtesy of Lenoir-Rhyne College.)

The original managers of the first five Carolina "Outlaw" League are pictured above. Top left is Emory "Stumpy" Culbreth, who managed the 1936 and 1938 Hickory teams. He stayed to manage and play in Hickory until the early 1940s. Others pictured from left to right include (front row) Mack Arnette, Shelby Cee Cees; Ginger Watts, Kannapolis Towelers; and Maurice Frew, Forest City Owls; (back row) Stumpy Culbreth and Blackie Carter, Charlotte Hornets. (Courtesy of Hank Utley.)

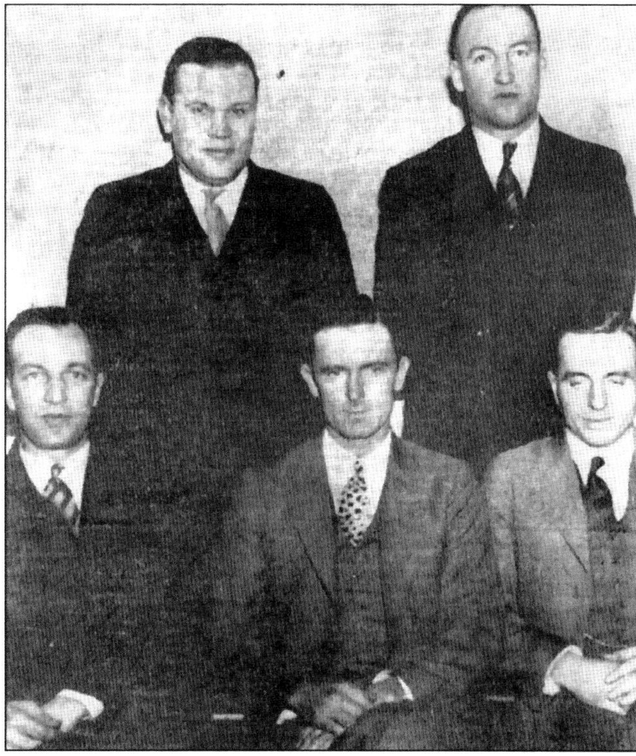

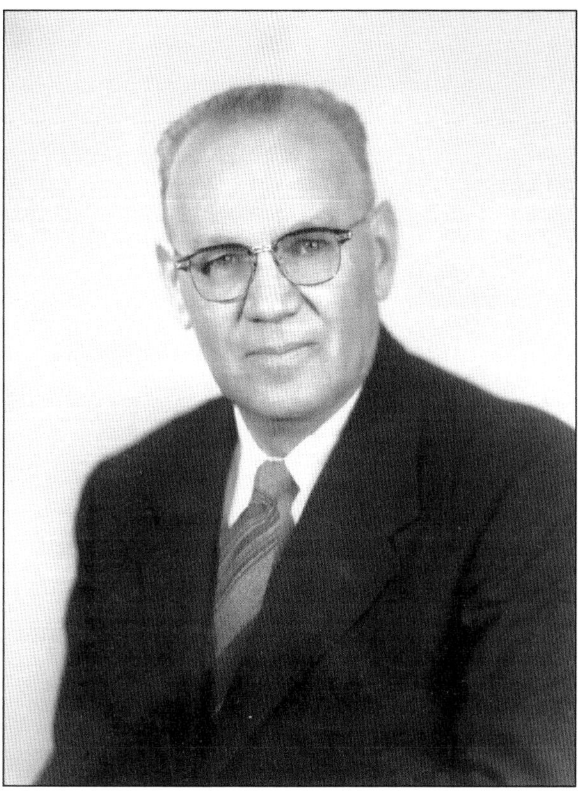

A textile executive from Brookford, M.A. "Mark" Bolick was the only Catawba County man to serve as an officer for the outlaw league. In 1936, he was the secretary-treasurer, and in 1937 and 1938, he was the vice-president. Bolick was a civic leader in the Hickory area for many years. (Courtesy of Naomi Taylor.)

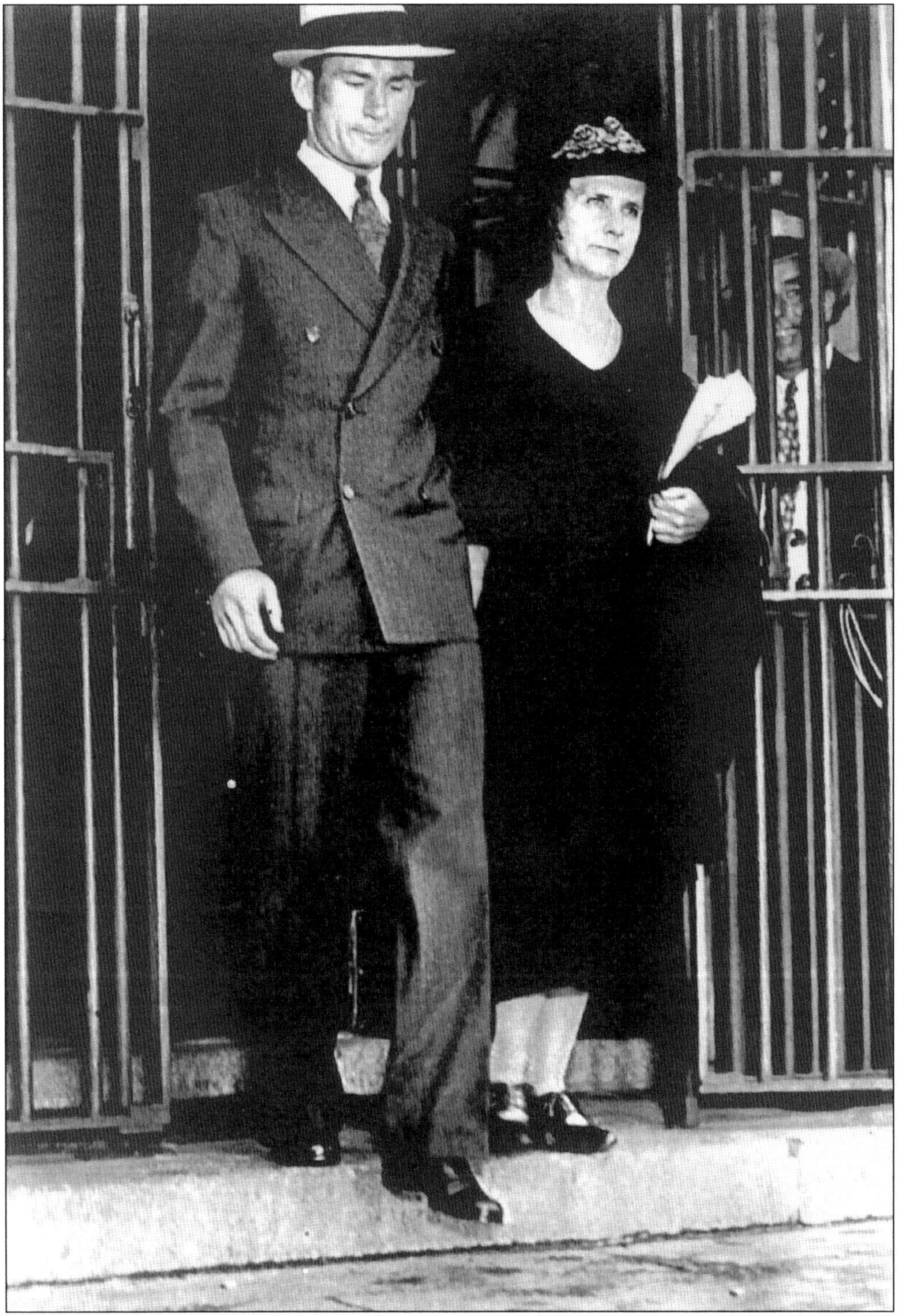

After serving five years for the armed robbery of a New York City grocery store, Edwin "Alabama" Pitts walks out of Sing Sing Prison with his mother, Mrs. Erma Rudd, on June 6, 1935. (Courtesy of Hank Utley.)

Vince Barton poses before a 1937 game. Barton, who played for Kannapolis that year, led the Hickory Rebels in 1938 with 26 home runs, 82 RBIs, and a .324 batting average. The Canadian-born player had a brief major-league career. Barton is not dressed because of a reported pulled muscle; however, he actually had a pistol shot wound in his side, sustained at a poker game the night before. (Courtesy of Bernie Edwards Jr.)

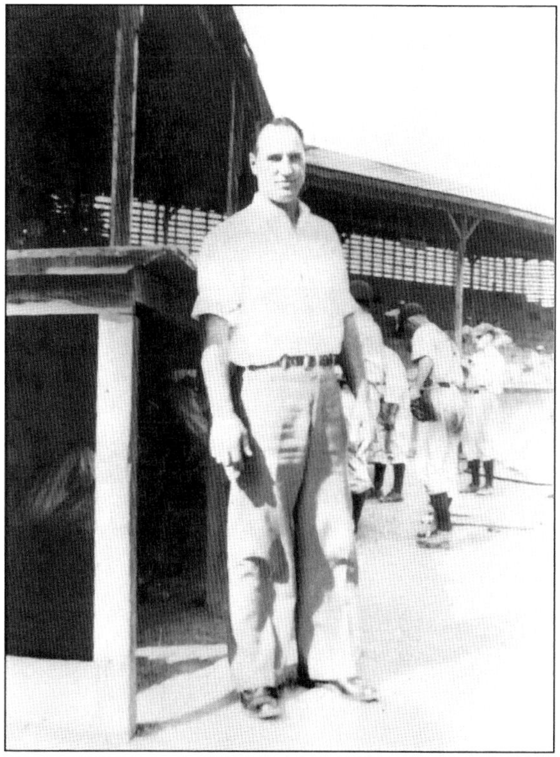

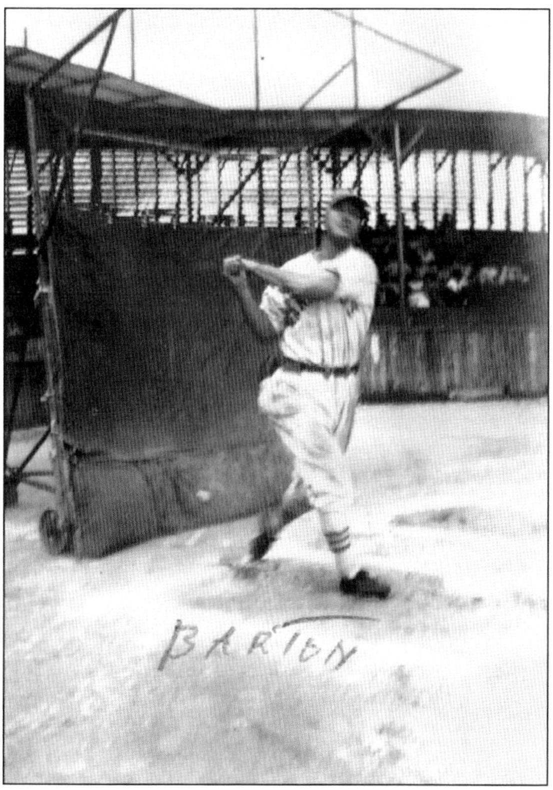

Vince Barton once hit five home runs in nine innings at College Field, and, according to Harold Lail, the area around the right field press box became known as Barton's Alley. (Courtesy of Bernie Edwards Jr.)

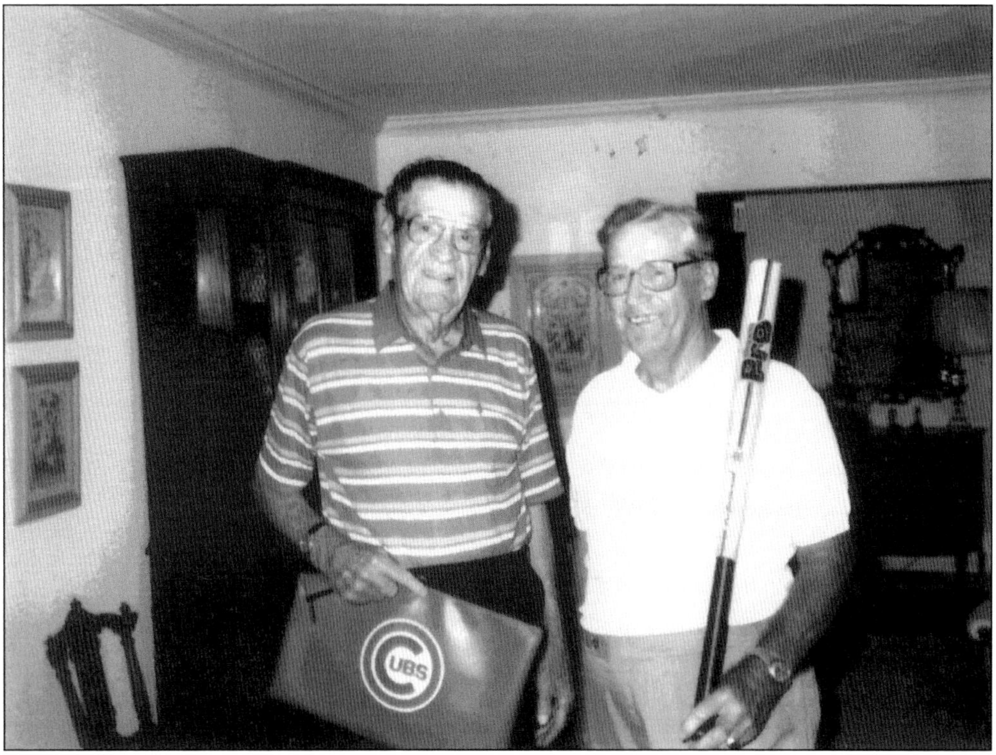

Rube Wilson and Hal Burris share memories in 1991. Wilson managed the 1937 Hickory Rebels outlaw team and the 1938 Newton-Conover Twins North Carolina State League team. Later he helped start Hickory Sporting Goods and worked as a scout for the Chicago Cubs. Burris caught for the 1935 Concord Weavers and for the outlaw Kannapolis Towelers in 1936. (Courtesy of Hank Utley.)

1937 Hickory, N. C.-Outlaw Carolina League-AB-246, R-63, H-83, 2B-27, 3B-7, HR-17, SB-10, RBI-62, BA-.337.

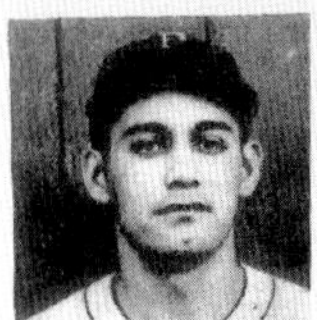

Prince Oana, outfielder-pitcher

HENRY KAUHANE (PRINCE) OANA
Born January 22, 1908 at Waipahu, Hawaii. Died June 19, 1976 at Austin, TX.
Batted right. Threw right. Height 6.02. Weight 193.
Became primarily a pitcher in the 1940s. See pitching record below. One of first Hawaiians to gain prominence in minor leagues.

Year	Club	League	Pos	G	AB	R	H	2B	3B	HR	RBI	SB	BA
1929	Globe	Ariz St	OF	85	340	81	127	26	10	18	-	18	.374
1930	Globe	Ariz St	OF	79	310	87	128	22	12	21	88	15	.413
	San Francisco	P C	OF	79	298	46	97	18	4	11	53	7	.326
1931	San Francisco	P C	OF	172	742	116	256	44	18	23	161	12	.345
1932	San Francisco	P C	OF-P	131	440	60	105	22	9	2	52	5	.239
1933	Portland	P C	OF	174	686	127	228	63*	11	29	163	11	.332
1934	Philadelphia	National	OF	6	21	3	5	1	0	0	3	0	.238
	Portland	P C	OF	11	43	6	10	0	0	1	5	0	.233
	Atlanta	South A	OF	127	480	65	143	21	8	17	102	11	.298
1935	Atlanta	South A	OF	57	218	35	63	7	3	5	34	8	.289
	Syracuse	Int	OF	87	320	46	96	21	8	12	52	4	.300
1936	Syracuse/Balt	Int	OF	115	418	53	117	23	4	7	66	5	.280
1937	Knoxville/LR	South A	OF	48	187	31	53	4	4	6	27	2	.283
1938	Jackson	SEastern	OF-P	143	513	104	164	39	7	26*	116*	10	.320
1939	Jackson	SEastern	OF-P	139	508	114	164	20	12	38*	127*	11	.323
1940	Ft. Worth	Texas	OF	159	594	80	157	28	6	14	75	13	.264
1941	Ft. Worth	Texas	O-1-P	140	478	50	121	23	4	5	76	18	.253
1942	Ft. Worth	Texas	OF-P	87	223	18	47	8	1	5	21	13	.211
1943	Detroit	American	P	20	26	5	10	2	1	1	7	0	.385
	Milwaukee	A A	P	20	34	8	14	1	1	0	4	0	.412
1944	Buffalo	Int	P	82	137	17	33	2	1	4	23	1	.241
1945	Detroit	American	P	4	5	0	1	0	0	0	0	0	.200
	Buffalo	Int	P	82	169	22	47	6	3	3	25	2	.278
1946	Dallas	Texas	P-OF	61	145	24	44	13	2	7	34	3	.303
1947	Dallas	Texas	P	38	48	5	18	4	1	1	16	0	.375
1948	Austin	Big St	O-P-1	60	149	16	40	10	0	2	20	2	.268
1949	Austin	Big St	P	24	46	7	16	3	0	3	18	0	.348
1950	Austin	Big St	P-1B	3	5	0	0	0	0	0	0	0	.000
1951	Texarkana	Big St	P	11	14	1	4	0	0	0	1	0	.286
	Majors			30	52	8	16	3	1	1	10	0	.308
	Minors			2214	7543	1210	2282	428	130	281	1300	171	.304

Pitching Record

Year	Club	League	G	IP	W	L	H	R	ER	BB	SO	ERA
1932	San Francisco	P C	3	6	0	0						
1938	Jackson	SEastern	1	1	0	0	0	0	0	0		0.00
1939	Jackson	SEastern	1	2	0	6	2	2	2	2	2	9.00
1941	Ft. Worth	Texas	7	14	0	0	7	9	6	9	9	3.86
1942	Ft. Worth	Texas	25	199	16	5	156	54	38	58	105	1.72
1943	Detroit	American	10	34	3	2	34	21	17	19	15	4.50
	Milwaukee	A A	14	84	3	5	59	35	29	20	32	4.08
1944	Buffalo	Int	38	211	13	13	199	100	85	103	112	3.63
1945	Detroit	American	3	11	0	0	3	2	2	7	3	1.64
	Buffalo	Int	31	242	15	14	200	134	113	117	138	4.20
1946	Dallas	Texas	38	284*	24*	10	253*	101	80	72	123	2.54
1947	Dallas	Texas	11	43	2	2	56	29	25	22	8	5.23
1948	Austin	Big St.	15	87	4	4	97	45	39	31	21	4.03
1949	Austin	Big St.	10	45	2	1	34	15	12	19	6	2.40
1950	Austin	Big St.	3	8	1	0	9	3		3		3.38
1951	Texarkana	Big St.	7	20	6	0	18	9	7	14	5	3.15
	Majors		13	45	3	2	37	23	19	26	18	3.80
	Minors		204	1229	89	84	1150	506	436	479	563	3.24

Hawaiian Henry "Prince" Oana was a leading hitter and popular player for the 1937 Rebels. His long career included brief stints with major-league teams both as a position player and as a pitcher. Note that his outlaw league record is not included. (Courtesy of Society of American Baseball Researchers.)

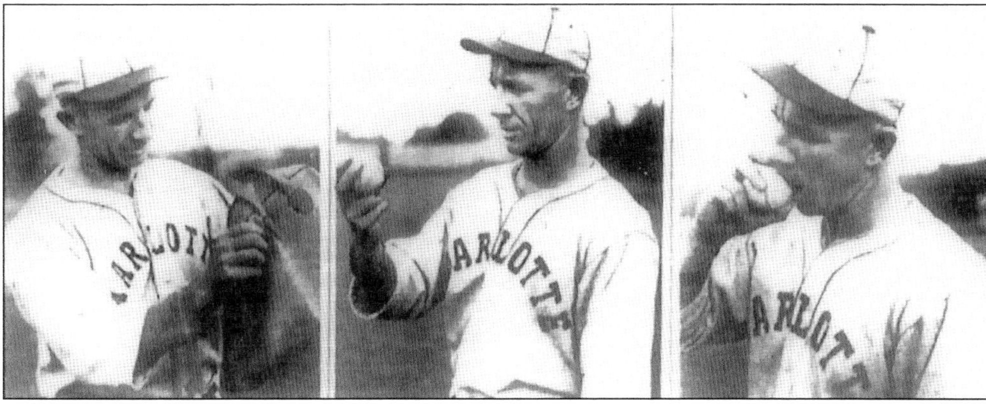

In 1936, Bud Shaney explains how he gets his pitches to break in this infamous outlaw league picture. He won his last game for the Asheville Tourists in 1954 at the age of 53. At the time, Shaney was the groundskeeper for the Tourists. (Courtesy of *The Charlotte Observer*.)

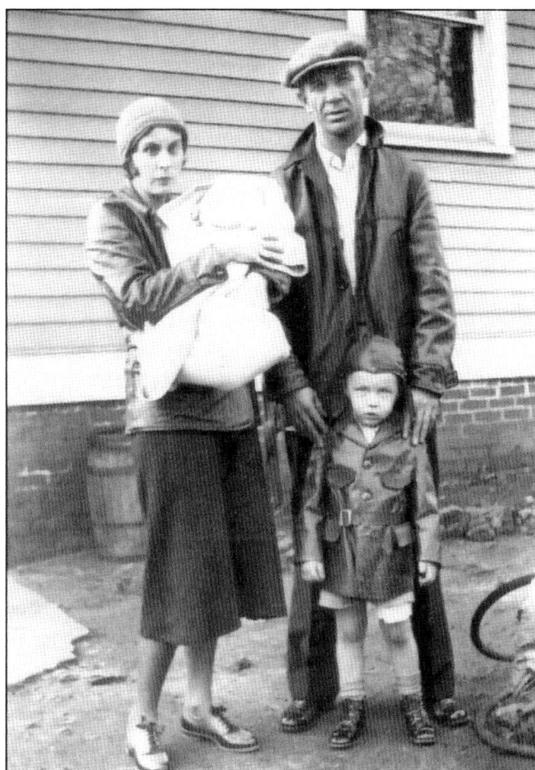

"Struttin" Bud Shaney is pictured with his young family in 1931. Shaney, an ace pitcher for the Charlotte Hornets, began the 1936 season with a 13-0 record. He managed the Hickory Rebels during their first year as a Class D minor-league team in 1939. Included in the photograph are Bud, Alice, and Charles R. Shaney; Richard Shaney is in his mother's arms. (Courtesy of Charles R. Shaney.)

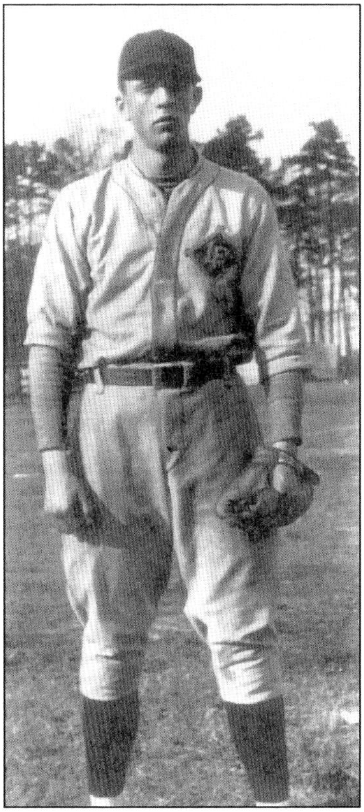

Glenn "Razz" Miller, the baseball player, is pictured in his Lenoir-Rhyne College days. Miller played in the outfield for the Kannapolis Towelers and was a leading hitter for all three outlaw years. (Courtesy of Lenoir-Rhyne College.)

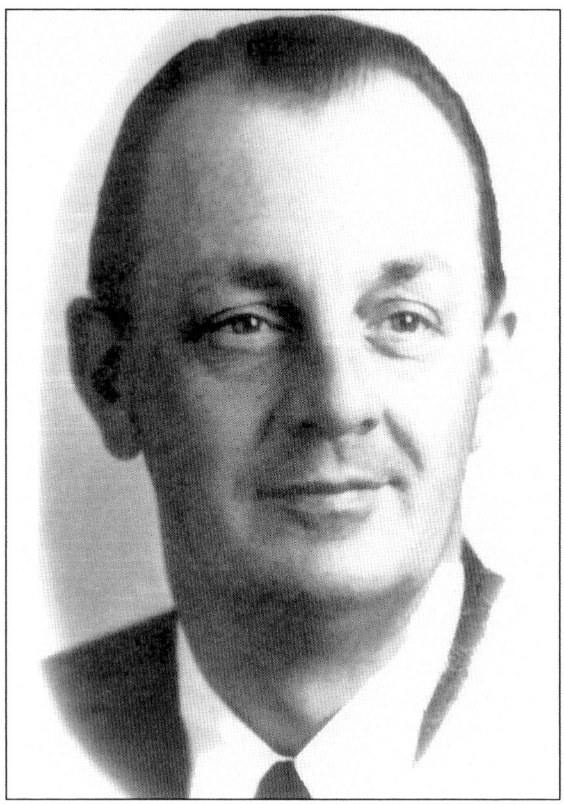

"Razz" Miller, the Lutheran minister, is pictured here. Miller gave up preaching for seven years because he could put more food on the table playing baseball and teaching high school during the off season. Eventually, he returned to a long distinguished career in the pulpit. (Courtesy of Mrs. Glenn Miller.)

Fireball pitcher Tracey Hitchner was the leading hurler for the 1936 Rebels with an 11-5 record and a league second 138 strikeouts. He also had an excellent year in 1937 under the assumed name of John Davis. (Courtesy of Tracey Hitchner.)

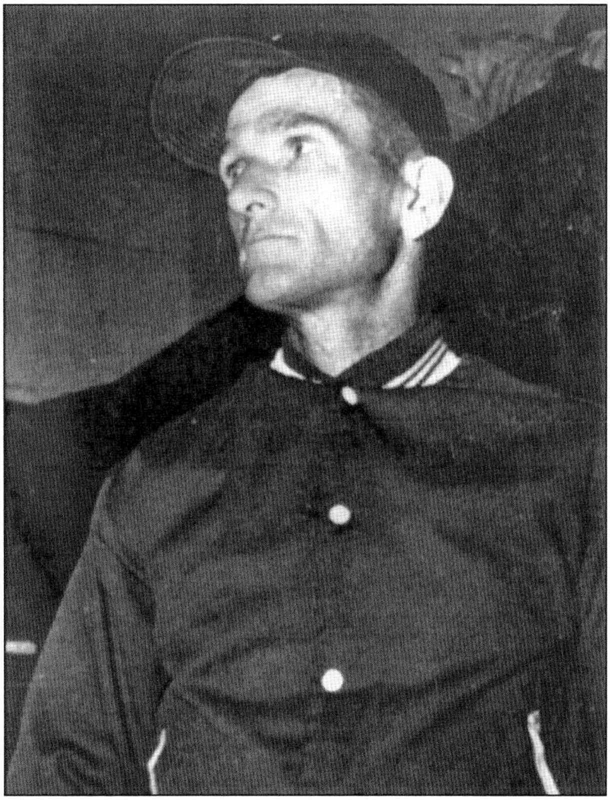

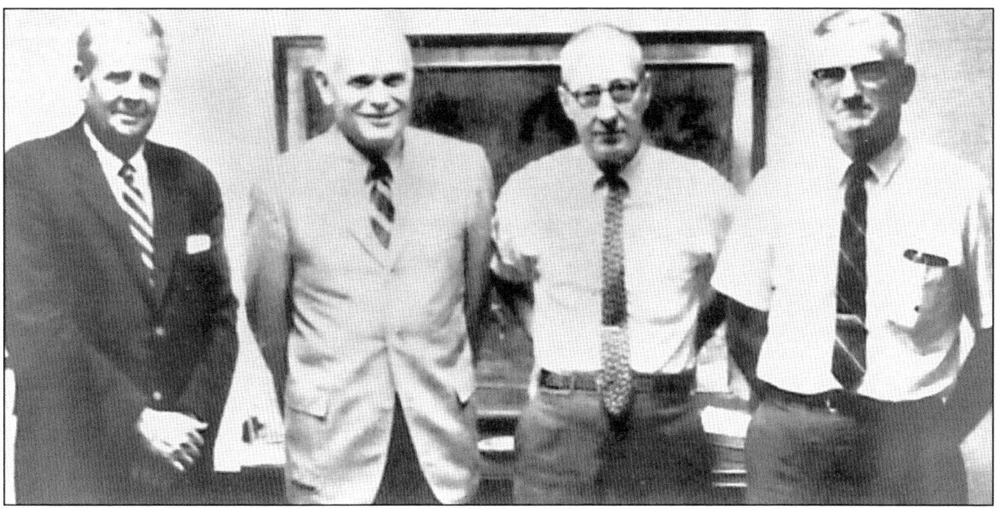

Tracey Hitchner pitched his last minor-league season for the 1947 Rebels. He then settled in the area and worked as a purchasing agent for Century Furniture. The following men are pictured from left to right: Harley Shuford, Century Furniture president; Samuel Hemphill; Ernest Woodary; and Tracey Hitchner. (Courtesy of Tracey Hitchner.)

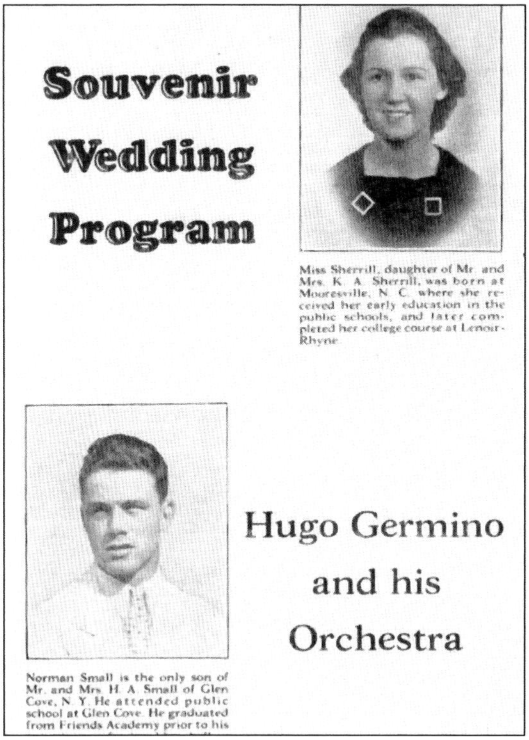

Souvenir Wedding Program

Miss Sherrill, daughter of Mr. and Mrs. K. A. Sherrill, was born at Mooresville, N. C. where she received her early education in the public schools, and later completed her college course at Lenoir-Rhyne.

Norman Small is the only son of Mr. and Mrs. H. A. Small of Glen Cove, N. Y. He attended public school at Glen Cove. He graduated from Friends Academy prior to his

Hugo Germino and his Orchestra

This is the souvenir program from the 1937 Durham Bulls game where Norman Small and Sara Sherrill were married on the field. (Courtesy of Norman Small.)

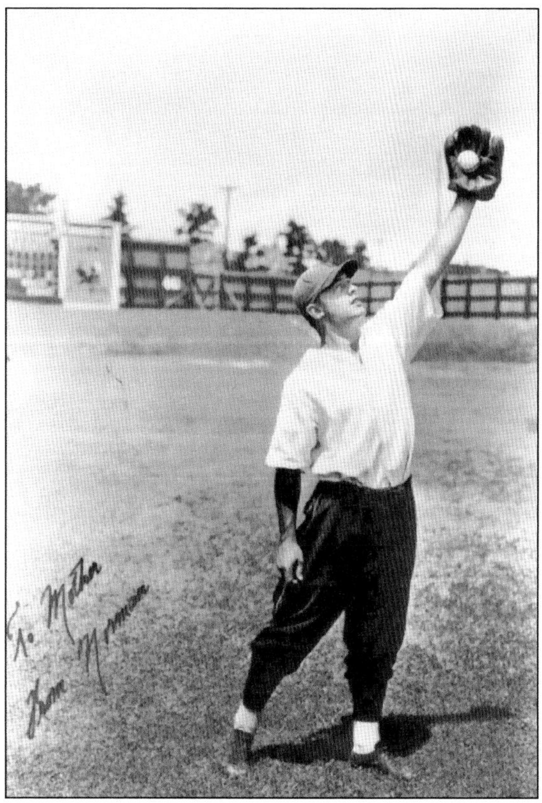

This is Norman Small's Durham Bulls "red pants" photo that he sent to his mother. Small, rated one of the top 100 all-time minor-league players, played for the outlaw Mooresville Moors. He later joined the Hickory Rebels as both manager and player. (Courtesy of Norman Small.)

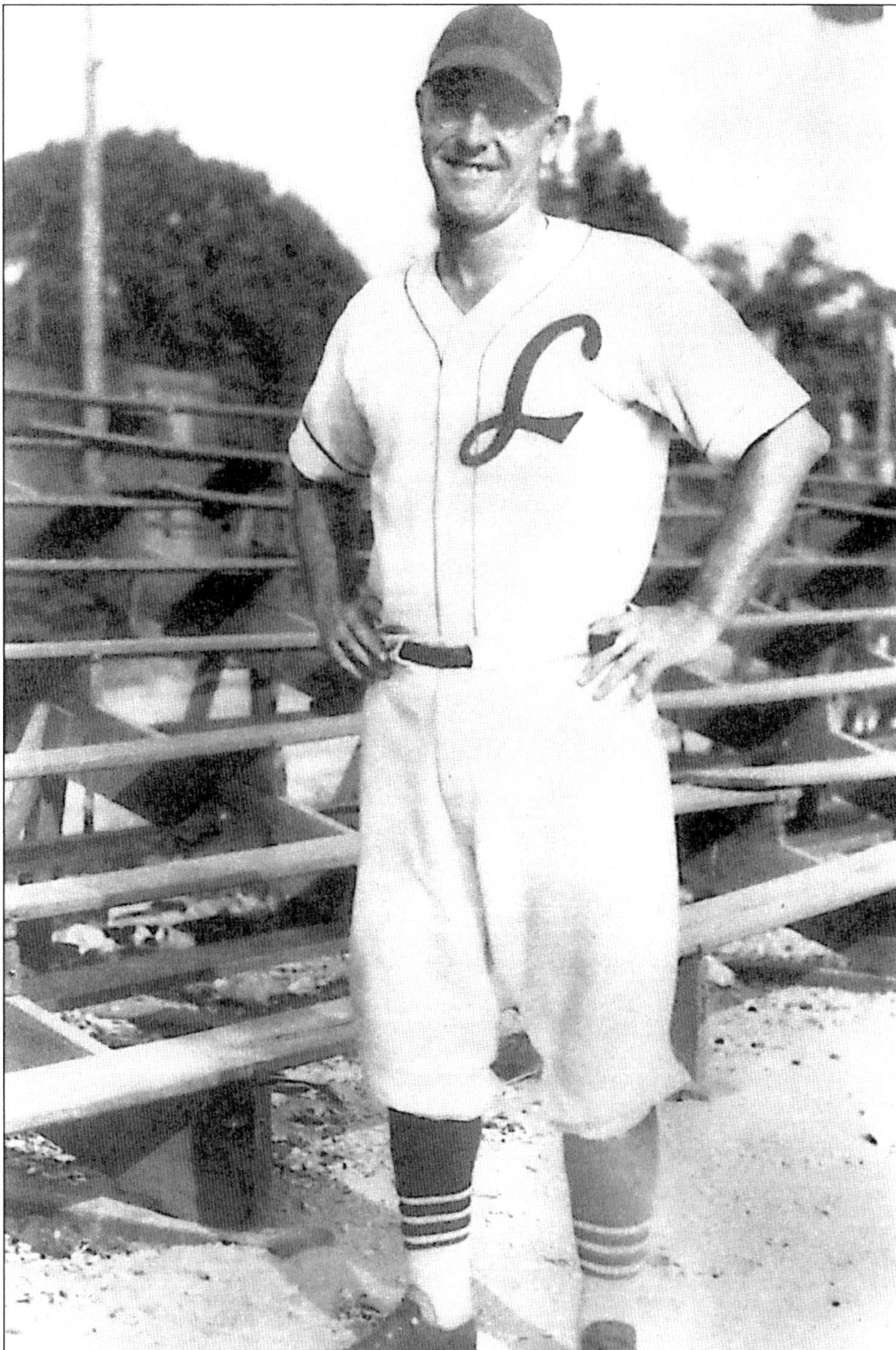

Seen here in his Landis uniform, Ed Cross was already a mainstay in the Textile League that preceded the independent Carolina League. Cross played shortstop for the 1936 Hickory Rebels, leaving halfway through the season with a .324 average. (Courtesy of Ed Cross family.)

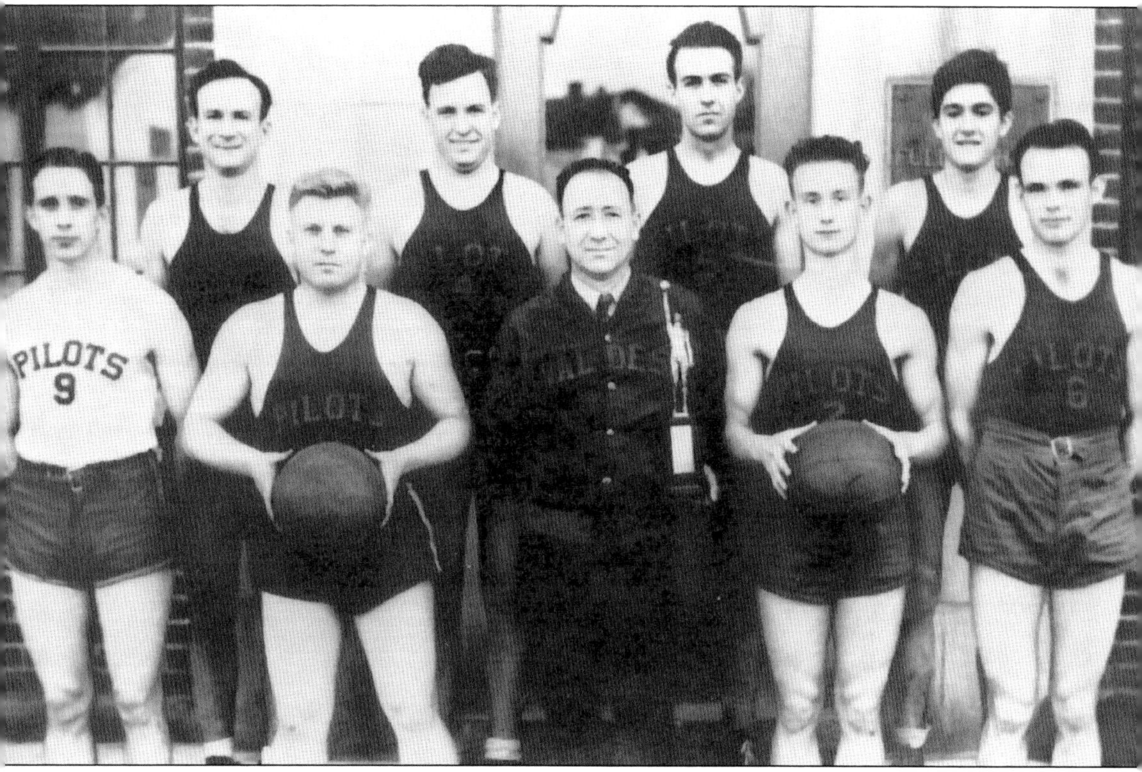

Edwin "Alabama" Pitts (top left in this rare photo) gained national attention in early 1935 when Johnny Evers (of Tinkers-Evers-Chance) attempted to sign him to his Albany Senators team in the International League. His battle with the National Association of Professional Baseball Leagues president Judge W.G. Branham was one of the hottest news items of the spring. When the commissioner of baseball, Judge Kennesaw "Mountain" Landis, intervened, the convicted felon was allowed to play. His first game drew nearly 8,000 fans. Pitts did not make it in the big leagues, and after his brush with fame (he also played briefly for the Philadelphia Eagles in the National Football League), he settled in Valdese in 1937, where he played for the outlaw Valdese Weaver team. (Courtesy of Hank Utley.)

Later Years

Back then it was so much fun—that's all people talked about. There was no television or outdoor theaters. There was only one thing to do in the spring and summer, and that was baseball.
—George Murphy

As the country emerged from the Depression and with the outlaw league out of the way, the National Association of Professional Baseball Leagues sought to broaden its strength in Western North Carolina. Hickory benefited from this process in 1939 as it was granted its first Class D minor-league franchise in the new Tar Heel League. Pinkie James, back from his tour as a high level minor-league player, helped recruit the players and led them in hitting with a .348 average and 105 RBIs. The team finished 48-62, although James and pitcher Bill Skinner, who struck out 212 batters, were named to the All-Star squad. The 1940 team improved to 54-52 but lost in the first round of the playoffs to Gastonia. Woody Traylor led them at the plate with a .316 average. Alabama Pitts played his last professional season that year, batting .302 in 64 games. The league folded at the end of the season, and Hickory was without a professional team in 1941.

Play resumed the next year, however, in the North Carolina State League. The 1942 season is remembered as the team's worst. Manager Bud Shaney posted a remarkable 8-9 record with a 2.92 ERA. This was remarkable given that the team's record, the third worst in minor-league history, was 18-80. Even Pinkie James could not help as he spent his last season of play in a part-time role.

The Rebels returned in a big way in 1945, finishing first by 11.5 games in the North Carolina State League with a record of 80-34. Outfielder Phil Alotta led the squad at the plate with 109 RBIs, while the popular Cuban Frank Hildago won 20 games on the mound. Again, the team lost in the first round of the playoffs. Charlotte native Sammy Bell, who had returned as a player in 1945, managed the Rebels for the next three seasons, amassing records of 55-56, 61-49, and 61-49. The 1946 team, led by Ohioan Dick Stoll, again failed to make it past the first round of the playoffs. Charlie Knight (.366) and Jim Thomas (.353, 31 home runs, 131 RBIs) played incredibly well in 1947, but they lost out in the first round again, this time to Norman Small's Mooresville club. The 1948 team, anchored by slugger Otis Stephens (.328, 32 home runs, 105 RBIs), made it to the playoff finals, where they lost to Statesville.

The next two years were tough ones for the Rebels. They fell to 50-74 in 1949 and to a woeful last place finish at 38-73 the following season. The highlight of the 1950 season was the return of local boy D.C. "Pud" Miller, who stayed around to manage and play the next year. This and the addition of slugger Norman Small made the difference in 1951. The team finished 72-54, and Miller won the league Triple Crown (.425, 40 home runs, 136 RBIs) and the Silver Bat for the highest batting average in the minor leagues. Small was not far behind at .340, 37 home runs, and 127 RBIs. Attendance swelled to over 53,000 as fans came out to see the long balls. Despite all this, the team again bowed out in the first round of the playoffs. Two more difficult years followed in 1952 and 1953. The teams lost (28-79 and 46-66), and a succession of managers saw the attendance drop into the 14,000 range. The 1954 season started well as the Rebel team sprinted to a 34-18 record, but the league folded June 21, leaving them forever in first place.

The final Rebel season was played in 1960 as the Hickory team participated in the resurrected Western Carolina League. They finished third with a 53-44 record. These Rebels, led by player-manager Joe Abernethy (.319) and the fantastic pitching of Danny Hayling (22-9, 2.00 ERA, 24 complete games), survived to the playoff finals but lost to the League Champion Lexington team. For the next 32 years, Hickory was without professional baseball.

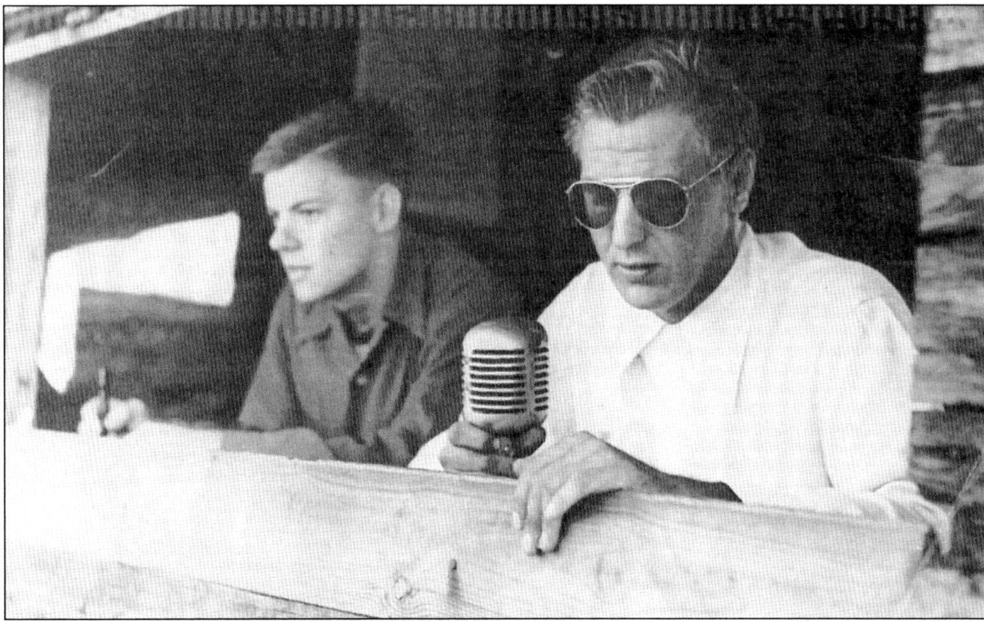

At 21 years old, George Murphy mans the microphone at a 1949 game. He is pictured with scorekeeper Bill Bass, whose own voice later became a staple at local baseball and football games. Murphy was the Rebels announcer from 1946 to 1953. Bass can still be heard at Hickory High School and American Legion contests. (Courtesy of *Hickory Daily Record*.)

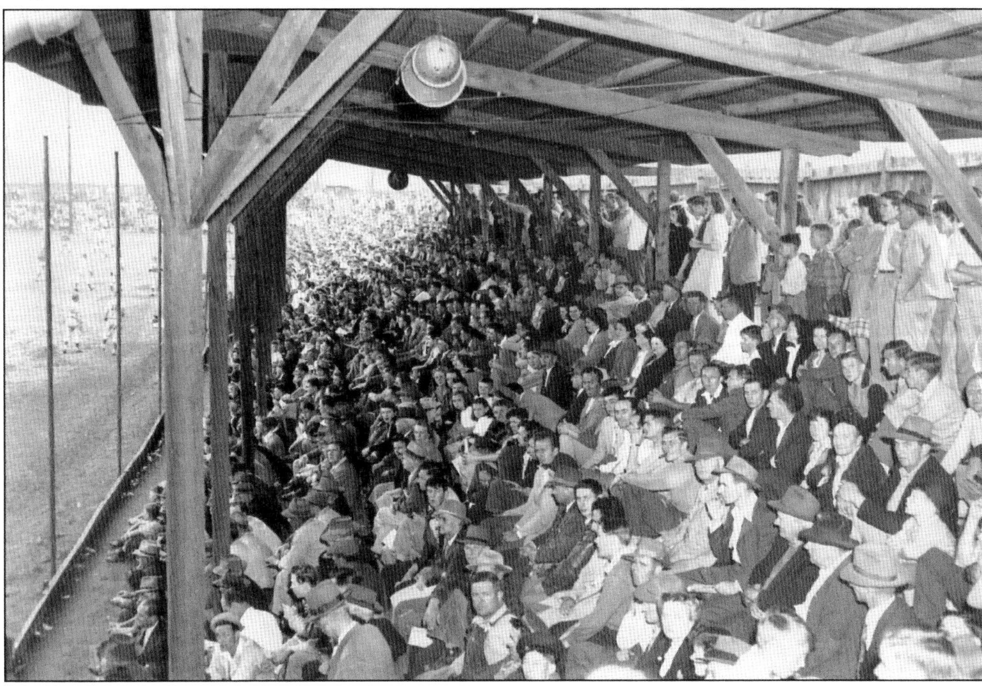

This photo, which was dated February 1947, is most likely rather the exhibition game in 1948 between the Indians and Giants. No exhibition game is mentioned in 1947 sports coverage. Fans traveled from a wide area to pack College Field for an up-close look at major-league players. (Courtesy of Catawba County Historical Museum.)

Harold Lail, an avid player for many years, was the batboy for the Rebels from 1940 to 1942. Lail recalls his favorite players: Norman "Pinkie" James, for whose equipment he was responsible at road games (James traveled separately and played part-time because of business), and Alabama Pitts, who gave Lail his Sing-Sing Prison uniform to wear in his Saturday sandlot games. (Courtesy of Penny Peeler.)

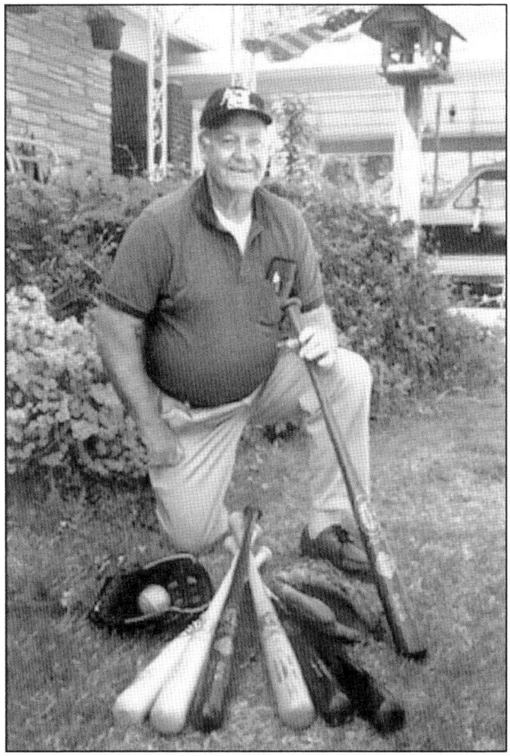

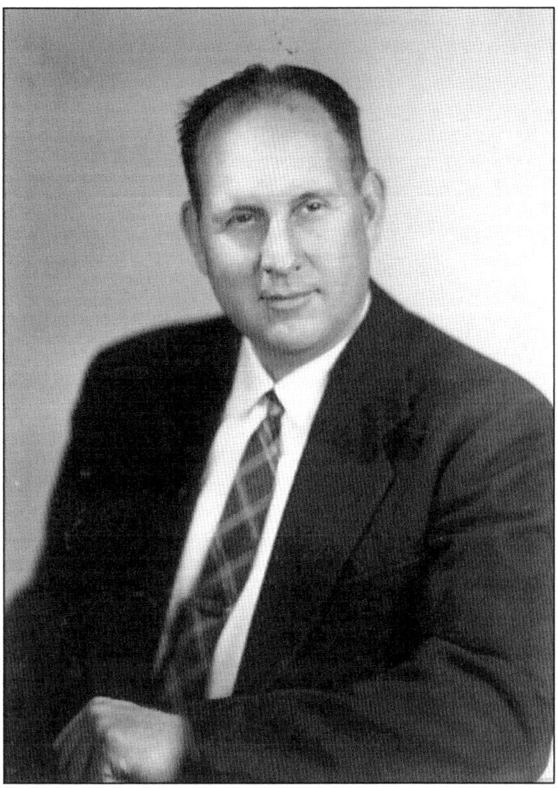

Pinkie James, a member of the Catawba County Sports Hall of Fame, was one of the greatest athletes ever in the Hickory area. He set records in football, basketball, track, and swimming. He was also an accomplished golfer, diver, and marksman. After his baseball career, he was a civic leader and a major advocate for area youth recreation. (Courtesy of Dicky James.)

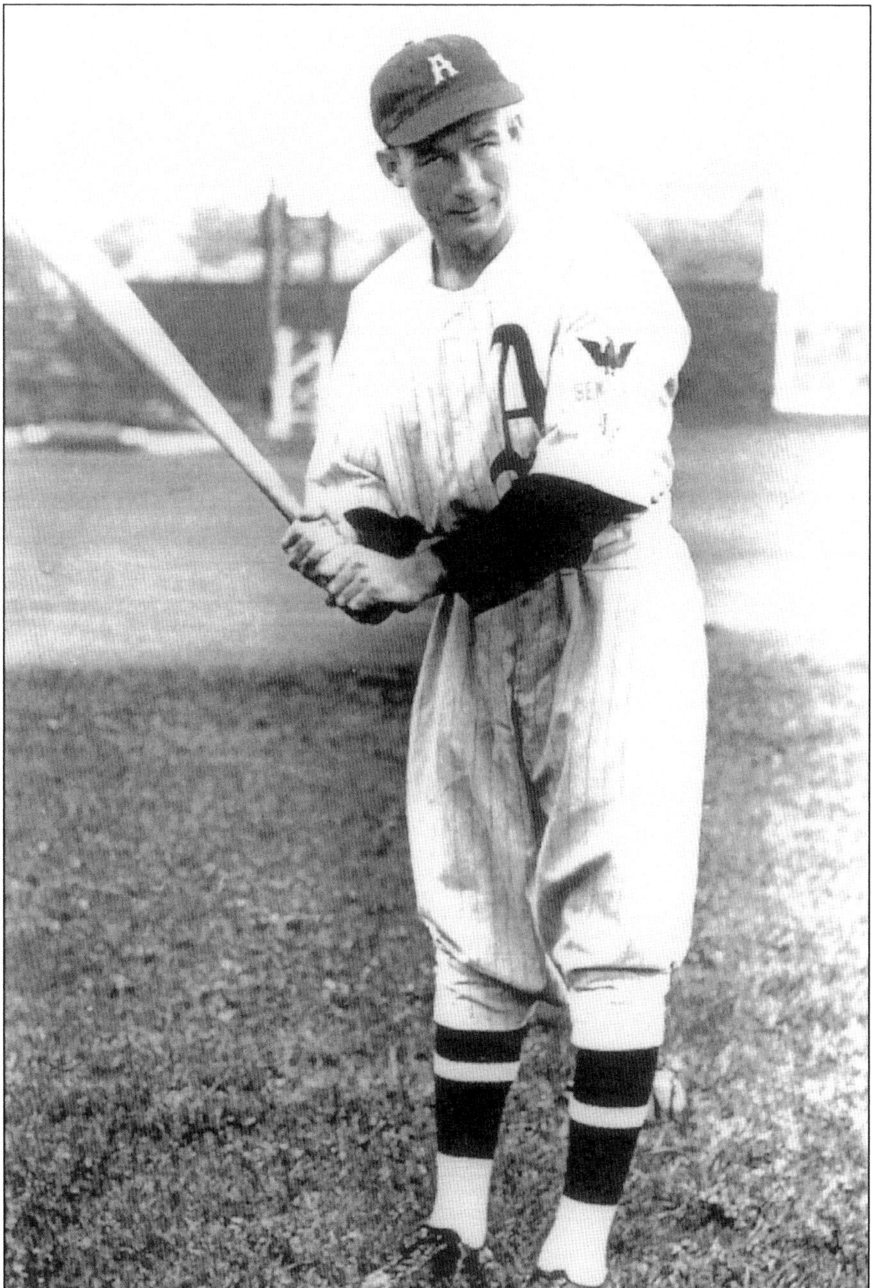

Alabama Pitts had one of his best "official" professional seasons with the 1940 Hickory Rebels. In 64 games he hit .302 with 39 RBIs and 14 doubles. Harold Lail remembers him as a quiet man and a fine player who could draw a crowd. The following season, Pitts played for a semi-professional team in Valdese. One night after a game in Morganton, where he had played for a House of David team and had hit a home run, he stopped at a roadside tavern in Valdese. There he got into a fight with Newland LeFevers, who slashed him across the arm; Pitts bled to death two hours later. (Courtesy of Joe Overfield.)

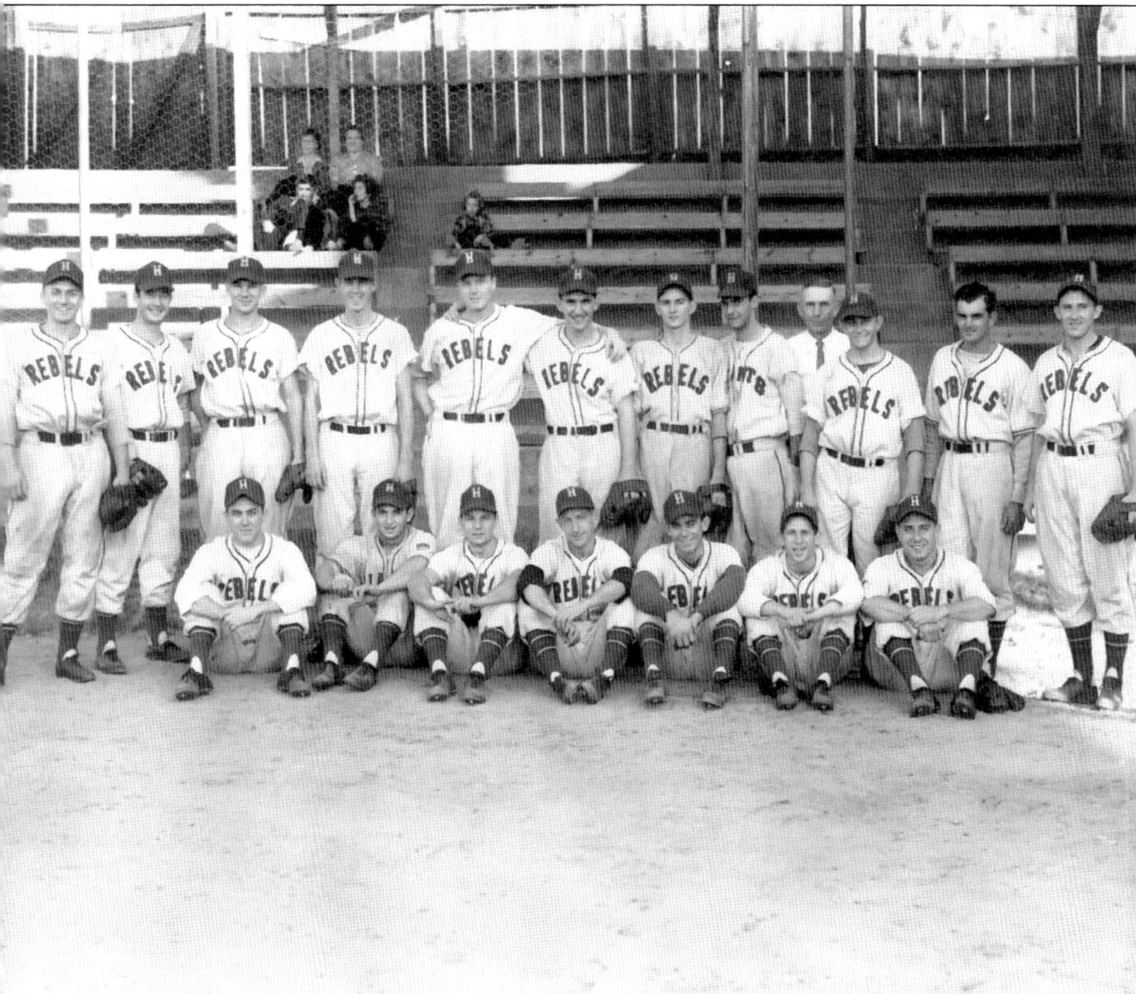

This 1946 photo of the Hickory Rebels is the one most often associated with the team. Several holdovers from the pennant-winning team from the previous year (80-34) remained, including Cuban pitcher Frank Hildago. Sammy Bell managed this team to a 55-56 record. Dick Stoll was their steadiest pitcher. The following players are pictured from left to right: (front row) Dick Stoll, Joe Frisina, Charlie Winstead, Sammy Bell, Presh Smith, Lou Bartilini, and Joe Salerno; (back row) Ernie Yellen, Jack Williams, Sam Herman, Charlie Knight, Patrick Earey, Bernie Weisman, Frank Hildago, Bill Harlein, Joe Hefner, James Lawing, and Ken Howard. (Courtesy of Dick Stoll.)

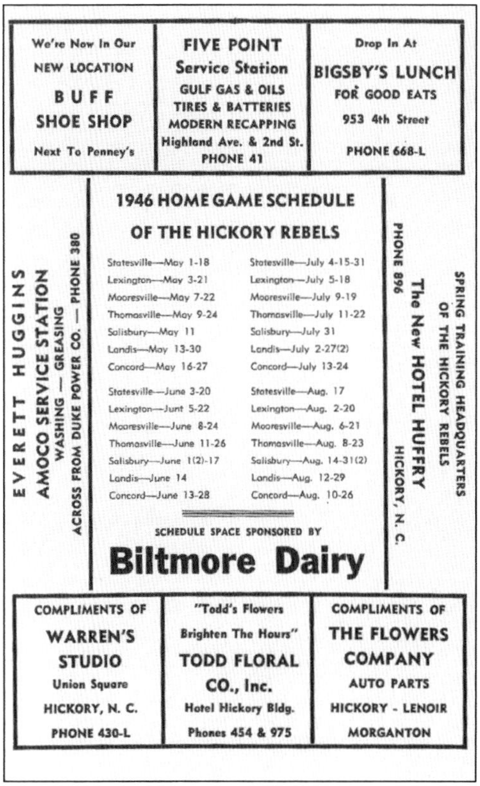
We're Now In Our NEW LOCATION
BUFF SHOE SHOP
Next To Penney's

FIVE POINT Service Station
GULF GAS & OILS
TIRES & BATTERIES
MODERN RECAPPING
Highland Ave. & 2nd St.
PHONE 41

Drop In At
BIGSBY'S LUNCH
FOR GOOD EATS
953 4th Street
PHONE 668-L

EVERETT HUGGINS
AMOCO SERVICE STATION
WASHING — GREASING
ACROSS FROM DUKE POWER CO. — PHONE 380

1946 HOME GAME SCHEDULE
OF THE HICKORY REBELS

Statesville—May 1-18	Statesville—July 4-15-31
Lexington—May 3-21	Lexington—July 5-18
Mooresville—May 7-22	Mooresville—July 9-19
Thomasville—May 9-24	Thomasville—July 11-22
Salisbury—May 11	Salisbury—July 31
Landis—May 13-30	Landis—July 2-27(2)
Concord—May 16-27	Concord—July 13-24
Statesville—June 3-20	Statesville—Aug. 17
Lexington—Junt 5-22	Lexington—Aug. 2-20
Mooresville—June 8-24	Mooresville—Aug. 6-21
Thomasville—June 11-26	Thomasville—Aug. 8-23
Salisbury—June 1(2)-17	Salisbury—Aug. 14-31(2)
Landis—June 14	Landis—Aug. 12-29
Concord—June 13-28	Concord—Aug. 10-26

SCHEDULE SPACE SPONSORED BY
Biltmore Dairy

The New HOTEL HUFFRY
PHONE 896
HICKORY, N. C.
SPRING TRAINING HEADQUARTERS OF THE HICKORY REBELS

COMPLIMENTS OF
WARREN'S STUDIO
Union Square
HICKORY, N. C.
PHONE 430-L

"Todd's Flowers Brighten The Hours"
TODD FLORAL CO., Inc.
Hotel Hickory Bldg.
Phones 454 & 975

COMPLIMENTS OF
THE FLOWERS COMPANY
AUTO PARTS
HICKORY - LENOIR
MORGANTON

This is the scorecard and schedule for the 1946 Hickory Rebels. (Courtesy of Dick Stoll.)

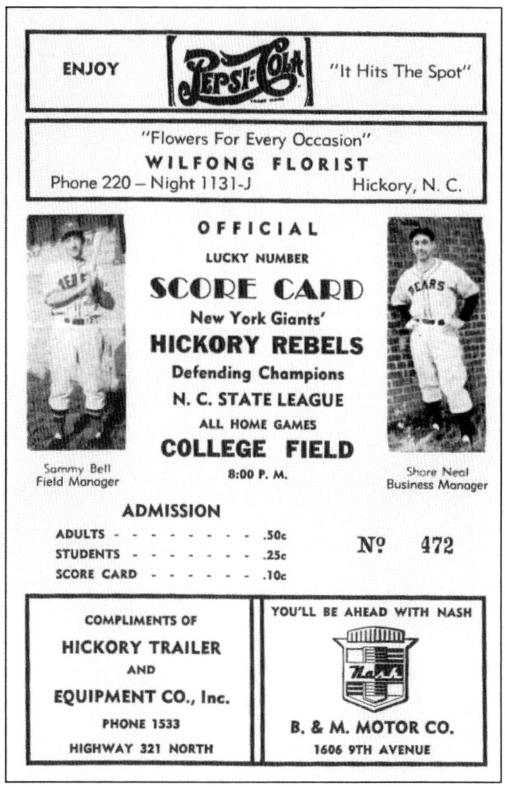
ENJOY Pepsi-Cola "It Hits The Spot"

"Flowers For Every Occasion"
WILFONG FLORIST
Phone 220 – Night 1131-J Hickory, N. C.

OFFICIAL
LUCKY NUMBER
SCORE CARD
New York Giants'
HICKORY REBELS
Defending Champions
N. C. STATE LEAGUE
ALL HOME GAMES
COLLEGE FIELD
8:00 P. M.

Sammy Bell
Field Manager

Shore Neal
Business Manager

ADMISSION
ADULTS .50c
STUDENTS .25c
SCORE CARD .10c

№ 472

COMPLIMENTS OF
HICKORY TRAILER AND EQUIPMENT CO., Inc.
PHONE 1533
HIGHWAY 321 NORTH

YOU'LL BE AHEAD WITH NASH
B. & M. MOTOR CO.
1606 9TH AVENUE

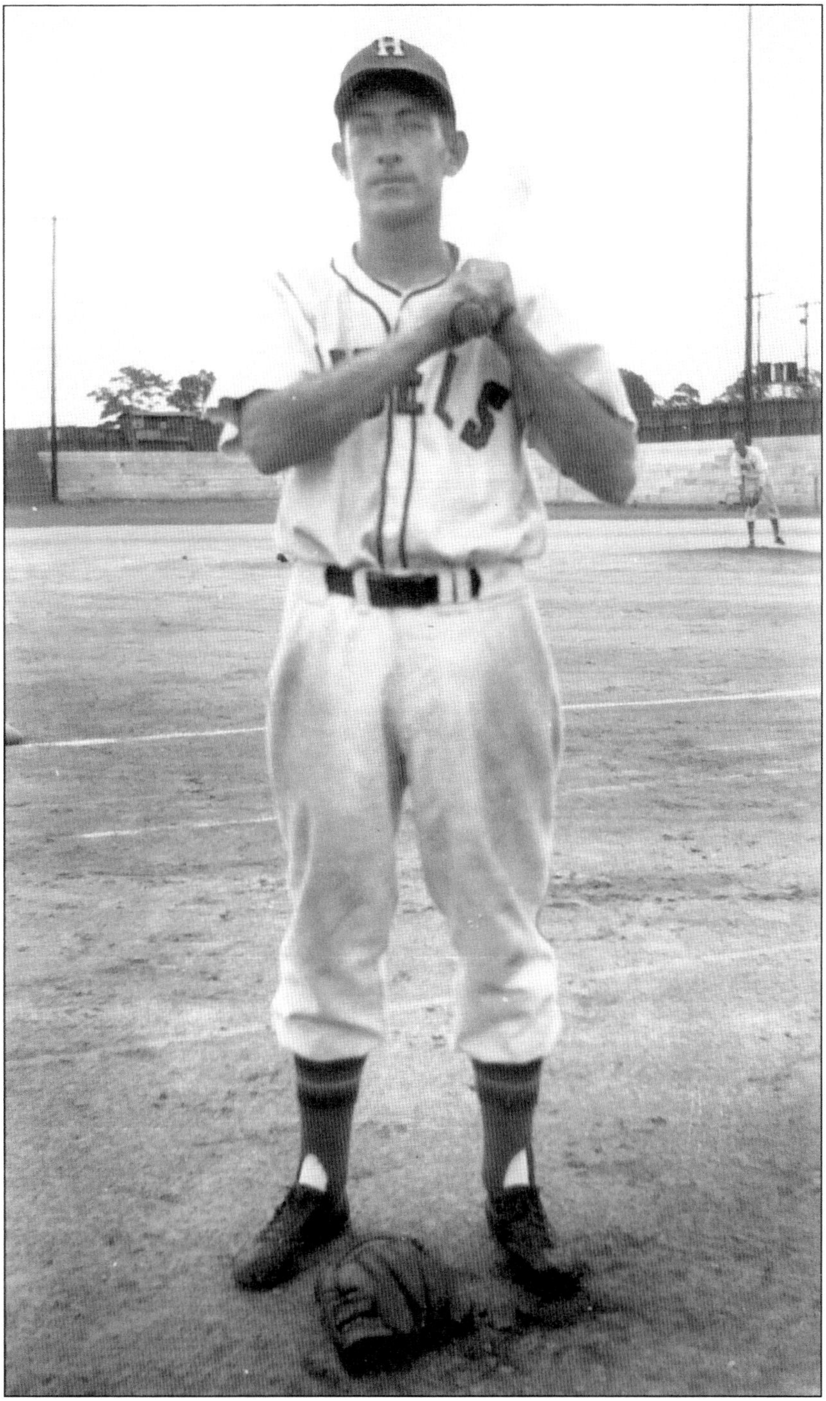

Sammy Bell first came to Hickory as a competitor for Central High of Charlotte. He returned with Pinkie James from Duke in 1933 to play for one of the first Rebel teams. After a minor-league career that included Triple-A ball, he returned to play for and manage the Rebels from 1945 to 1948. Bell was an excellent second baseman and hitter who unfortunately got caught behind Jackie Robinson in the Dodger organization. (Courtesy of Dick Stoll.)

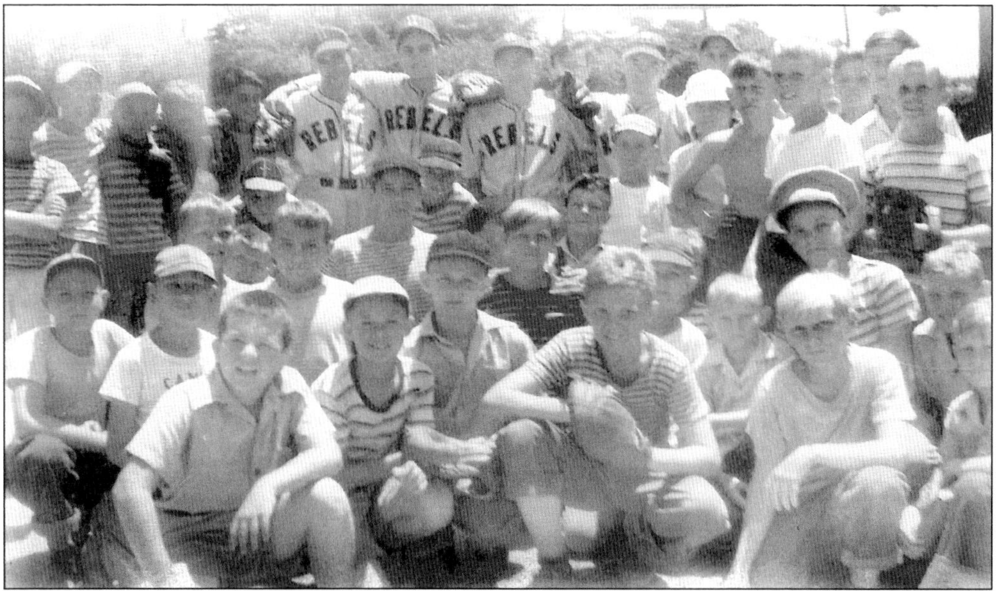

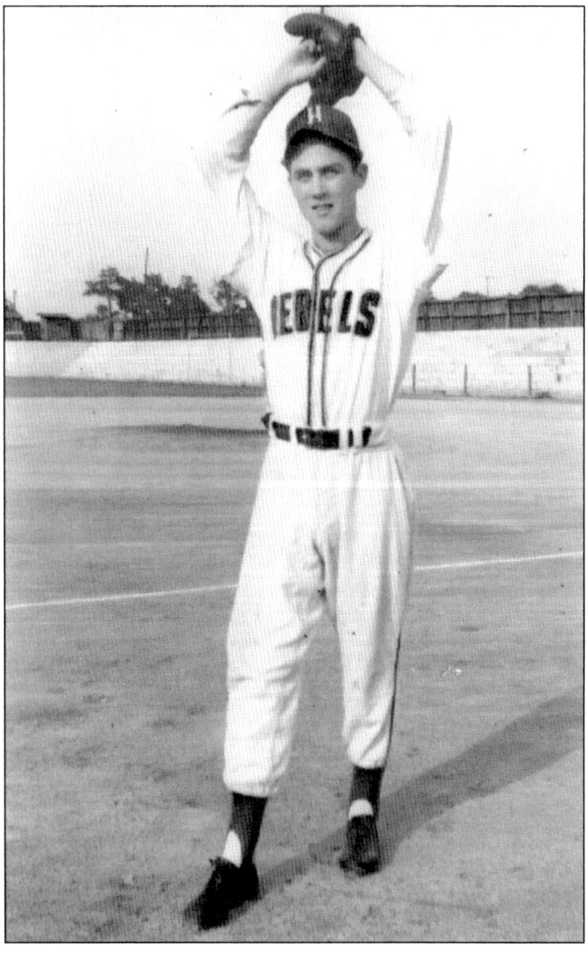

The 1946 Hickory Rebels players pose with future diamond stars. The summer baseball camp was held at Hickory High School on a field behind what is now the Arts Center. (Courtesy of Dick Stoll.)

In 1946, Dick Stoll, a native of Ohio, stopped in Hickory en route to Bristol, Tennessee. After a pitching tryout, Sammy Bell convinced him to stay on with the Rebels, where he became the team's top starter. (Courtesy of Dick Stoll.)

Lou Bartalini of New York was an excellent third baseman and a clutch hitter for the 1946 Rebels. (Courtesy of Dick Stoll.)

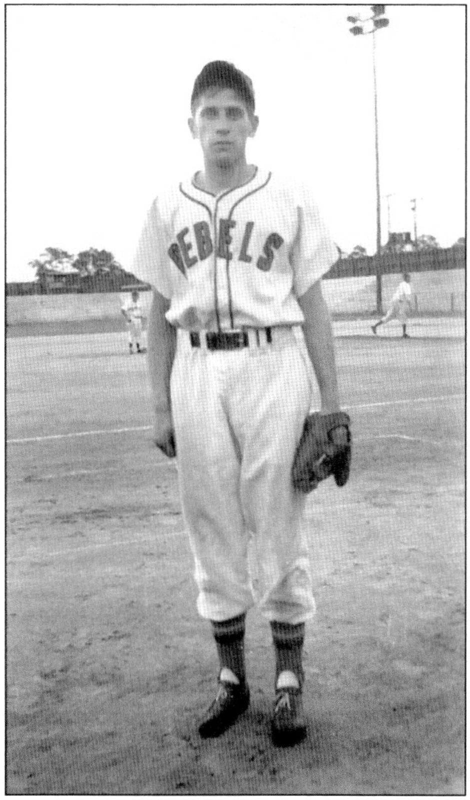

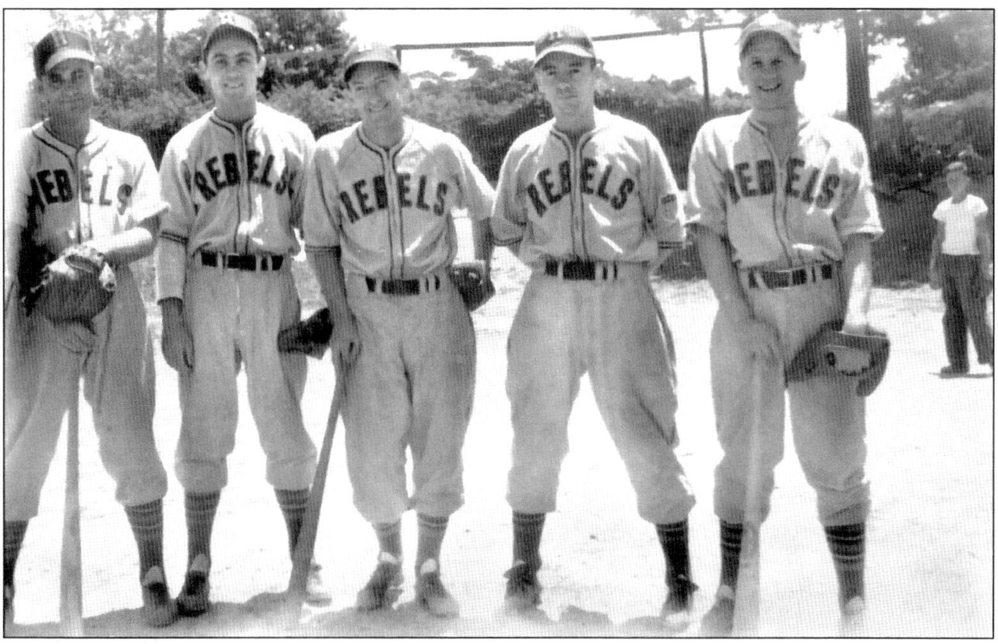

Rebel players and the manager relax during a break at the 1946 baseball camp. (Courtesy of Dick Stoll.)

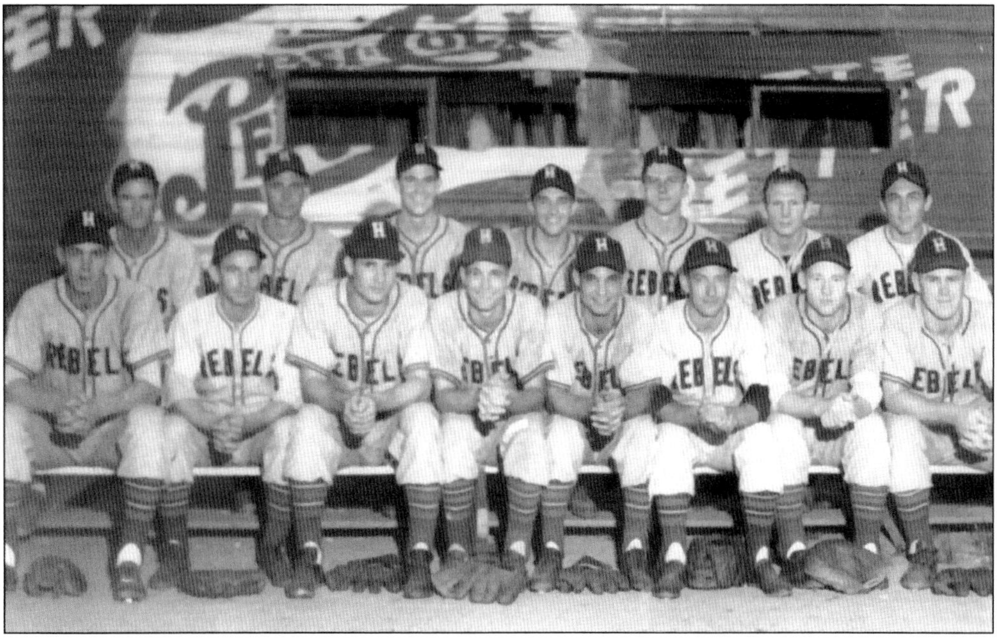

This shot of the 1947 Rebels was taken in the dugout at Mooresville after a game. This team was led by Charlie Knight and Jim Thomas, who hit 31 home runs and drove in 131 RBIs. Their 61-49 record was good enough for third place, but they lost in the playoffs to League Champion Mooresville. (Courtesy of Dick Stoll.)

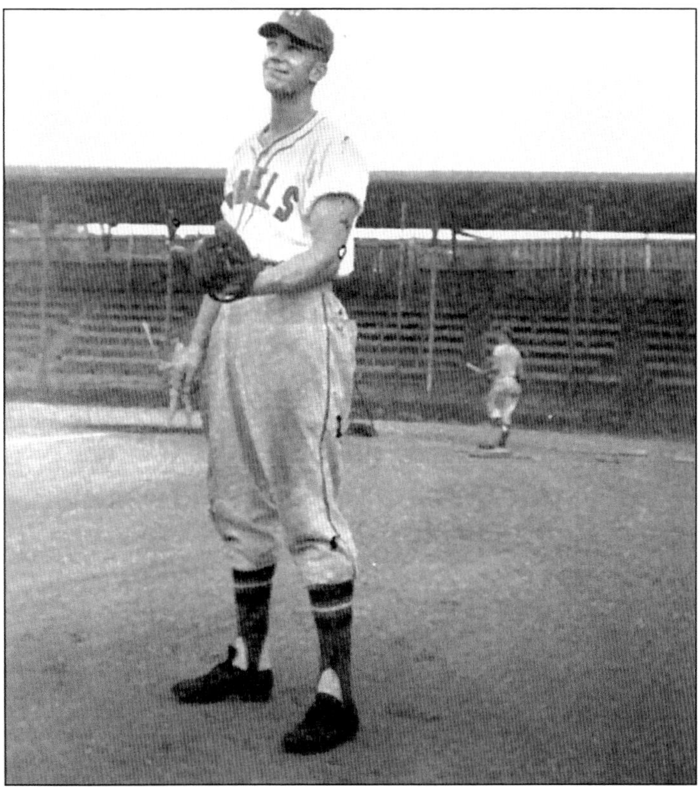

Ken Howard was a left-handed slugger and center fielder for the 1946–1947 Rebels. He loved the low pitches. (Courtesy of Dick Stoll.)

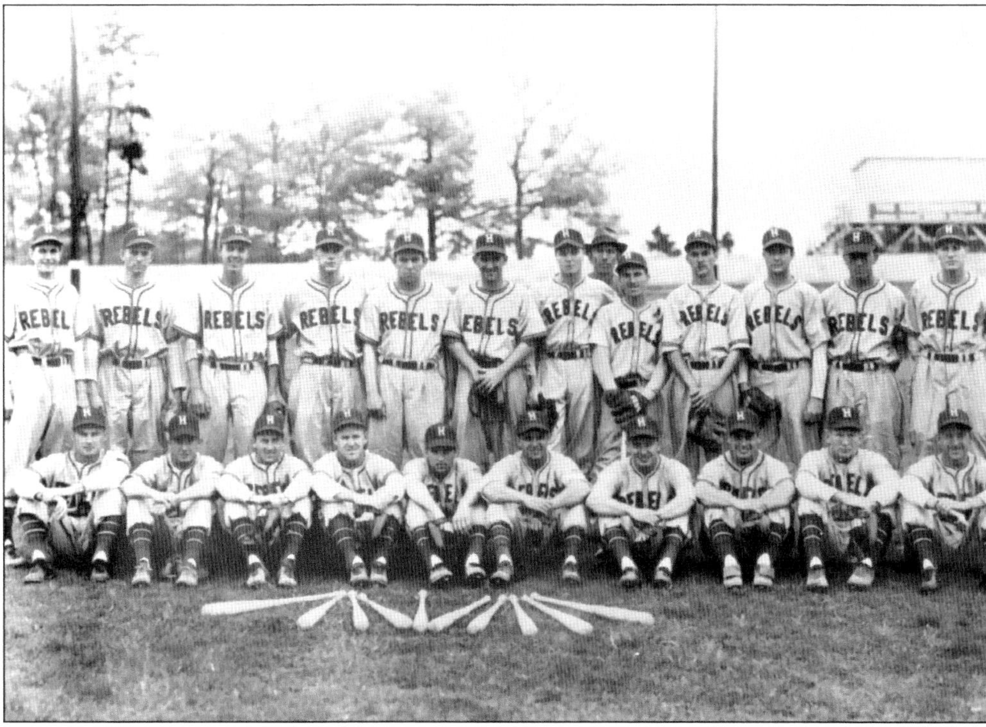

This is the 1947 pre-season team picture that was taken before players had been reassigned. (Courtesy of Charlie Bost.)

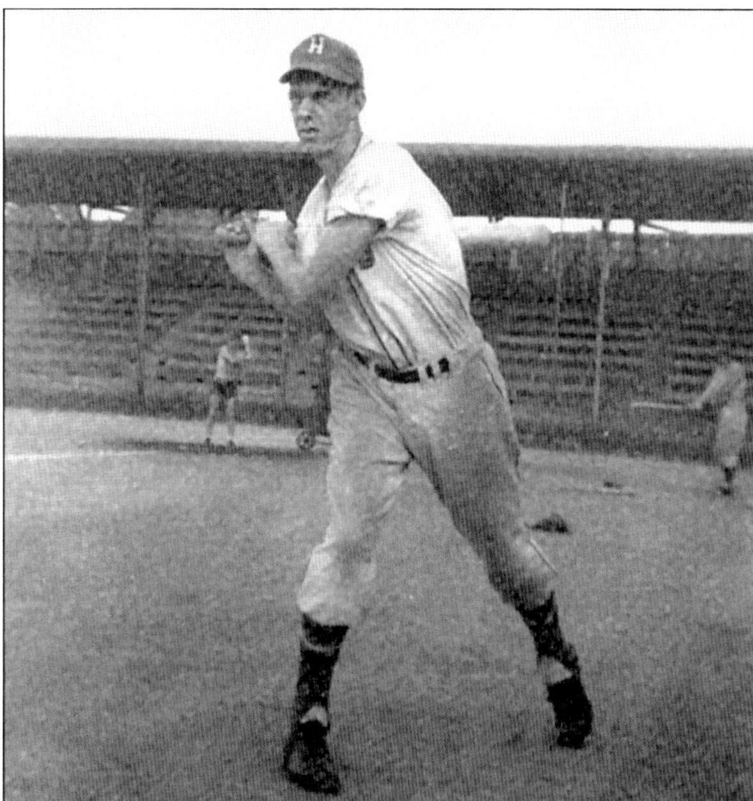

First baseman Charlie Knight led the 1947 Rebels with a .366 average. (Courtesy of Dick Stoll.)

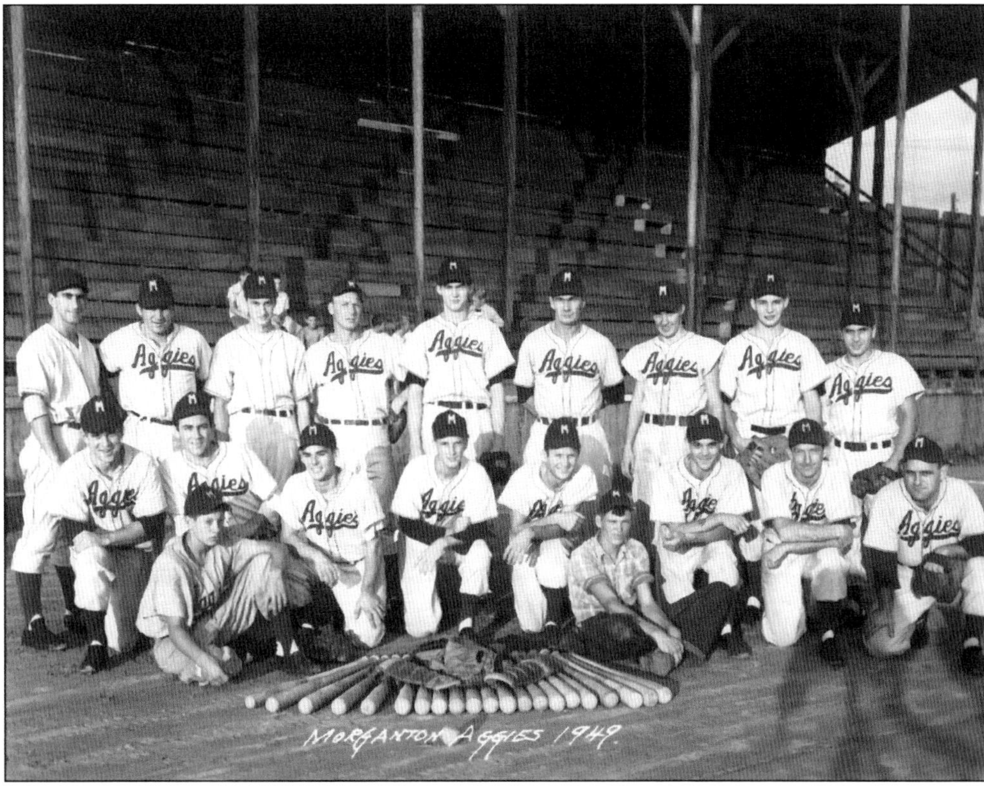

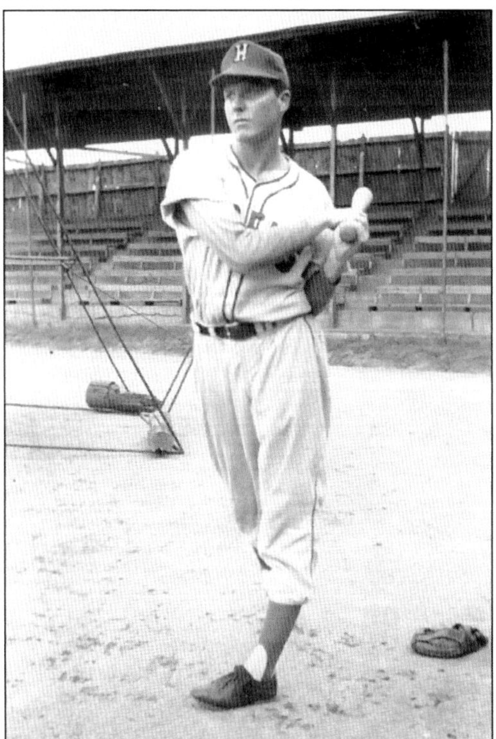

Dick Stoll (second from the left on front row) finished his professional career with the Morganton Aggies. The 1949 and 1950 teams, which featured outstanding players like Radio James and Jack Harvey, were managed by the ubiquitous Sammy Bell (second from the right on front row). (Courtesy of Dick Stoll.)

Pitcher Patrick Earey was known as "Big Red Pat." (Courtesy of Dick Stoll.)

A fine catcher for the 1946 Rebels, Ernie Yellen was the most popular of that year's players with the female fans. (Courtesy of Dick Stoll.)

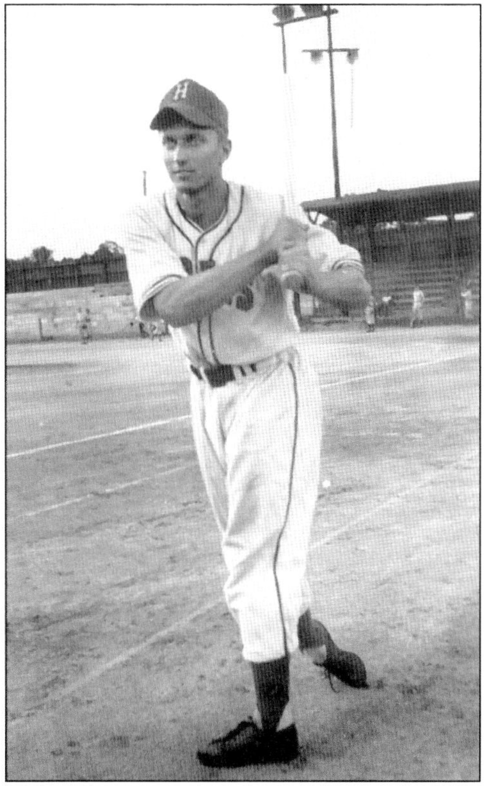

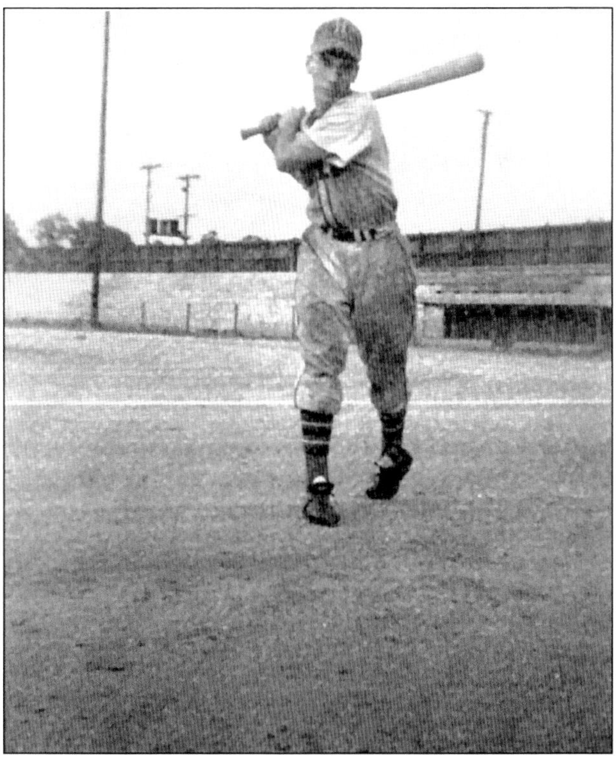

Johnny Allen led the 1945 Rebels with a .325 average while scoring 140 runs. A year later, he was traded to Lexington. He was released after the 1948 season because he had played his limit in Class D ball as a three-year player. When a manager's job fell through and no playing opportunity presented itself, the despondent Allen committed suicide with a shotgun. (Courtesy of Dick Stoll.)

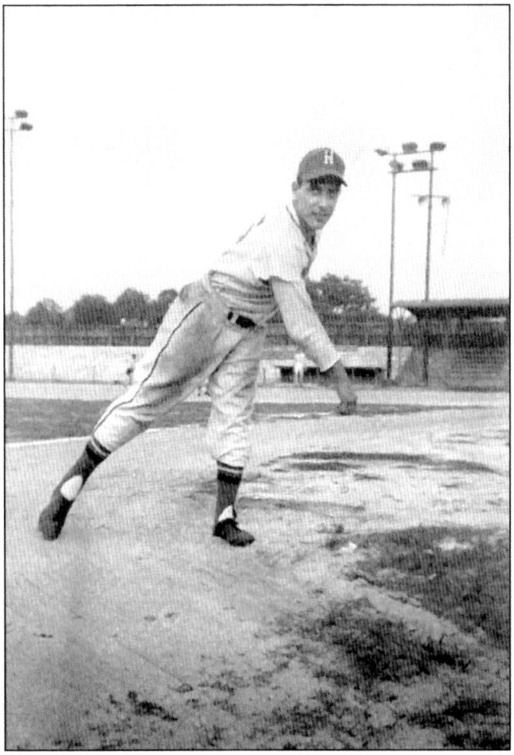

Joe Salerno was a hotshot pitcher from New York City. (Courtesy of Dick Stoll.)

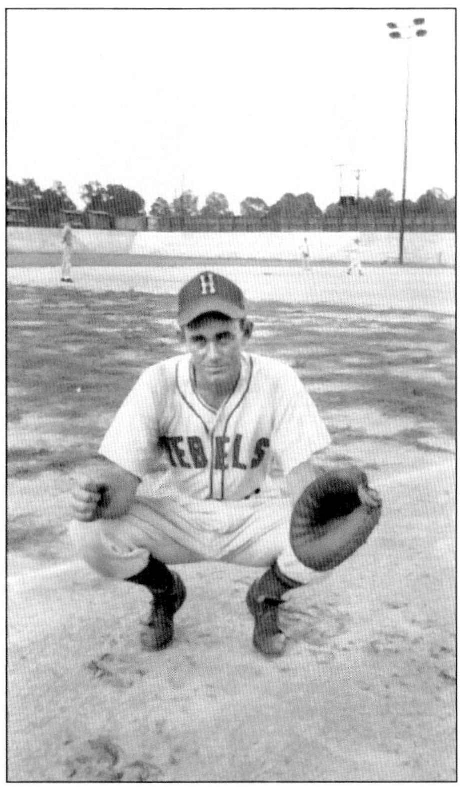

Presh Smith was a popular catcher and assistant manager. (Courtesy of Dick Stoll.)

The great Bob Feller pitched in an exhibition game in Hickory in 1948. An estimated 11,000 people gathered for the game, filling the stands and all the areas along the foul lines. What most people remember are the two mammoth home runs hit off of Feller in the first inning by Johnny Mize and Mel Ott. (Courtesy of Hickory Crawdads.)

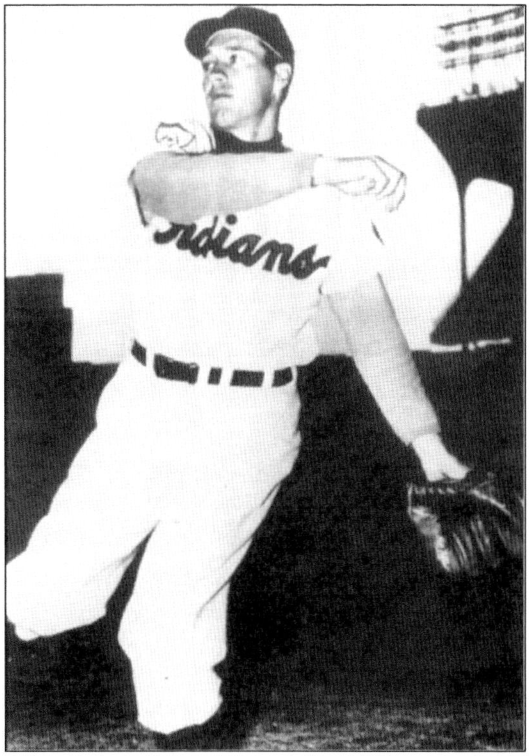

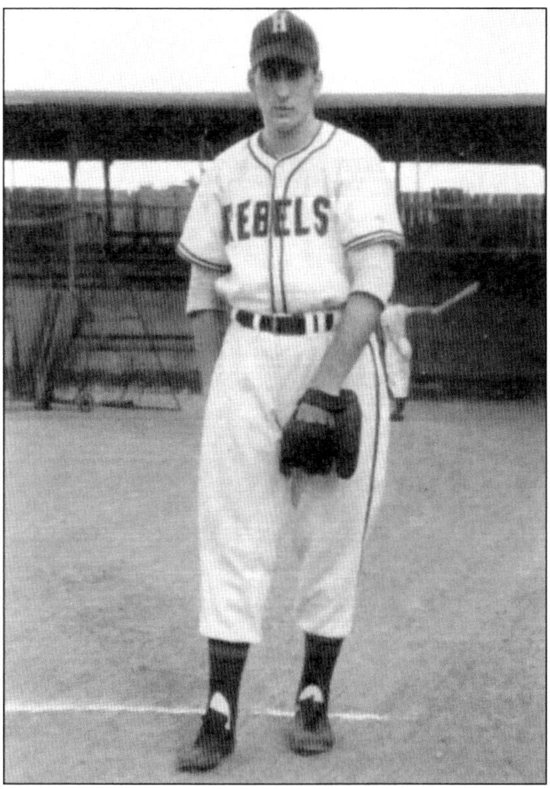

During parts of 1948 and 1949, Lee Postove was a regular hurler for the Rebels. His 14-7 record in 1948 earned him a spot on the All-Star team. However, he was suspended by Manager Bell late in the season for refusing to dress out for a game. (Courtesy of Hickory Crawdads.)

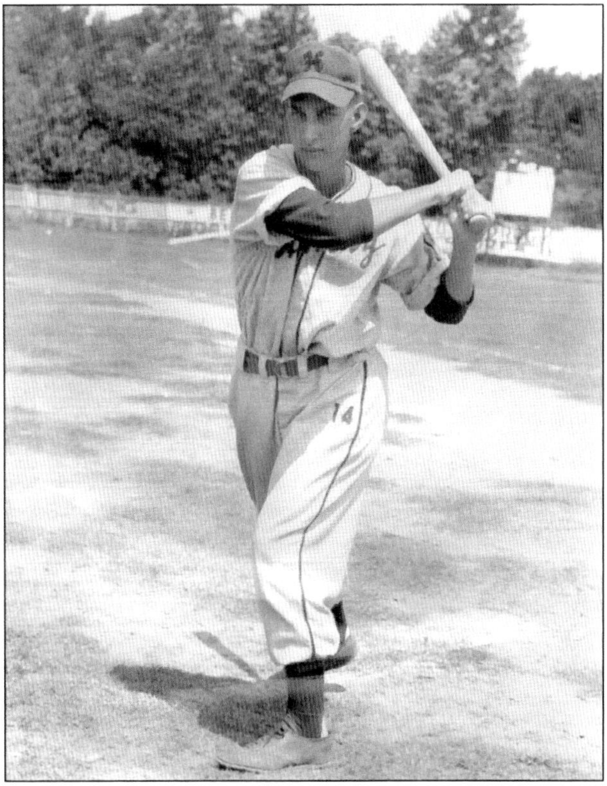

A local boy in every sense of the word, Ted Hefner played first for Hickory High, then the Hickory American Legion team, and then the Hickory Rebels. (Courtesy of Ted Hefner.)

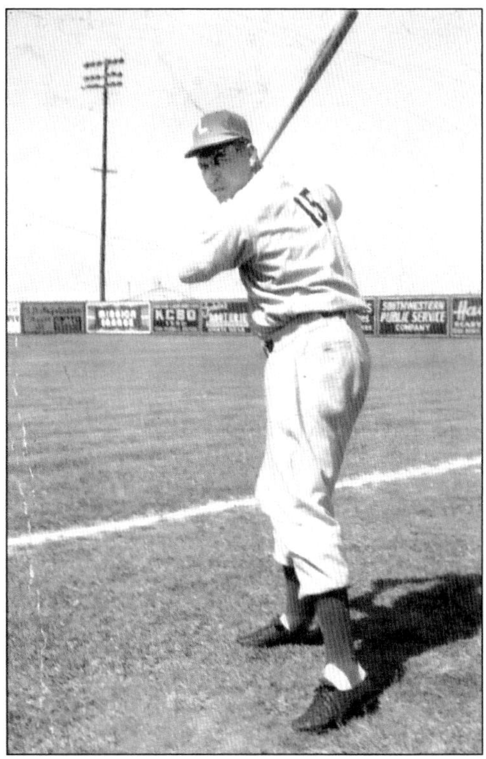

D.C. "Pud" Miller, seen here in Lemesa, Texas, in 1949, returned home to Hickory in 1950, where he managed and gave new life to the Rebels from 1950 to 1953. (Courtesy of Betty Miller.)

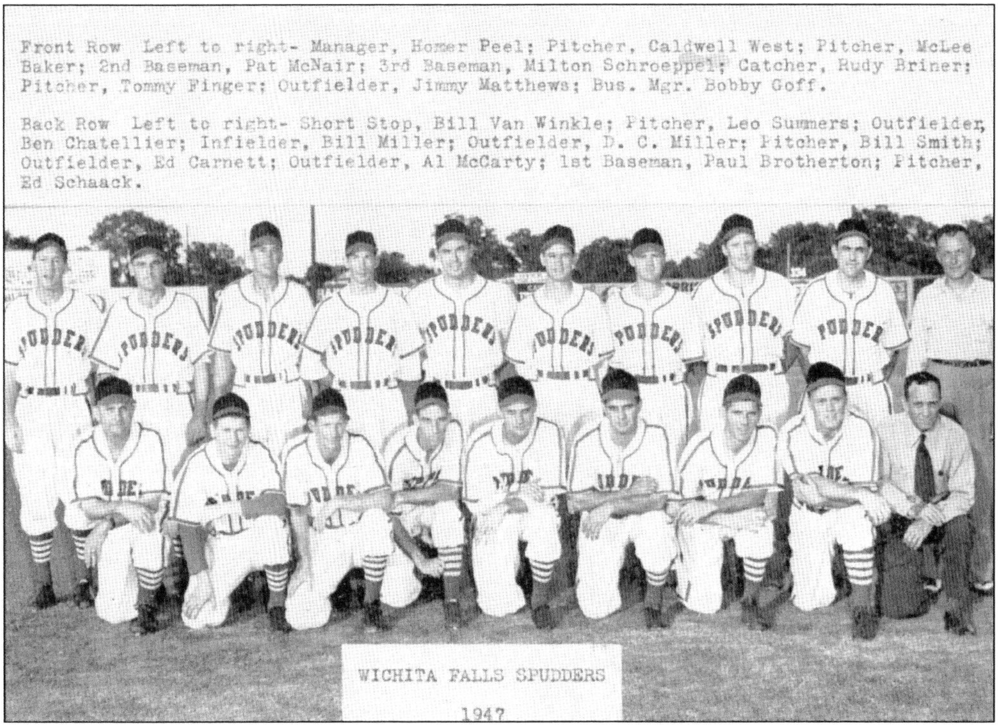

D.C. "Pud" Miller, who is rated by the Society of American Baseball Researchers as a top 100 all-time minor leaguer, had his most incredible year in 1947 for the Wichita Falls Spudders. The slugger led his team with 57 home runs, 196 RBIs, and a .356 average. (Courtesy of Betty Miller.)

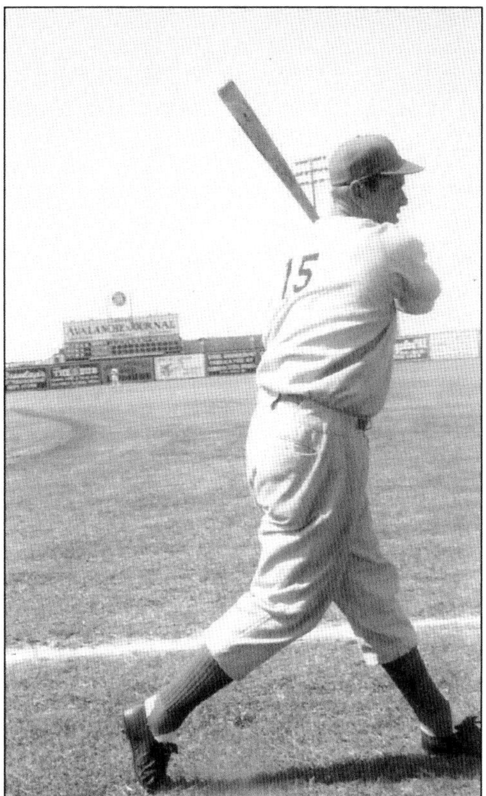

This is another shot of Miller's awesome swing. (Courtesy of Betty Miller.)

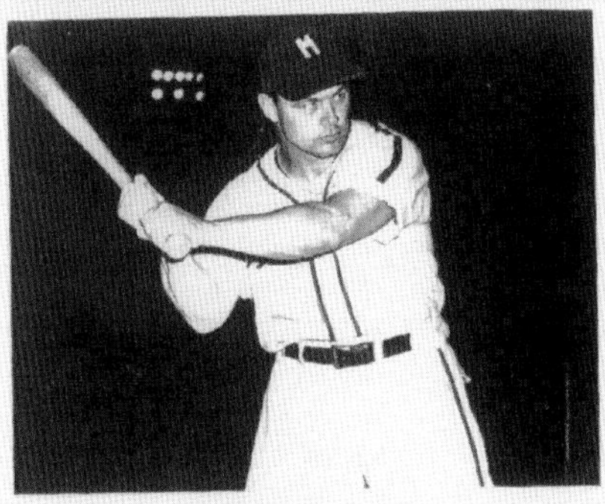

Norman Woodnut Small

Born November 6, 1913 at Glen Cove, NY.
Batted right. Threw right. Height: 5-10. Weight: 176.
Manager for Mooresville, North Carolina State, 1947-1948; Hickory, North Carolina State, 1951.

YEAR	CLUB	LEAGUE	POS	G	AB	R	H	2B	3B	HR	SB	RBI	AVG
1934	Martinsville	Bi-State	of	40	123	24	37	12	3	2	–	–	.301
1935	Asheville	Piedmont	of	15	58	14	11	3	0	3	–	11	.190
	Greenwood	East Dixie	of	16	49	2	8	2	0	0	–	3	.163
	Martinsville	Bi-State	of-3b	47	135	12	33	5	1	1	–	–	.244
1936	York	New York-Pennsylvania	of	2	7	1	1	0	0	0	–	0	.143
1937	Mooresville	North Carolina State	of	35	148	44	58	12	2	12	5	51	.392
	Durham	Piedmont	of	88	318	49	87	18	7	2	8	42	.274
1938	Durham	Piedmont	of	69	276	40	76	9	9	5	6	43	.275
	Waterloo	Three I	of	9	29	3	2	0	0	0	0	2	.070
	Columbia	SALLY	of	21	78	10	32	6	1	2	1	16	.410
1939	Columbia	SALLY	of	111	455	60	123	24	10	6	5	54	.270
	Meridian	Southeastern	of	11	39	9	11	2	0	4	–	7	.282
1940	Mooresville	North Carolina State	of	103	437	95	151	41	6	25	5	115	.346
1941	Mooresville	North Carolina State	of	95	386	75	128	22	8	18	3	73	.332
1942	Mooresville	North Carolina State	of	100	383	91	144	35	6	20	7	107	.376
1943	Jersey City	International	of	53	168	21	42	10	1	4	0	19	.250
1944-45							Military service						
1946	Mooresville	North Carolina State	of	99	388	100	135	31	10	18	8	69	.348
1947	Mooresville	North Carolina State	of	104	398	106	143	36	2	31	3	102	.359
1948	Mooresville	North Carolina State	of	110	431	103	154	32	4	33	7	130	.357
1949	Mooresville	North Carolina State	of	124	456	115	157	20	4	41	7	182	.344
1950	Mooresville	North Carolina State	of	98	350	73	103	23	0	32	4	104	.294
1951	Hickory	North Carolina State	of	126	485	106	165	38	6	37	4	127	.340
1952	Hickory	Western Carolina	of	20	82	15	28	10	2	2	0	13	.341
	Raleigh	Carolina	of	112	419	59	113	25	4	12	1	68	.270
1953	Mooresville	Tar Heel	of	95	385	75	131	31	1	14	6	87	.340
			Minors	1703	6483	1302	2073	443	87	336	80	1395	.320

1936 after Norman Small left York in the Class A New York/Penn League,
joined the Mooresville Moors of the outlaw Carolina League. In 127
es at bat he hit 10 hone runs with a .315 BA.
to courtesy Norman Small

Norman Small joined fellow power hitter Pud Miller on the 1951 Rebels team. Small hit 37 home runs, drove in 127 runs, and batted .340 in 126 games. The 1951 team finished second with a 72-54 record as Miller won the Triple Crown and the Silver Bat with a .425 average, 40 home runs, and 136 RBIs. Small began the following season as manager but was released when the team failed to win. (Courtesy of Society of American Baseball Researchers.)

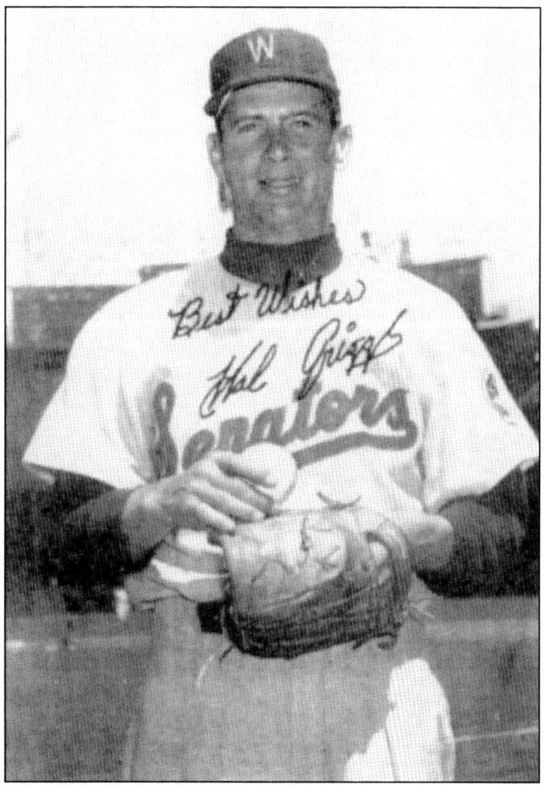

Hal Griggs pitched several years for the Rebels in the early 1950s before moving on to a four-year stint with the Washington Senators. In 1952, he posted a 14-13 record when the Rebels only won 29 games. Griggs was married on the diamond at College Field. (Courtesy of Hickory Crawdads.)

Three

Twins

You throw the ball and run as fast as you can to back up third base, hoping you can hold him to a double.
—Dick Stoll, on how to pitch Don Stafford

On April 9, 1926, baseball made its way into Newton by way of the newly founded Newton Indians. The Indians were set to hook up with teams from Lincolnton, Hickory, Shelby, Lenoir, and Morganton to form the Western North Carolina League.

Wade Lefler, a member of the 1925 World Champion Washington Americans, was selected as the team's first manager and also served as a first baseman for the squad. With the arrival of the new team came a need for a ballpark. At a local town meeting, a committee was formed to find a place for the ballpark; the field was eventually set up in the South Newton area.

After a successful run, the Indians put their gloves down for good in 1936. It was then, on January 8, 1937, that Newton joined Conover to create the beloved Newton-Conover Twins. The Twins, who had a working agreement with the Cleveland Indians, became part of the newly formed Class D North Carolina State League. Two years later, the Twins switched from the North Carolina State League to the brand-new Class D Tar Heel League. The team remained in this league until they dropped out of baseball completely on July 19, 1940, midway through the season. The league also closed its doors at the end of the season.

After the collapse of the Newton-Conover Twins, the two towns went without professional baseball until 1948, when Newton-Conover reformed and joined the Class D Western Carolina League. That year, the Twins had their best season as an organization up to that point, finishing second with a record of 67-43. The return of baseball to the area was highlighted by star players such as Eddie Yount, Don Stafford, and Ray Lindsey.

The 1949 and 1950 teams each won the league pennant with records of 72-36 and 69-41, respectively. The 1951 season saw the Twins finish with a 63-48 record, leaving them in fourth place, just high enough to receive their fourth consecutive playoff berth. The team eventually lost in the first round to Shelby. After four solid seasons, the Twins and the entire league folded because of financial problems. The team's attendance that year had dropped to less than half of what it was in 1950.

In 1960, the Twins gave it one more go as the old Western Carolina League was revamped. The team struggled in the opening season with a record of 47-52. In 1961, for the second time in the history of the organization, the Twins signed a working agreement with a major-league ball club—this time with the Milwaukee Braves. Unfortunately, the team finished in the cellar with a record of 36-58. The fan base began to decline quickly during the season, and that eventually led to the end of professional baseball in Newton and Conover after the 1962 season.

Despite the rough times for the team as an organization, the Twins provided the people of Newton and Conover with wonderful entertainment and left them with many memories. Players like Charlie Bost, Joe Plick, George DePillo, Bill Cooke, Jimmy Sweezy, John "Hom" Isaac, and the aforementioned Don Stafford, Ray Lindsey, and Eddie Yount all became household names across the area.

Included here are photographs of some of the team's heroes and legends from the short but great run of the Newton-Conover Twins.

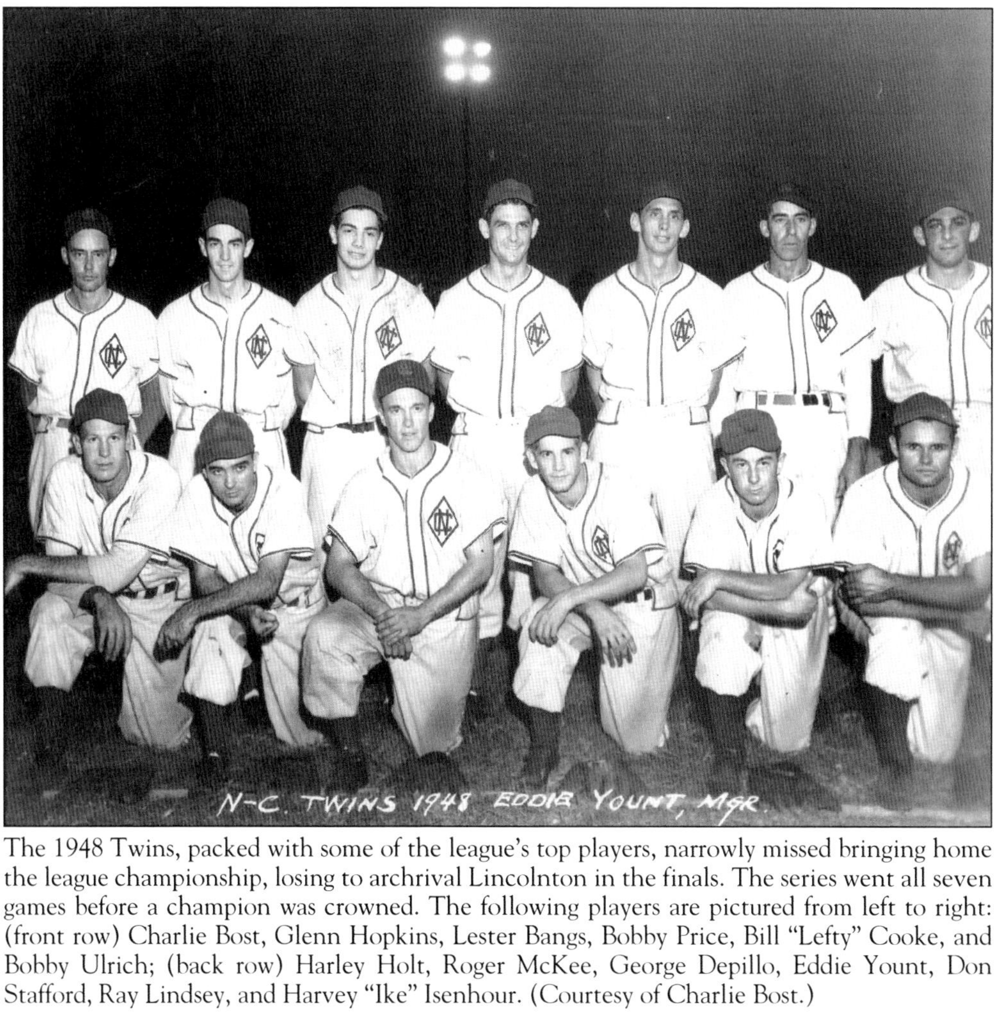

The 1948 Twins, packed with some of the league's top players, narrowly missed bringing home the league championship, losing to archrival Lincolnton in the finals. The series went all seven games before a champion was crowned. The following players are pictured from left to right: (front row) Charlie Bost, Glenn Hopkins, Lester Bangs, Bobby Price, Bill "Lefty" Cooke, and Bobby Ulrich; (back row) Harley Holt, Roger McKee, George Depillo, Eddie Yount, Don Stafford, Ray Lindsey, and Harvey "Ike" Isenhour. (Courtesy of Charlie Bost.)

Earl Holder was the voice of the Newton-Conover Twins for seven seasons. He broadcasted every home game and most of the Twins away games on WNNC radio in Newton. Holder's name quickly became as popular as the players' names. (Courtesy of Jackie Dellinger.)

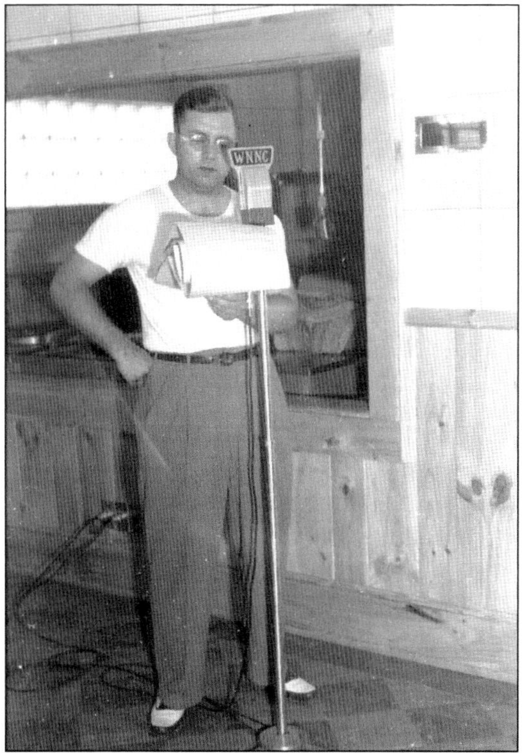

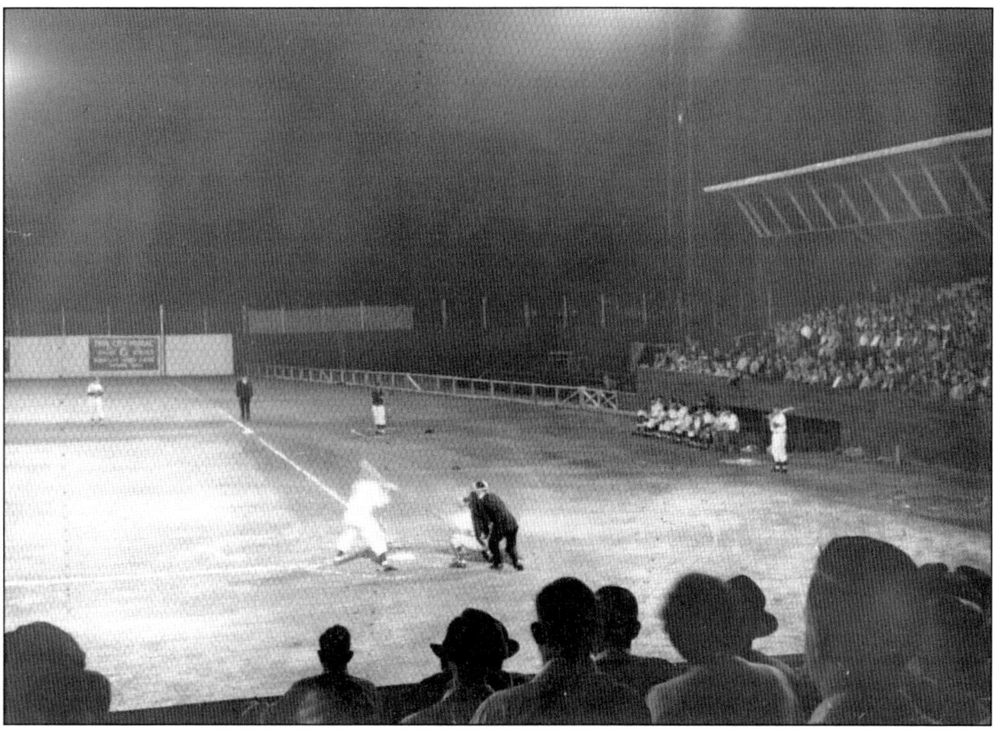

In this rare action shot, Charlie Bost gets ready to take a swing in front of a packed house at Newton's Legion Park. (Courtesy of Charlie Bost.)

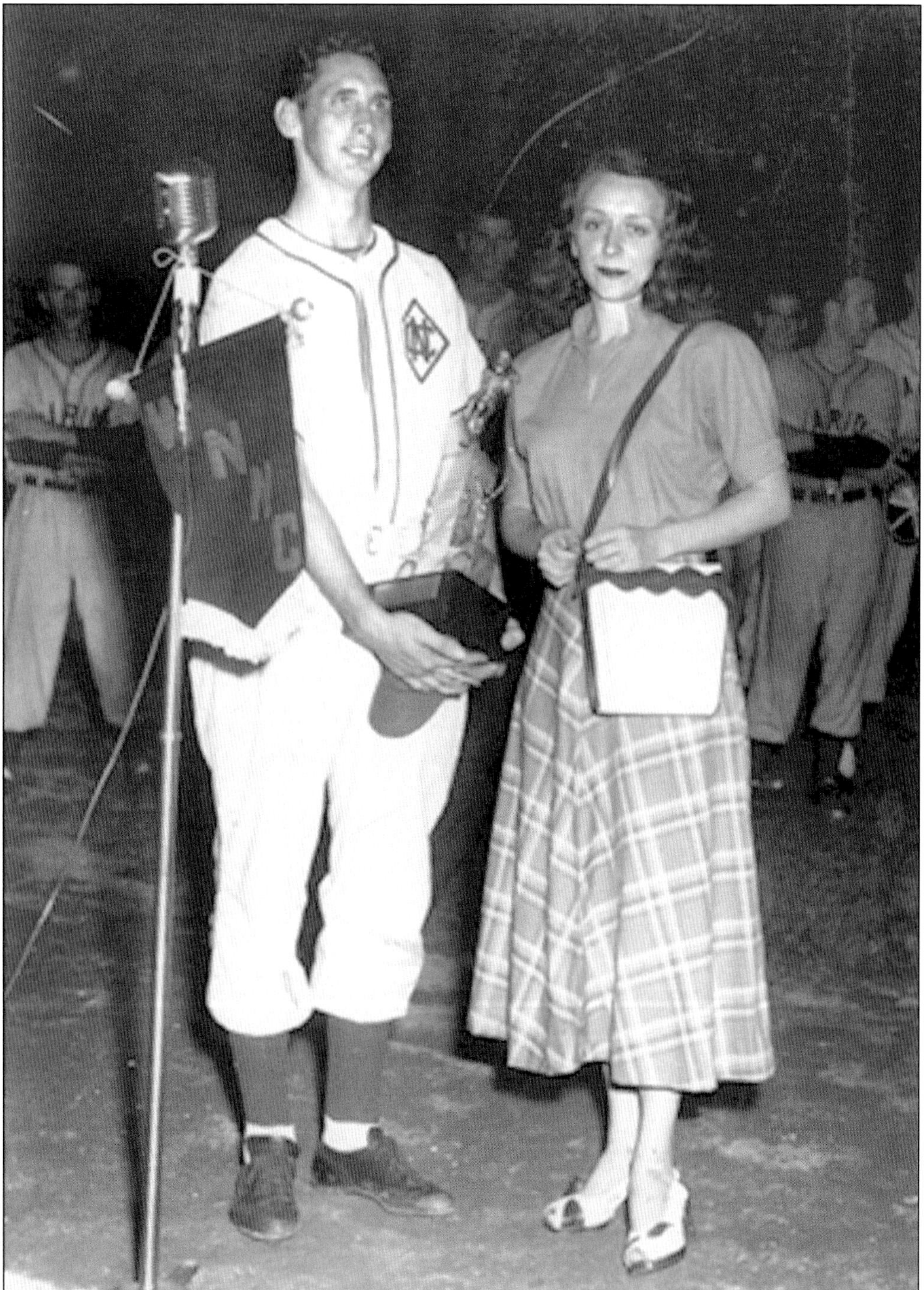

Don Stafford, seen here with his wife, Vivienne, poses with the A.G. Spaulding trophy. Judge Wilson Warlick presented Stafford with the award that honors the best hitting rookie in minor-league baseball. The Twins first baseman had a .390 average, 23 home runs, and 109 RBIs in his award-winning 1948 season. (Courtesy of Don Stafford.)

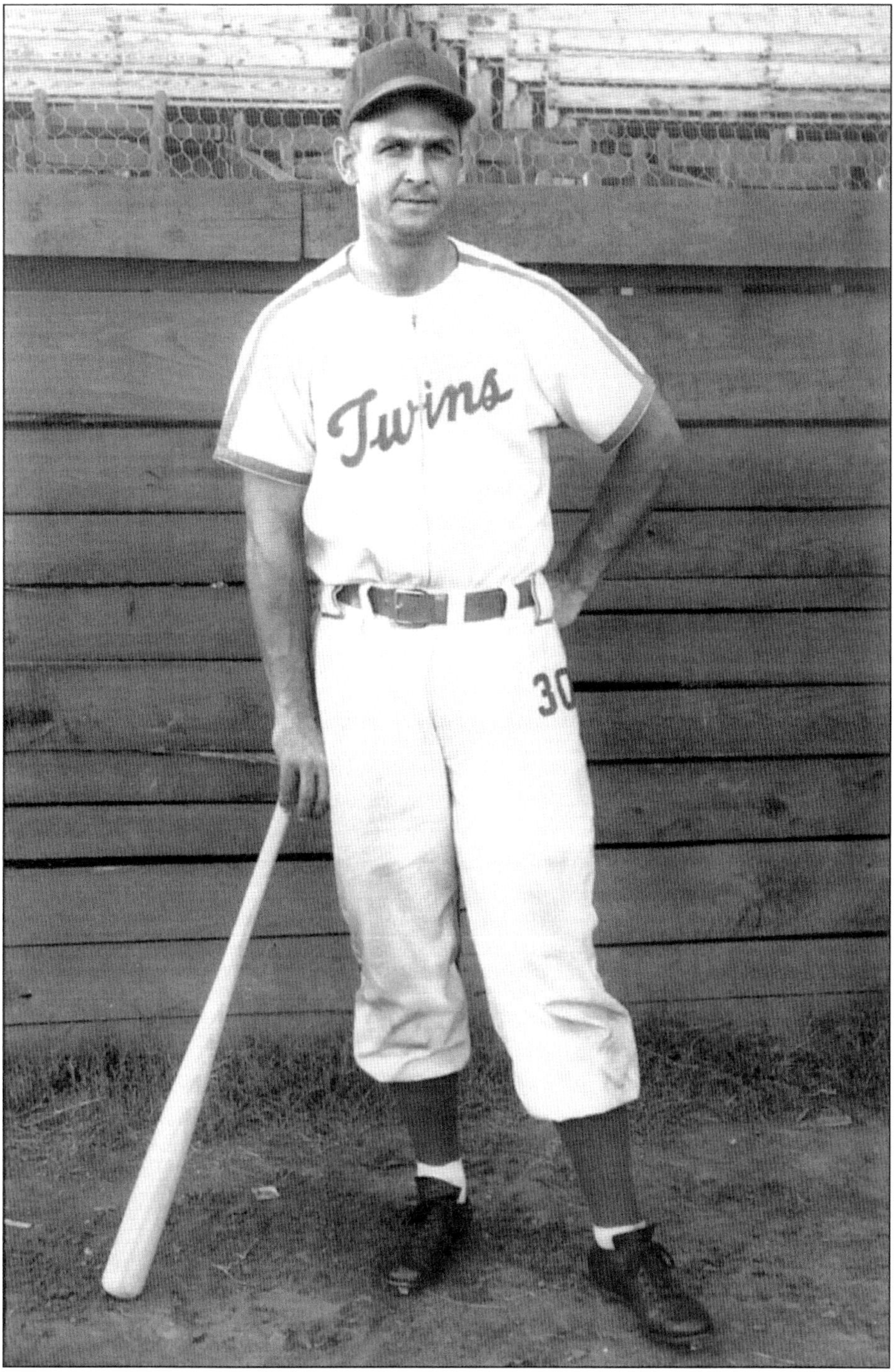

Eddie Yount, one of the Twins' and Western Carolina League's all-time greats, dominated the league in almost every offensive category during the 1948 season. Yount, the team manager and catcher, hit 43 home runs, 140 RBIs, had 169 hits, scored 139 runs, and notched a batting average of .420. He fell just short of Wes Ferrell's league-leading .425 average. (Courtesy of Chris Holaday.)

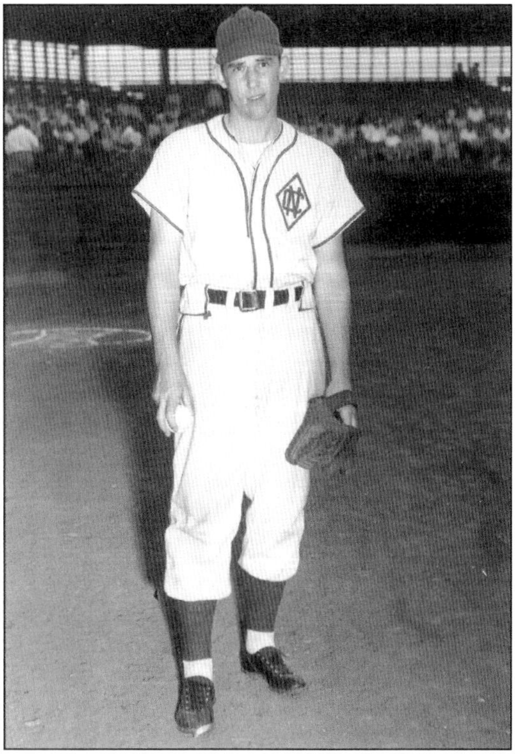

Pictured at left is right-handed hurler Boyce Stone. (Courtesy of Charlie Bost.)

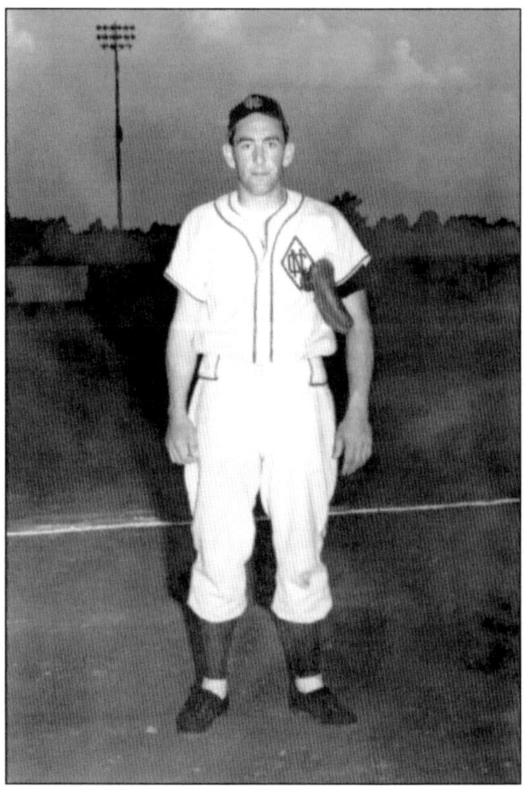

Harvey "Ike" Isenhour, labeled by a local newspaper as a Mooresville "castoff," took advantage of his newfound opportunity with the Newton-Conover Twins. When the Moors released Isenhour, the Twins quickly signed him. The right fielder and catcher showed his appreciation by hitting .320, with 18 home runs, and 81 RBIs. (Courtesy of Charlie Bost.)

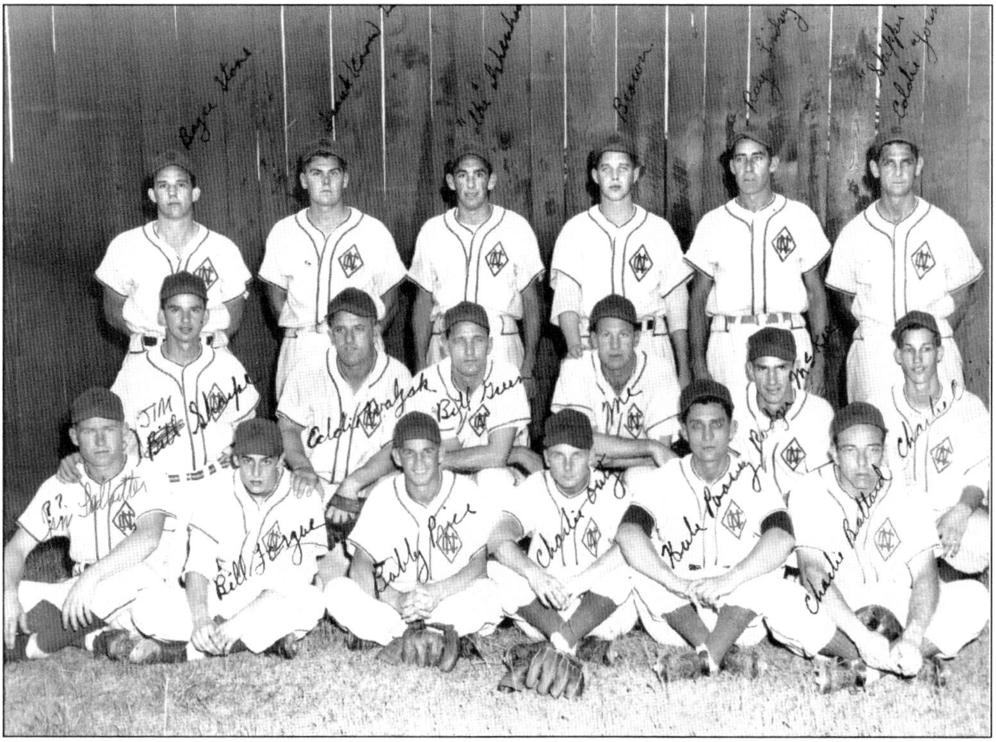

Pitchers Ray Lindsey (above, fifth from left on the back row) and Bill Greene (at right) led the way for the 1949 pennant-winning Twins. Lindsey, one of Newton-Conover's all-time best pitchers, retired after 11 seasons with a record of 154-98, an ERA of 2.97, and an astounding 1,904 strikeouts. Greene had his best season as a Twin that year, going 17-6. (Courtesy of Charlie Bost.)

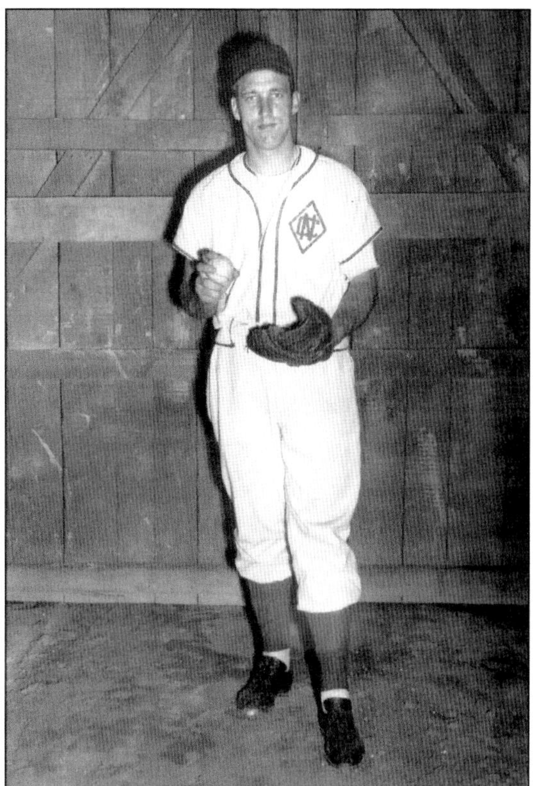

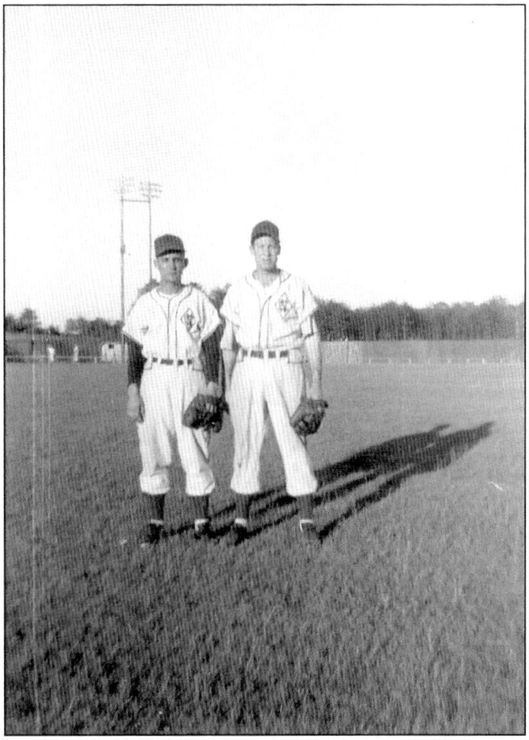

Charlie Bost, seen here with Hugh Poovey (left), covered the gamut of Catawba County baseball; he played for the Lenoir-Rhyne Bears, the Hickory Rebels and Spinners, and the Newton-Conover Twins. (Courtesy of Charlie Bost.)

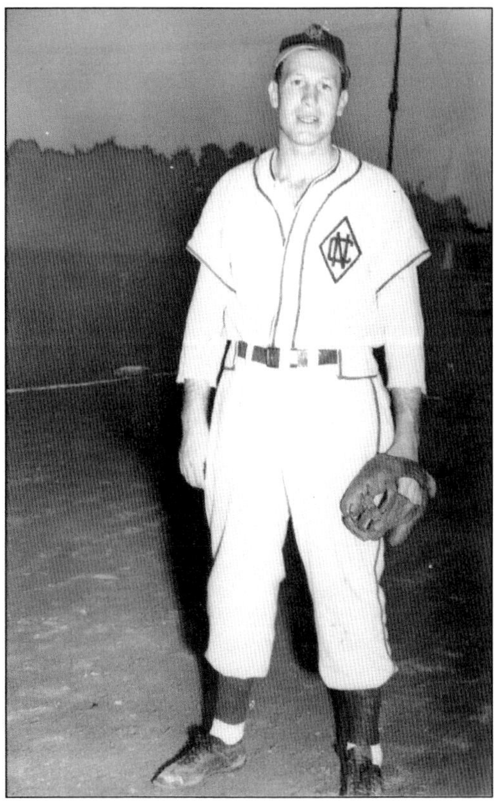

Charlie Bost played four seasons with the Twins and had one of his best years in 1948, when he posted a .322 batting average, 20 home runs, and 76 RBIs. (Courtesy of Charlie Bost.)

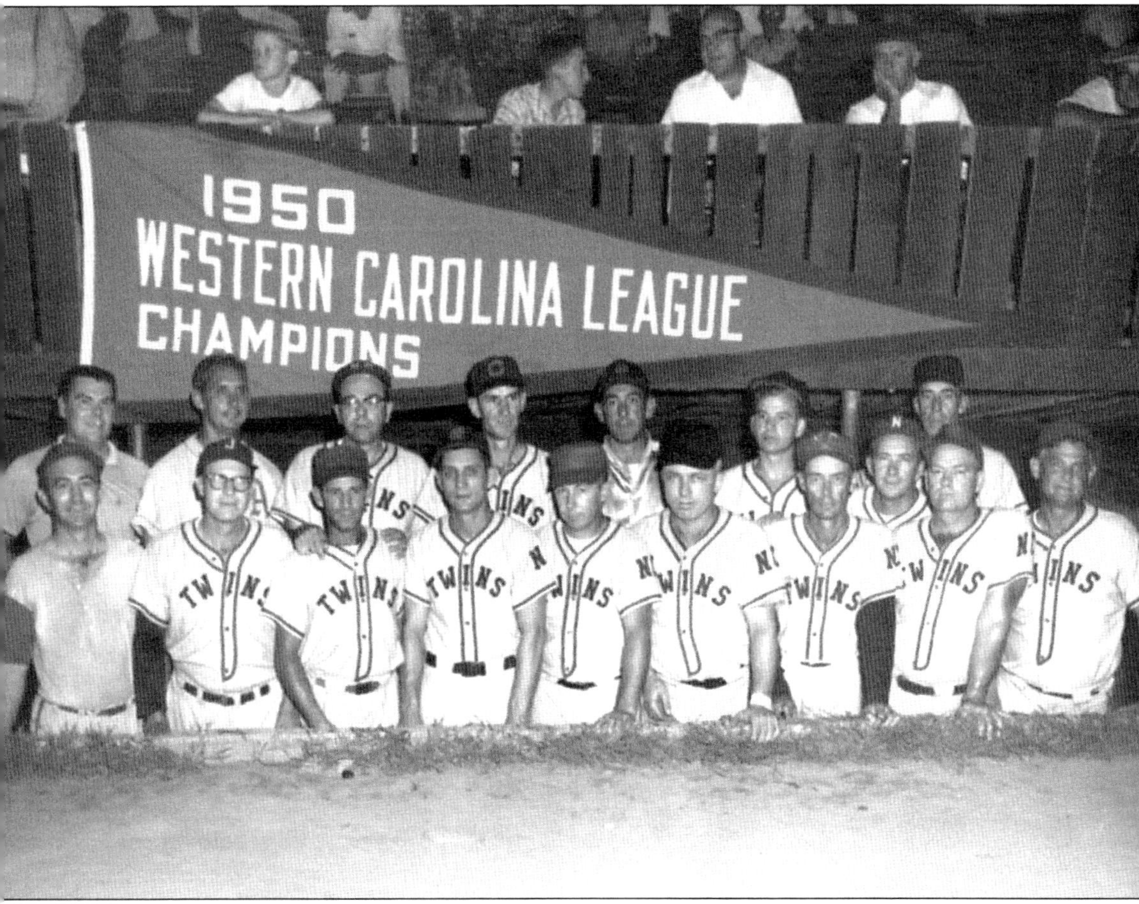

The 1950 Newton-Conover Twins finished with a record of 69-41, winning their second league pennant in a row. George DePillo and Eddie Yount were two of the league's top hitters. (Courtesy of Gary Yount.)

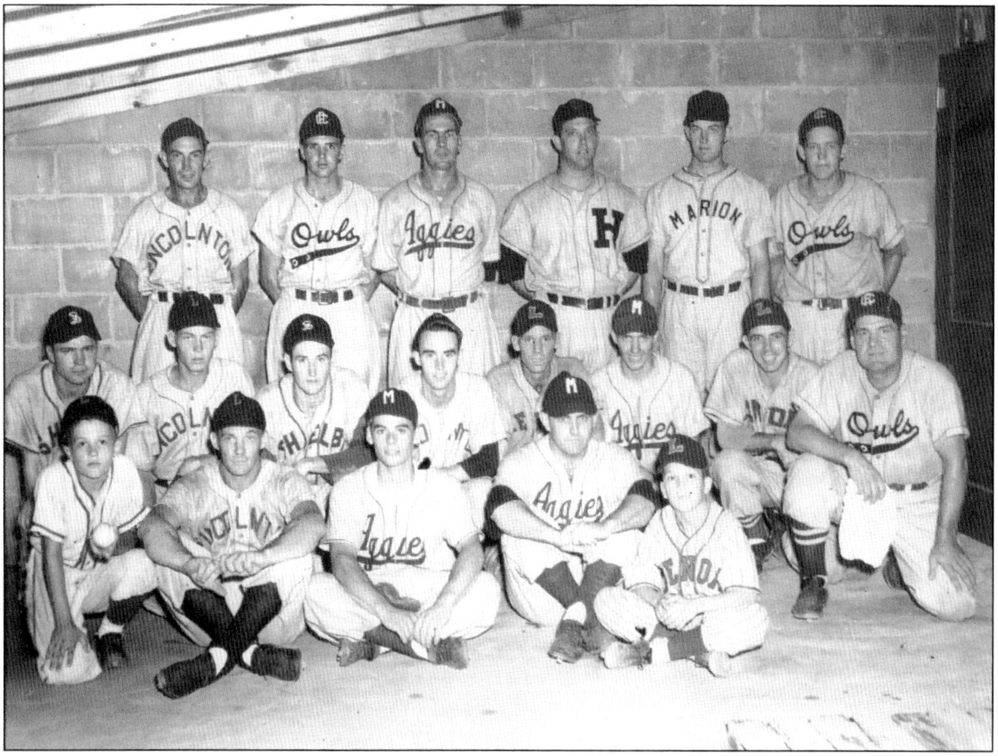

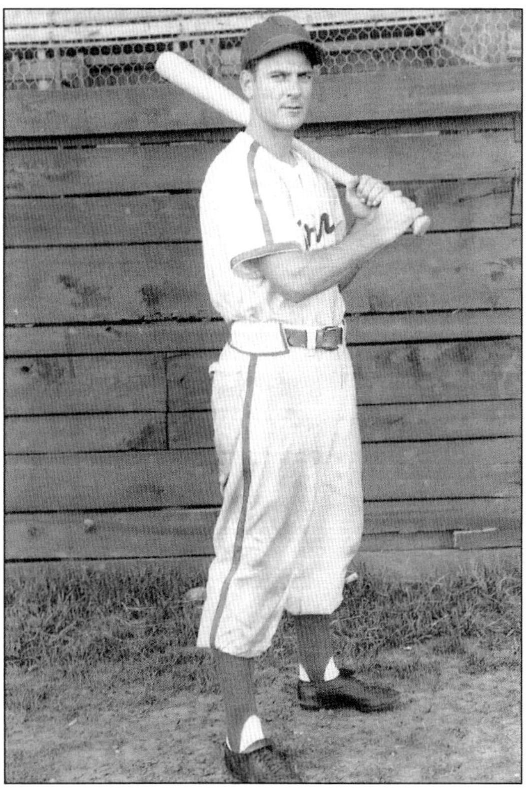

This All-Star team, made up of players from the Western Carolina League, played the League Champion Newton-Conover Twins in an exhibition game in 1950. (Courtesy of Charlie Bost.)

First baseman Joe Plick was one of the top players in the Western Carolina League during the 1950 and 1951 seasons. (Courtesy of Chris Holaday.)

Don Stafford was one of the most dangerous hitters that Catawba County has ever produced. Although Stafford had two brilliant seasons with the Twins, one of his best came in a Salisbury Pirates uniform. In 1952, he won the John A. "Bud" Hillerich Silver Bat for being the top hitter in minor league baseball. (Courtesy of Hickory Crawdads.)

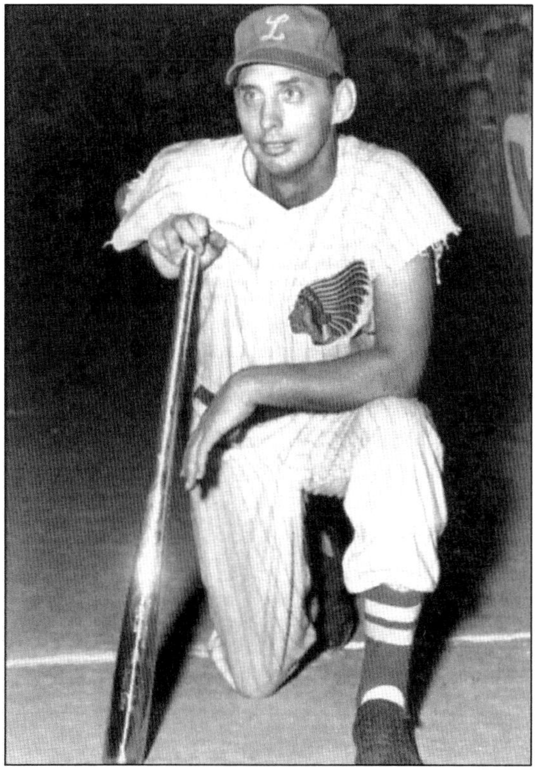

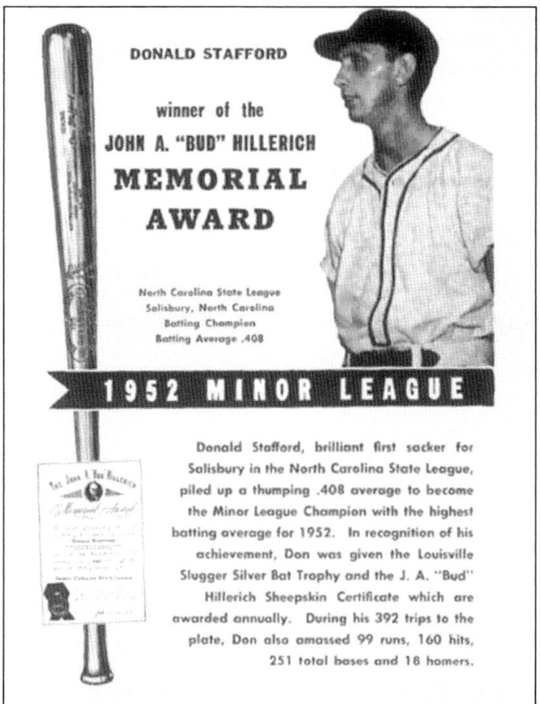

Reprinted from the *1953 Hillerich & Bradsby Famous Slugger Yearbook.*

Former Morganton Aggies and Hickory Rebels pitcher Dick Stoll remembered being asked how you pitch to Stafford; his response was, "You throw the ball and run as fast as you can to back up third base hoping you can hold him to a double." (Courtesy of Hickory Crawdads.)

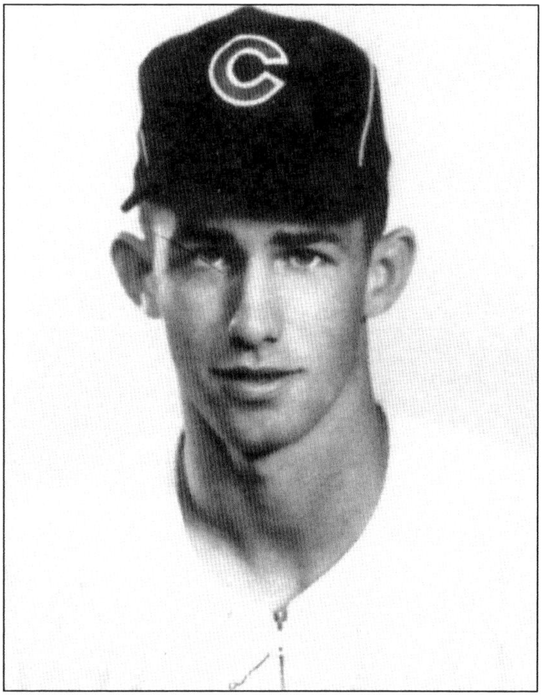

Steve Bolick spent two seasons in the Chicago Cubs organization before suiting up as a Newton-Conover Twin in 1961.

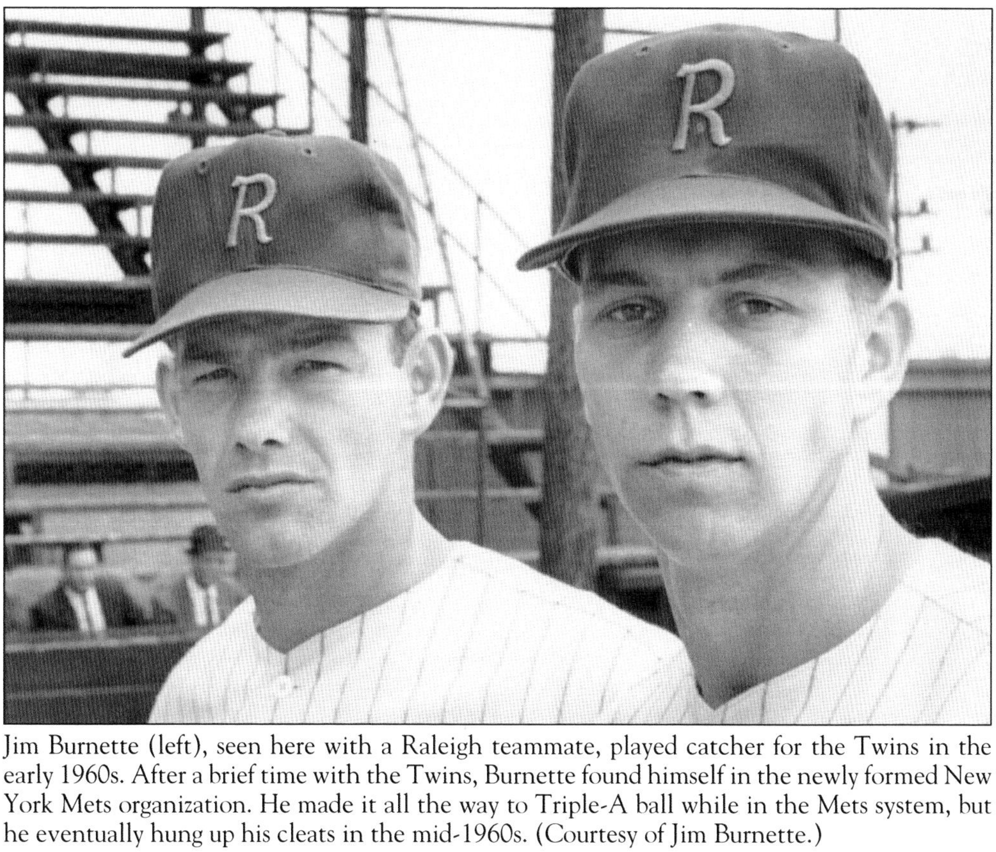

Jim Burnette (left), seen here with a Raleigh teammate, played catcher for the Twins in the early 1960s. After a brief time with the Twins, Burnette found himself in the newly formed New York Mets organization. He made it all the way to Triple-A ball while in the Mets system, but he eventually hung up his cleats in the mid-1960s. (Courtesy of Jim Burnette.)

Burnette participated in the Mets 1962 spring training in St. Petersburg, Florida. He had the opportunity to play with the likes of Gil Hodges and Don Zimmer and to be managed by names such as Casey Stengel and Rogers Hornsby. (Courtesy of Jim Burnette.)

NEW YORK NATIONAL LEAGUE BASEBALL CLUB
OPERATED BY
METROPOLITAN BASEBALL CLUB INC.

EXECUTIVE OFFICES
680 FIFTH AVENUE
NEW YORK 19, N. Y.
TEL: LT 1-2300

January 29, 1962

Mr. James Burnette
1016 N. Ashe Avenue
Newton, North Carolina

Dear James:

It gives me a great deal of pleasure to inform you that Casey Stnegel has requested that we invite you to our major league Spring Training Camp in St. Petersburg, Florida.

However, before you will be able to report it will be necessary for you to sign your 1962 contract with Syracuse Club. You will soon be receiving this from Mr. Bill Bergesch our Farm Director.

Pitchers and Catchers are to report to St. Petersburg, Florida on February 18th, ready for the first workout on Monday, Feb. 19th. It will be required that you be housed at the Colonial Inn, St. Petersburg Beach, Florida. It will not be permissable for your wife, if any, to accompany you to the camp during major league Spring Training season.

I am assuming that you will have no difficulty in coming to terms on your Syracuse contract and therefore, would suggest that you start making necessary transportation arrangements for arrival at St. Petersburg, Florida. You should buy your own ticket and will be reimbursed upon arrival. You can fly either to the Tampa airport or St. Petersburg airport, then take a cab from the airport to the Colonial Inn. A bulletin is enclosed which outlines the information I have given in this letter.

Please let me know by return mail, if you will be able to accept this invitation.

Sincerely,

John J. Murphy
Administrative Assistant

JJM:t
Enc.

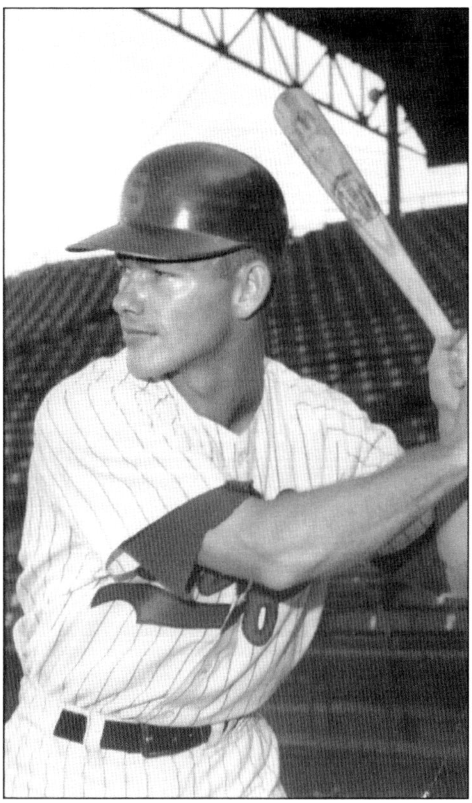

Burnette poses for a picture while in Syracuse. (Courtesy of Jim Burnette.)

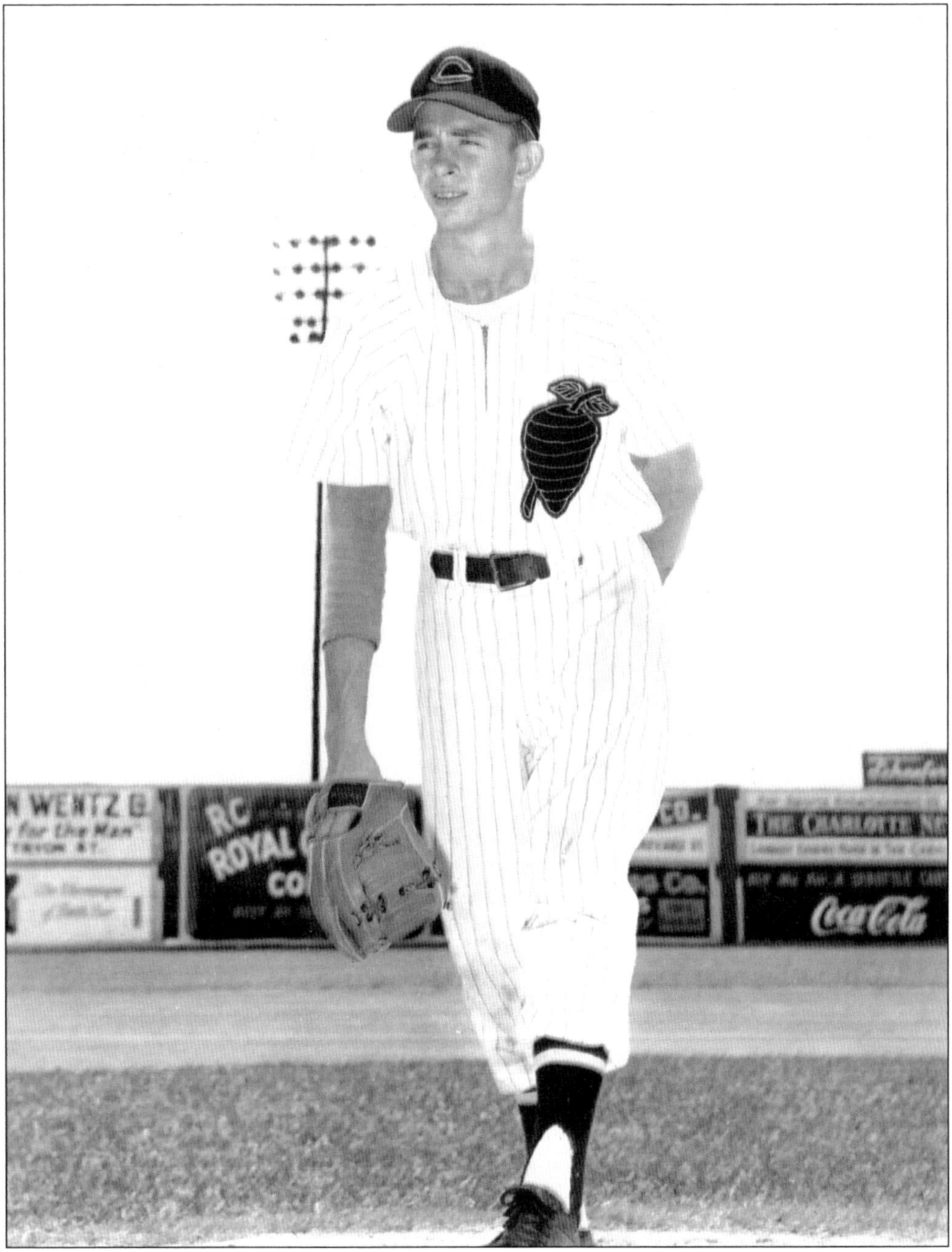

John "Hom" Isaac, seen here in his Charlotte Hornets uniform, played two seasons with the Newton-Conover Twins. His best season in Newton came in 1960 when the manager and pitcher went 16-9 and posted an incredible 1.60 ERA. Isaac joined Jim Burnette as the only two Twins to be selected to the All-Star team that season. (Courtesy of John Isaac.)

FOUR

Bears

[T]he Lenoir-Rhyne team came charging out of the dugout like mountain bears charging forth from their haunts.
—Raleigh News and Observer

Baseball was the first intercollegiate sport to begin at the Lutheran college known then as Lenoir College. There was a great deal of debate over whether it was advisable to bring attention to sports like at many larger colleges. Finally on January 30, 1903, the faculty voted to offer a scholarship for a pitcher and a catcher. The school newspaper reported that on March 17, 1903, Catawba College (of Newton) and Lenoir College "crossed bats at the Lenoir College athletic park." So began a tradition that has produced many excellent teams, players, and coaches for the area.

The 1924 baseball team is responsible for the nickname that the school's athletic teams still carry. Covering their April 9 game at Atlantic Christian College in Wilson, a *Raleigh News and Observer* sportswriter declared that "after a slow start, the Lenoir-Rhyne team came charging out of the dugout like mountain bears charging forth from their haunts in the Western North Carolina mountains."

During most of the Lenoir-Rhyne baseball history, the sport has remained a minor one. Few scholarships were ever made available, and players were generally football players who were recruited in part because they could play both sports. Nevertheless, Lenoir-Rhyne has had many fine players and competitive teams, many of which will be featured in the following pages.

One of the most successful coaches in college history was a former Bear player, Troy Washam. Washam's teams won 70 and lost 23 and garnered several Conference Championships. Over time, Washam also established himself as a great American Legion and high school baseball coach and became a powerful influence in the lives of many young men. In 2004, he was selected as a member of the Catawba County Sports Hall of Fame.

In 1988, John Hamilton took over the Lenoir-Rhyne baseball program and began to shape it into a frontline sport by adding games and a fall schedule. His assistant Frank Pait assumed the helm in 1997 and continued the course that Hamilton had set. Pait's teams have won 30 or more games three times, and he began the 2004 season as the winningest coach in school history with 181 wins. Today's Bears play an exciting brand of baseball and the program seems to be headed for continued success.

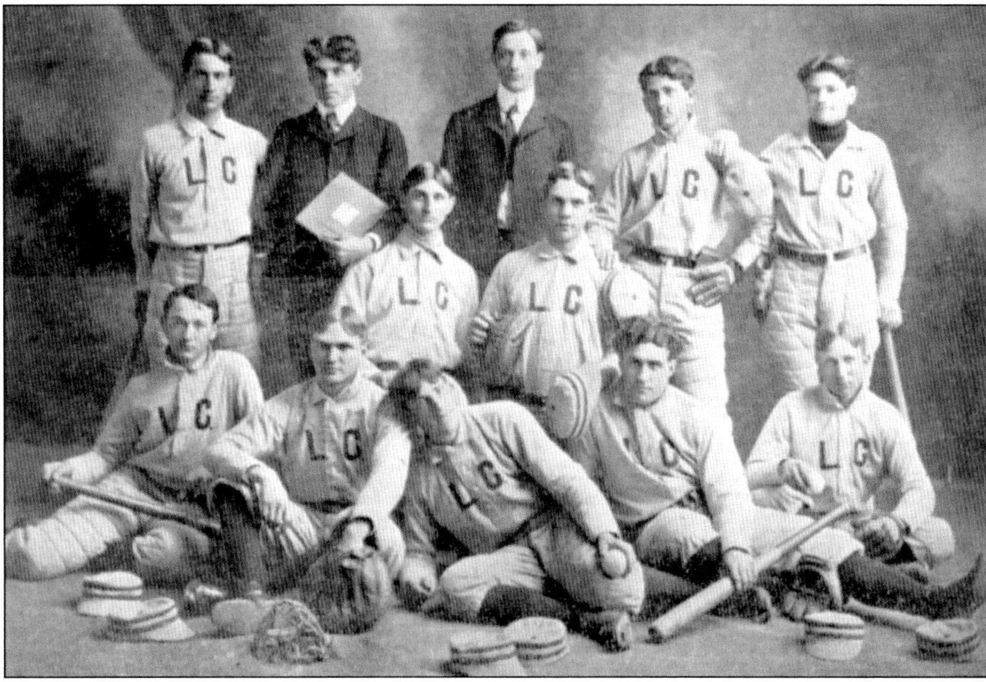

The 1903 Lenoir College baseball team was the first athletic team in the school's history. (Courtesy of Lenoir-Rhyne College.)

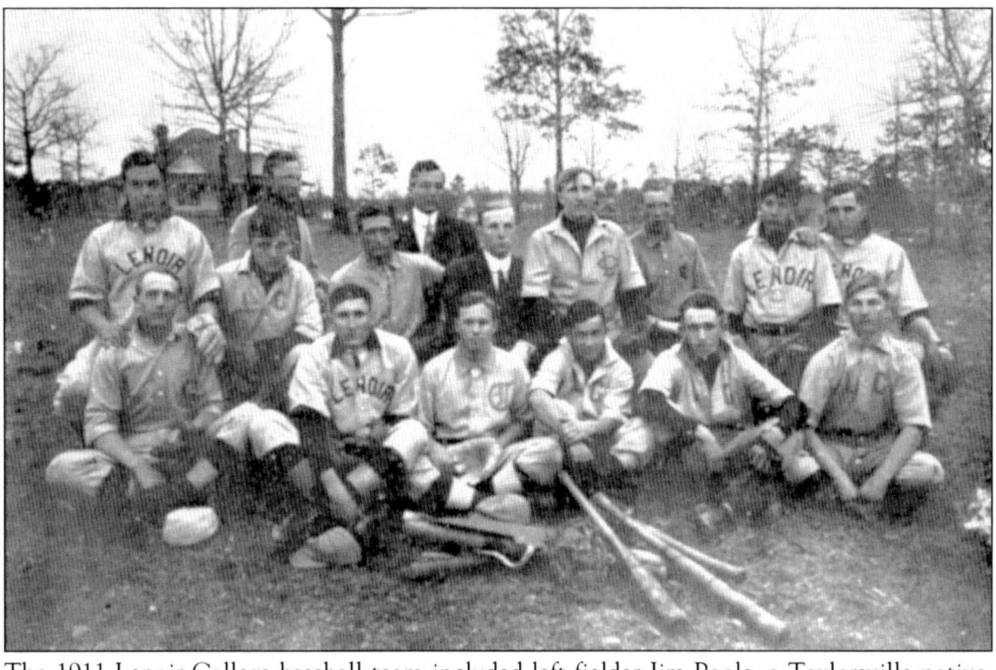

The 1911 Lenoir College baseball team included left-fielder Jim Poole, a Taylorsville native, who later played three seasons for Connie Mack's Philadelphia Athletics. Poole had a major-league career average of .288 with 13 home runs. He was a star hitter for the outlaw Mooresville Moors while in his mid-40s. Poole played and managed Class D minor-league teams into his early 50s. (Courtesy of Lenoir-Rhyne College.)

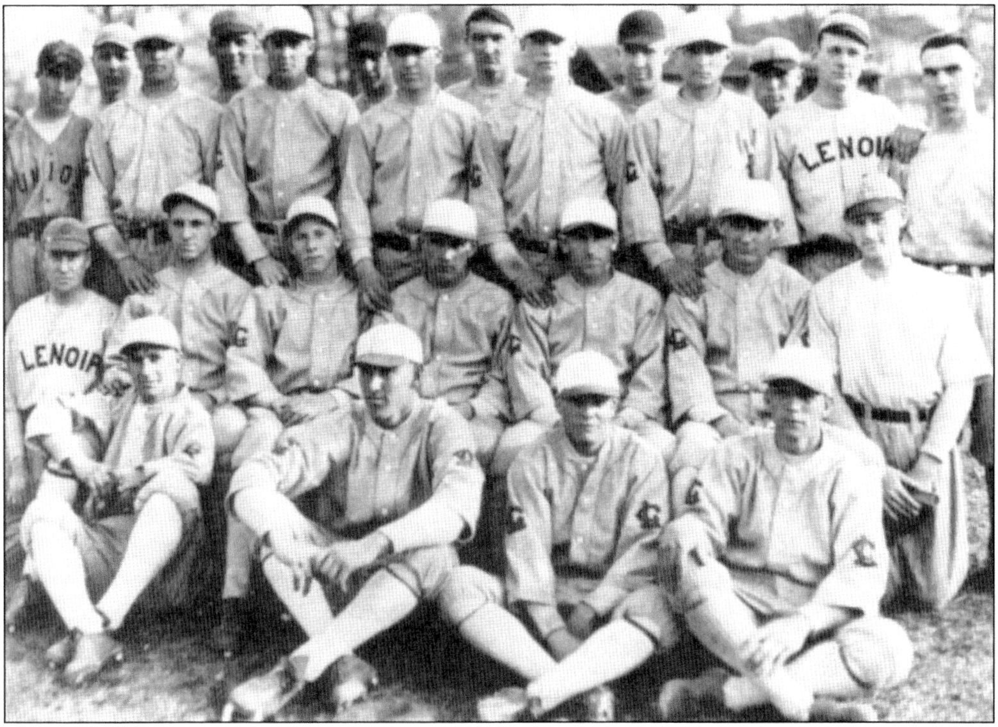

The 1924 team was considered to be the finest in school history. They boasted a 12-2 record with wins over University of North Carolina, University of South Carolina, and Duke. This team, which inspired the school's athletic nickname, was led by Paul Deaton, Toby Hawn, and Baxter Moose. (Courtesy of Lenoir-Rhyne College.)

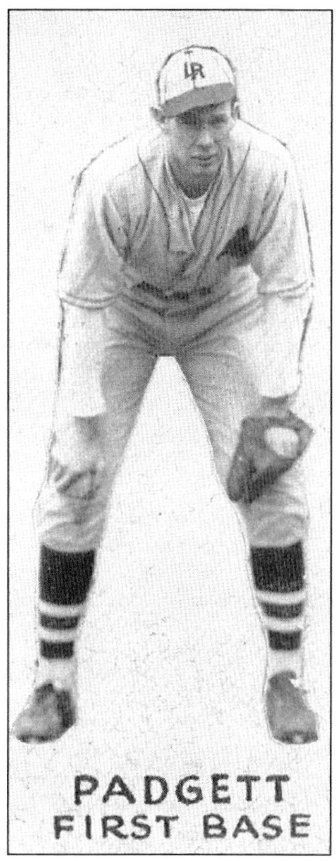

Although Padgett only played for one season, Pat Shores rated Don Padgett as one of his best all-time players. Padgett left to play professional baseball and spent eight seasons with four major-league teams: the Cardinals, Dodgers, Braves, and Phillies. He ended his career, which was interrupted by World War II, with 37 home runs and a career .288 average. (Courtesy of Lenoir-Rhyne College.)

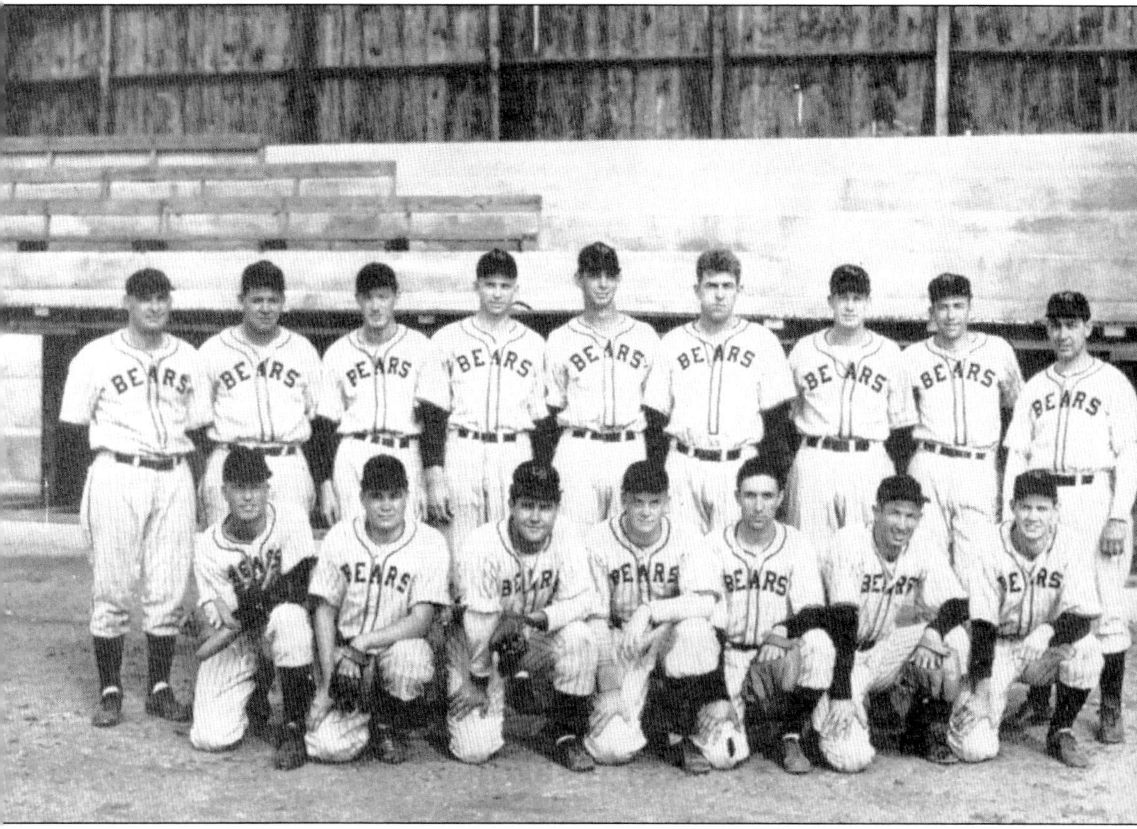

After World War II, a full schedule of baseball returned to Lenoir-Rhyne in 1946. This gifted group of athletes won the Conference Championship for Coach Shore Neal with a 12-3 record. (Courtesy of Lenoir-Rhyne College.)

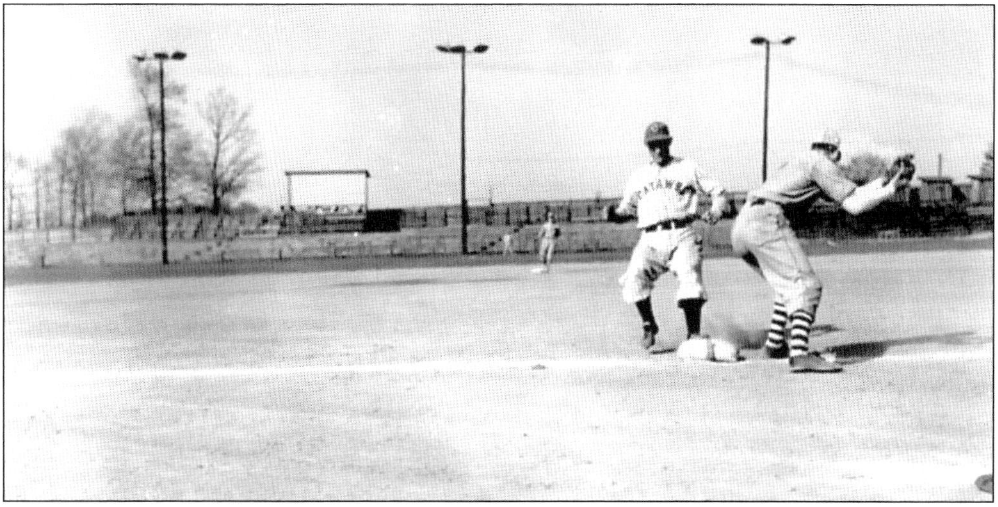

These are action shots from this 1930s game with Catawba. Even after the school left its Newton location, it remained the biggest rival for Bear teams. (Courtesy of Catawba County Historical Museum.)

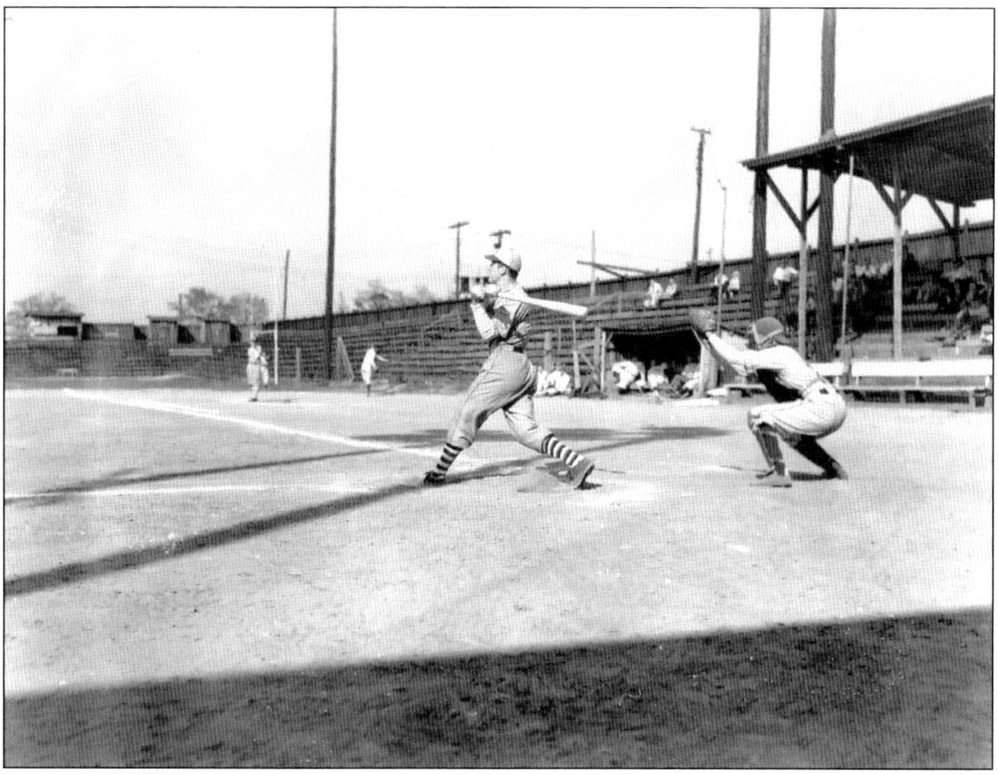

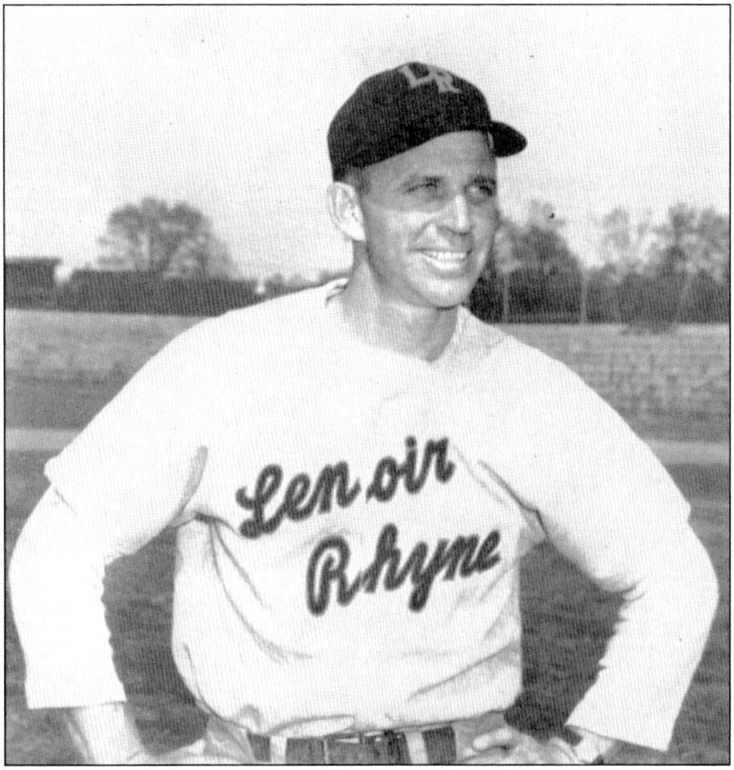

Troy Washam, a 2004 Catawba County Sports Hall of Fame inductee, is seen in this 1952 photo. At 70-23, he holds the best winning percentage of all Lenoir-Rhyne baseball coaches. He also coached the 1948 Hickory American Legion team to the national semi-finals. A member of the American Legion Hall of Fame, he won nine Conference Championships at Hickory High School. The current Hickory High School baseball field bears his name. (Courtesy of Lenoir-Rhyne College.)

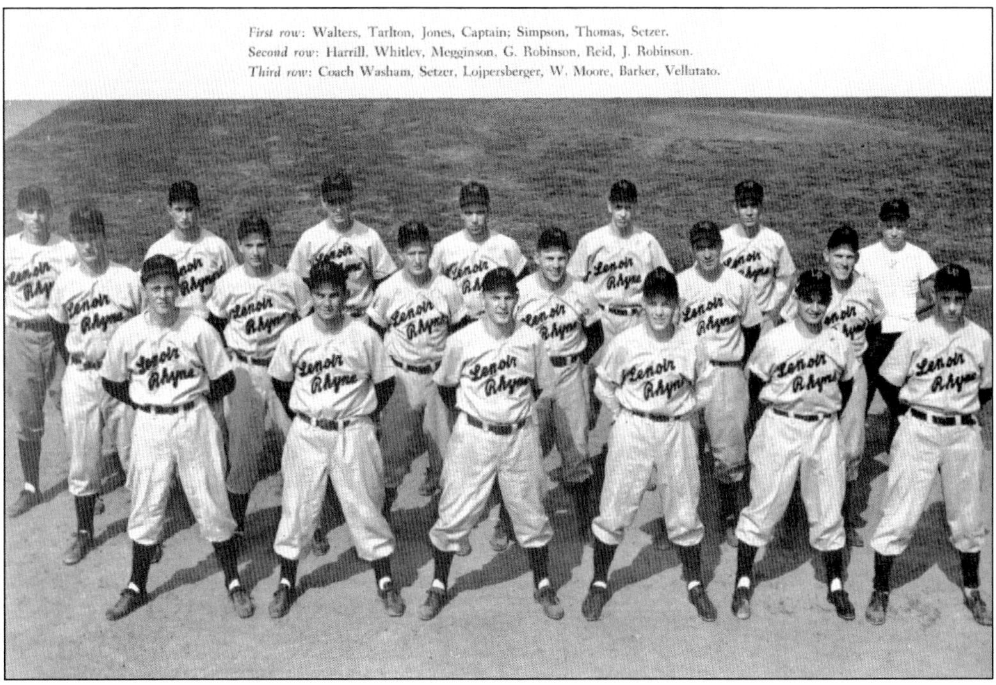

The 1952 squad was one of Coach Washam's best. With a record of 16-2, they won the conference with a team that featured captain Archie Simpson, Massachusetts natives the Robinson brothers, and local star Giles Setzer. (Courtesy of Lenoir-Rhyne College.)

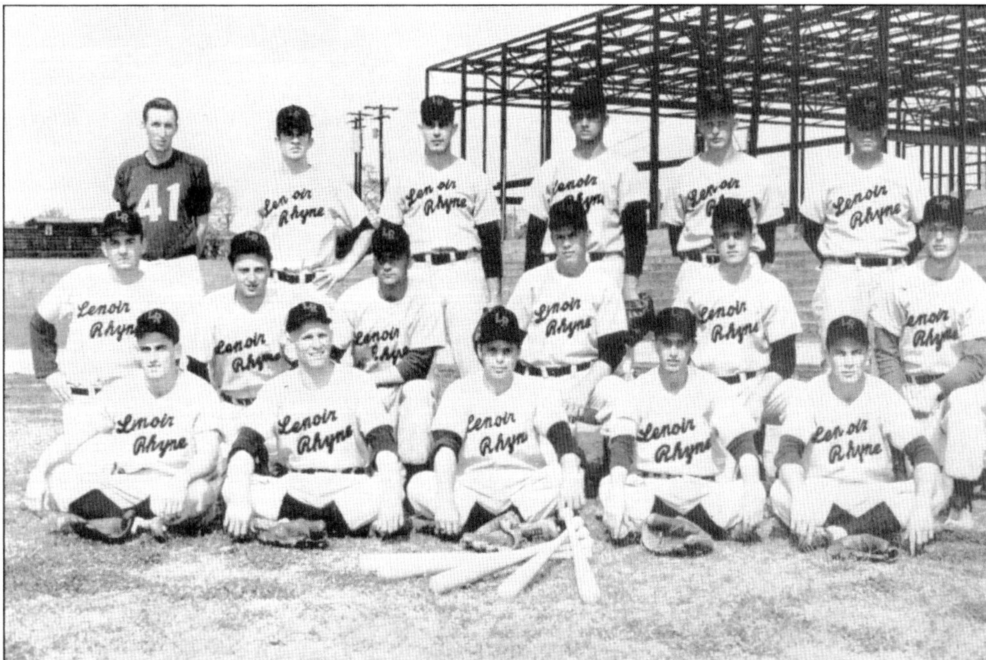

Front row: Buff, Cornwell, Kimmell, Peeler, Glover. *Second row:* Lovingood, Barkley, Carswell. Fox, Brawley, Johnson. *Third row:* Sifford, *Manager*, Baird, Coulter, Weber, James, Erwin.

The 1956 team finished with a record of 13-9 under Coach Mac Erwin. The steel structure of Shuford Memorial Gymnasium rises in the background. (Courtesy of Lenoir-Rhyne College.)

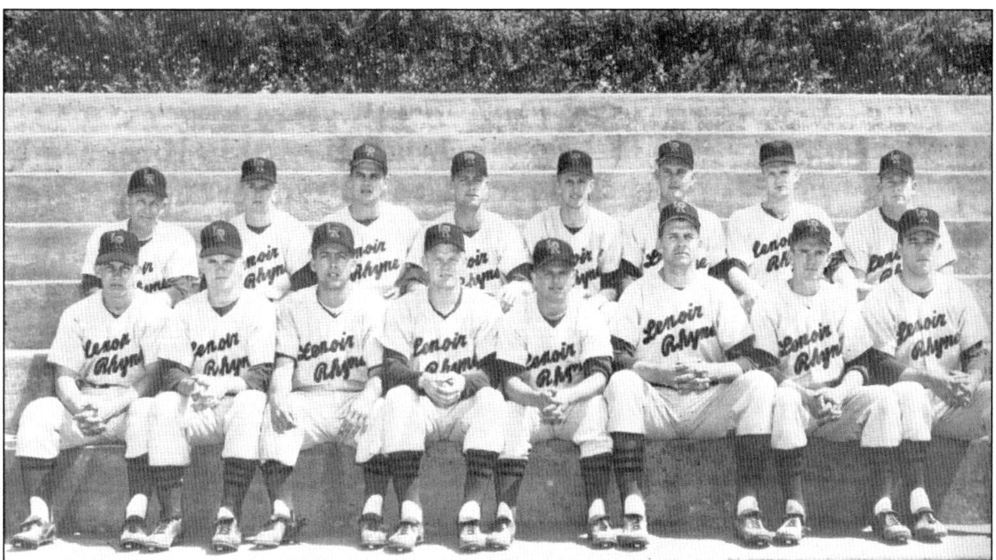

Captained by shortstop Danny Thompson, the 1962 team with a record of 16-3 featured the power hitting of David Dale, Jim Kilby, and one of Lenoir-Rhyne's most successful pitchers, Gary Hinkle. (Courtesy of Lenoir-Rhyne College.)

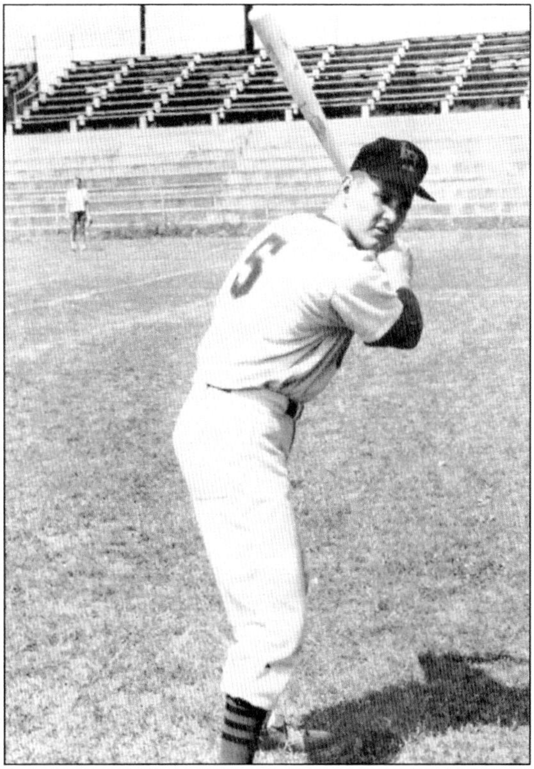

Jim Kilby, an excellent all-around athlete, helped power the Bears to their successful 1962 season. (Courtesy of Lenoir-Rhyne College.)

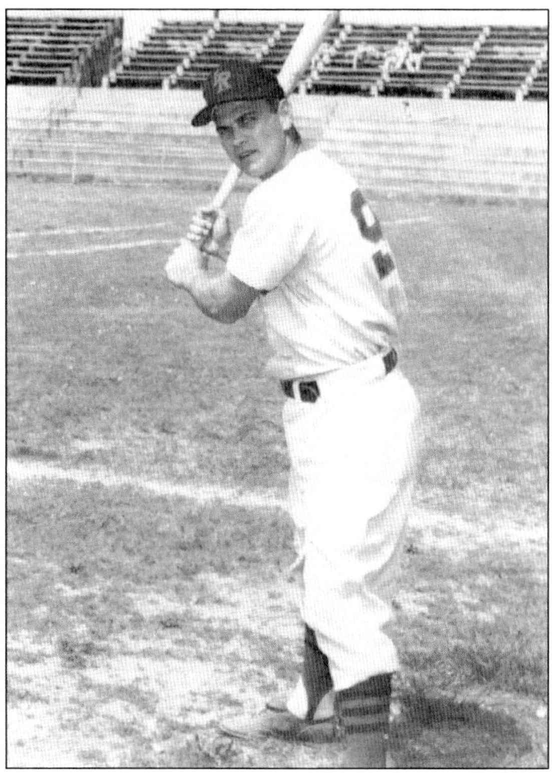

David Dale, a member of the Longview family associated with the Hickory Spinners, was a leading hitter for the Bears of the early 1960s. (Courtesy of Lenoir-Rhyne College.)

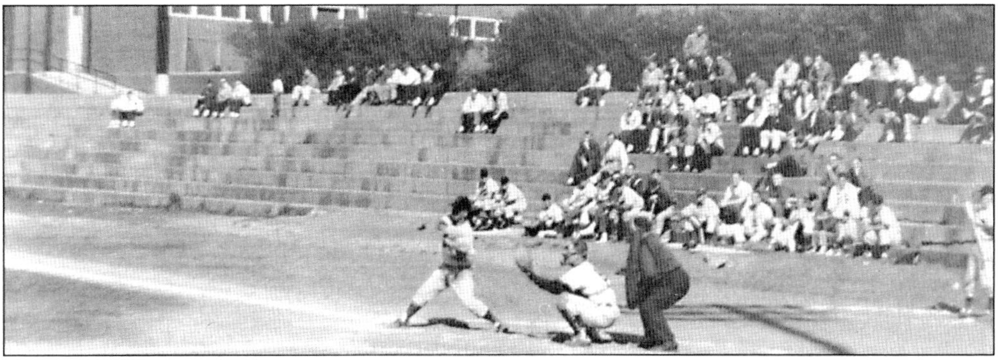

This image features the Catawba game of 1962, an important 5-4 win for Coach Odell Moose's Bears. (Courtesy of Lenoir-Rhyne College.)

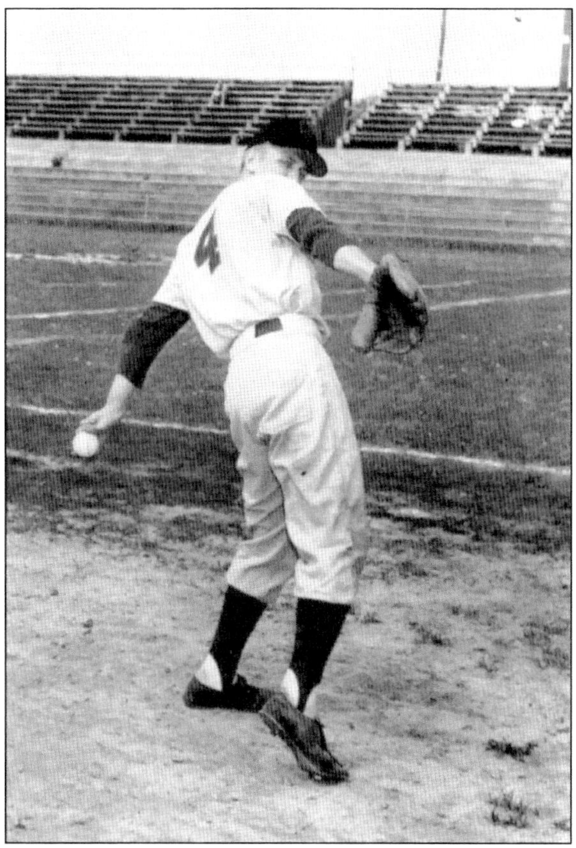

Gary Hinkle is pictured at right. His 8-0 record as a pitcher in 1961 is still the benchmark for the school. (Courtesy of Lenoir-Rhyne College.)

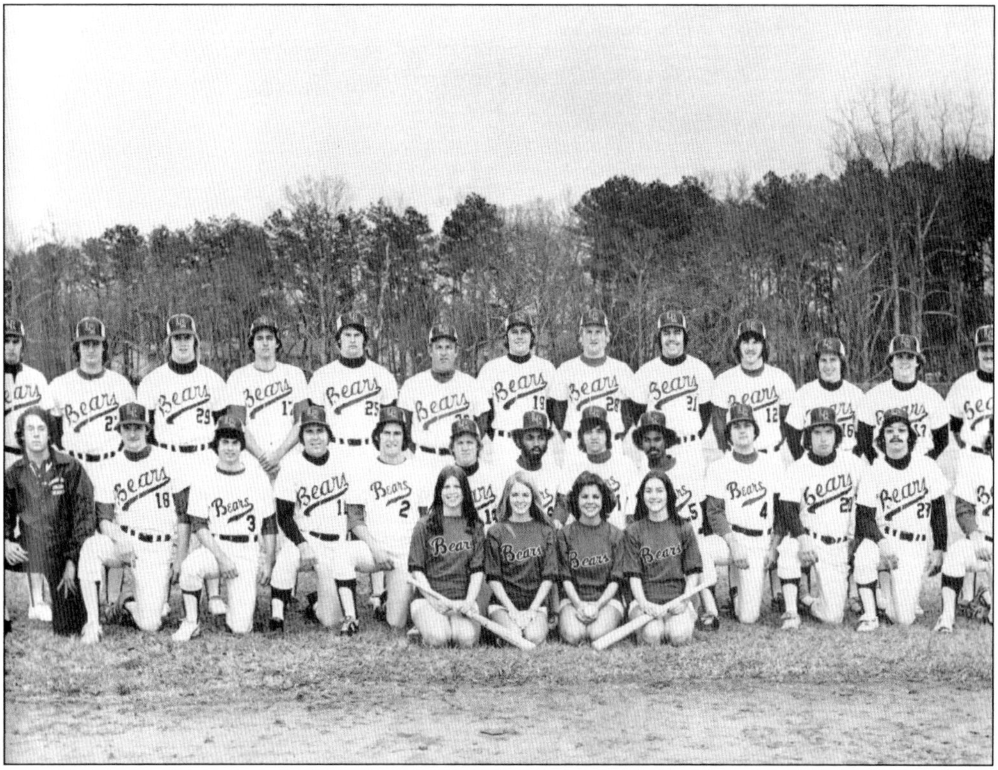

Coach Curtis Threatt led the 1976 team to a 12-13 record. The bat girls were a popular addition to the teams of the 1970s. (Courtesy of Lenoir-Rhyne College.)

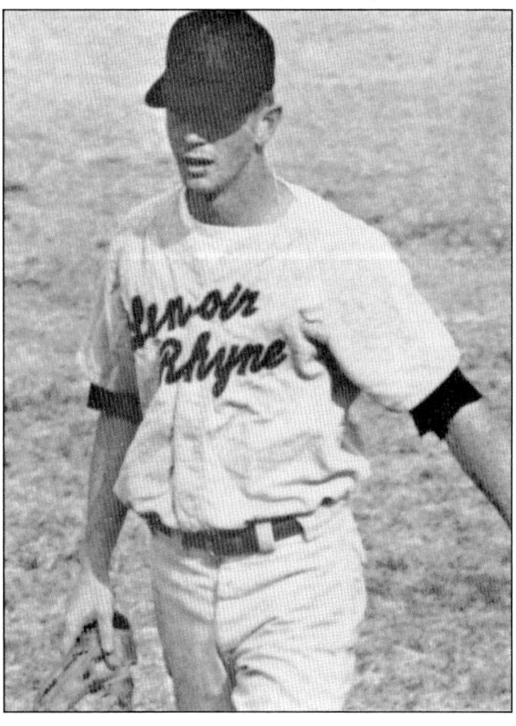

Also an outstanding football player, Kelly Rudisill was the center fielder and leading hitter for the 1969 team. (Courtesy of Lenoir-Rhyne College.)

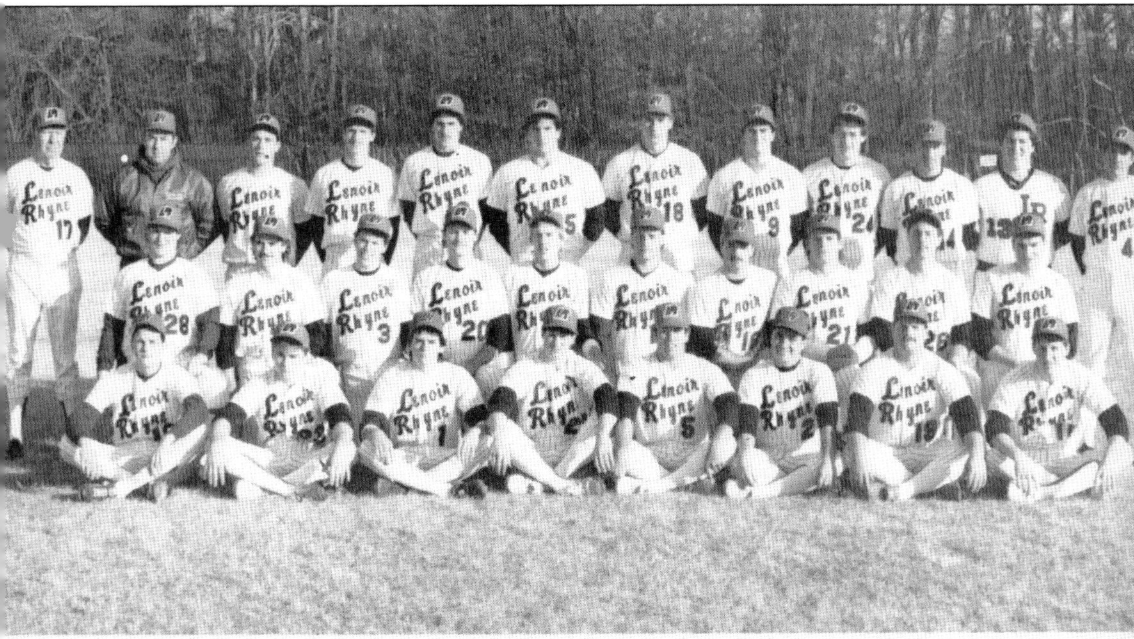

row: Bill Johnson, Doug Hayes, Jeff Cox, Bryan Boyson, Eddie Hickman, Jeff Thompson, Mike Wheless, Carl Hearn. Second row: H
n, Keith Beam, Bill Volk, Tommy Gilliam, David Fox, James Ham, Bobby Hannon, Neil Kivett, Roy Albright, Kirk Palmer. Back
ant Coach Charlie Bowles, Coach P.D. Fowler, Tim Bader, Rick Gragg, Tommy Price, Carl Tillitson, Steve Richter, Scott Ran
on Sellers, Benny Harris, Keith Kazanjian, Head Coach Danny Thompson.

The 1985 team broke the streak of 12 straight losing seasons for the Bears. The squad finished 20-14 for longtime Recreation Director Danny Thompson. The assistants included veteran recreation coach P.D. Fowler and former major-leaguer and Hickory Rebels manager Charlie Bowles. (Courtesy of Lenoir-Rhyne College.)

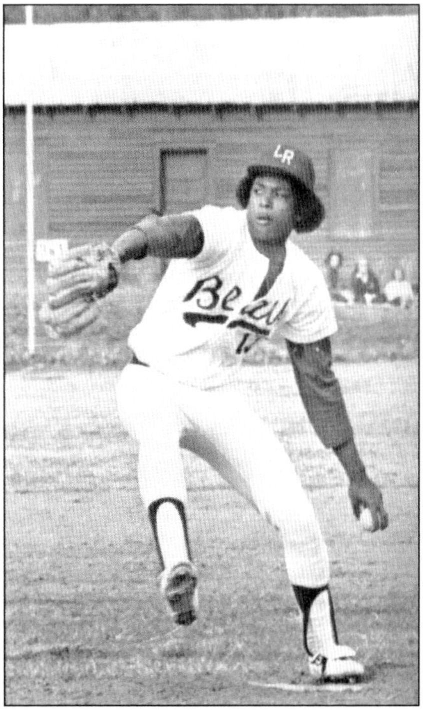

Danny Browner shows the form that made him a top pitcher for Lenoir-Rhyne in the mid-1970s. Notice the barn that stood behind the outfield fence at the current college field. (Courtesy of Lenoir-Rhyne College.)

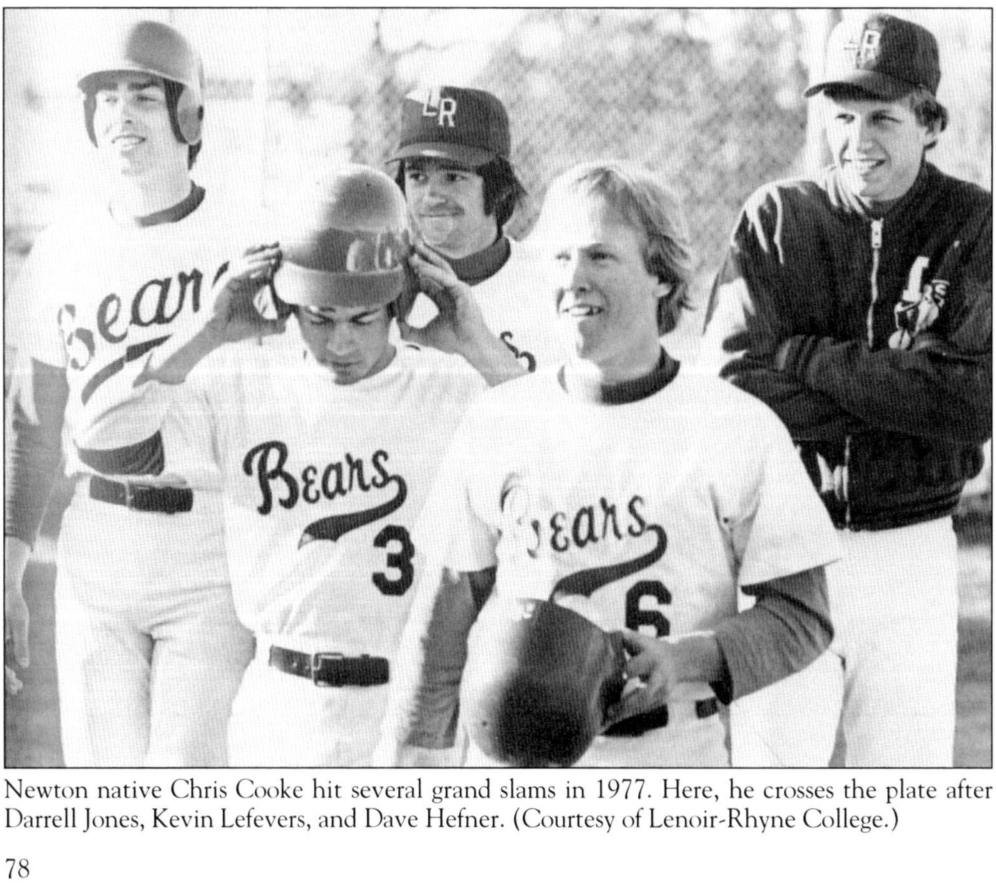

Newton native Chris Cooke hit several grand slams in 1977. Here, he crosses the plate after Darrell Jones, Kevin Lefevers, and Dave Hefner. (Courtesy of Lenoir-Rhyne College.)

Catcher Joel Fender shows the swing that set the single-season batting record of .464 in 1978. (Courtesy of Lenoir-Rhyne College.)

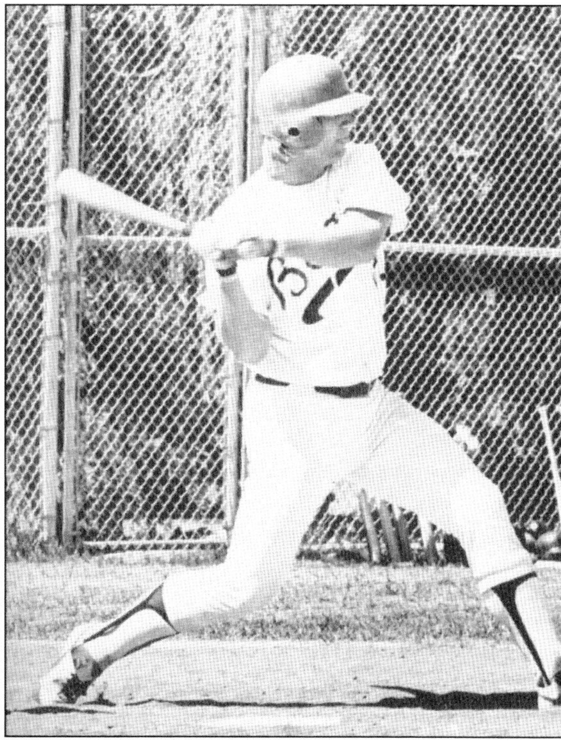

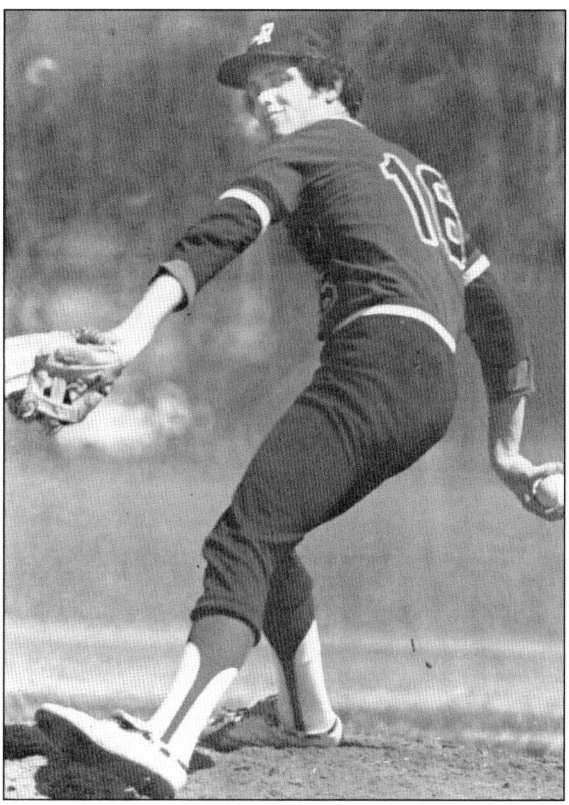

Benji Rowe delivers a fastball for Bill Alton's 1978 team. (Courtesy of Lenoir-Rhyne College.)

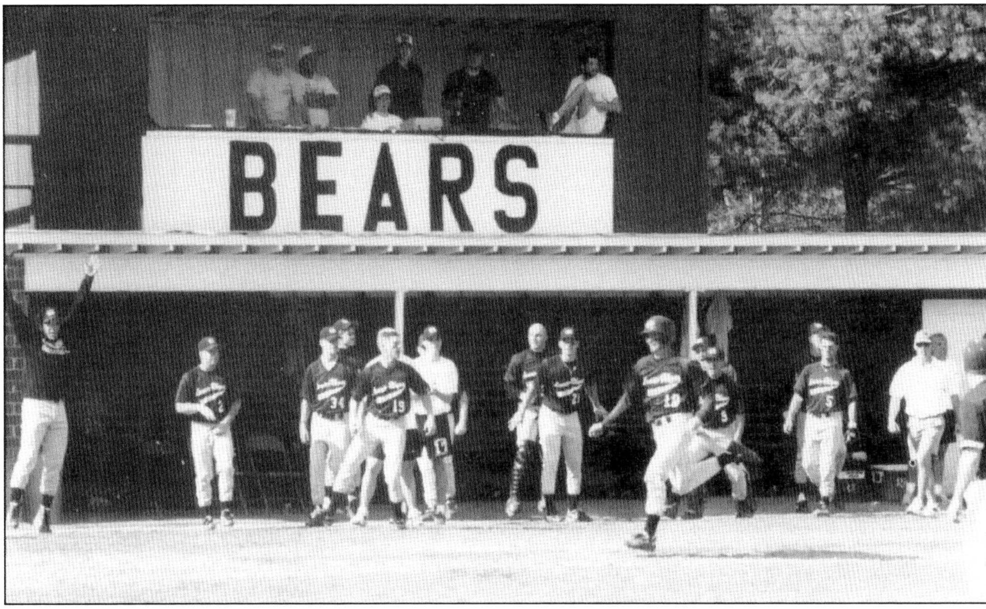

Robert Gray scores the winning run for the home team in a 1996 game. (Courtesy of Lenoir-Rhyne College.)

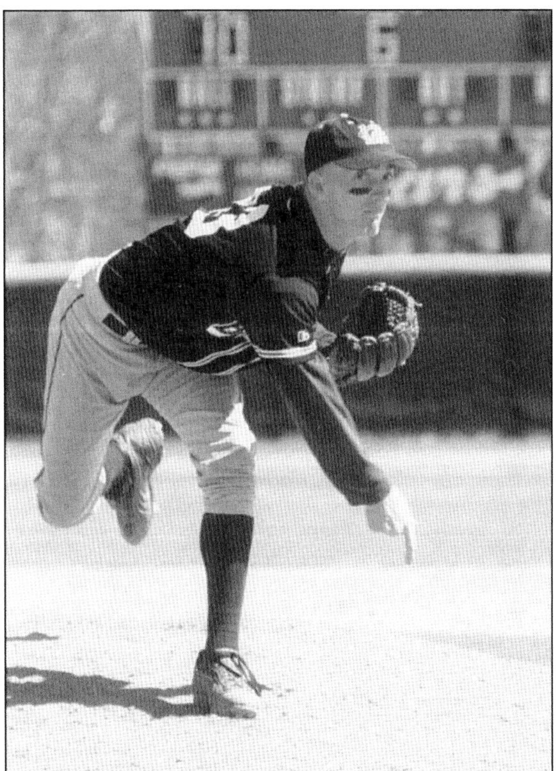

Israel Campbell brings the heat for the 2001 Bears. (Courtesy of Lenoir-Rhyne College.)

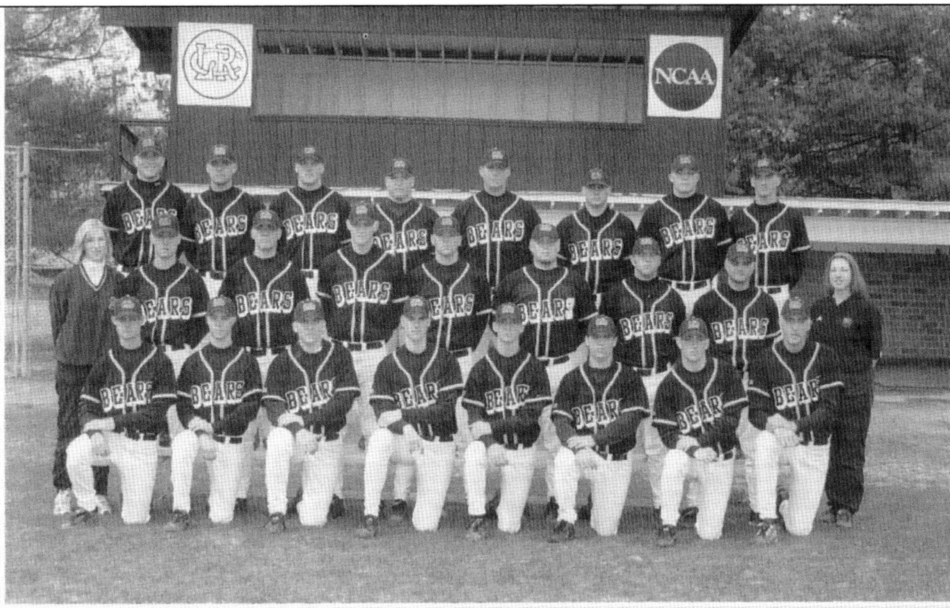

2001 Baseball Team

Dustin Day, Brandon Blake, Brian Neill, Adam Whicker, Drew Lindley, Jarred Caputo, Billy Ashby, Patrick Price, Dan Futrelle, Craig Sizemore, Brett Yates, Jeremy Krech, Will Combs, Brent Nichols, Michael Clontz, Chip Bradford, Matt Howell, Joe Nichols, Israel Campbell, Andy Cauble, Brandon Earp, Alan Payne, David Porter, Paul Pope, Jason Raines, Ryan Mumy, Head Coach Frank Pait, Assistant Coach Kelly Haynes, Athletic Trainer Tracy Crincoli

The 2001 Lenoir-Rhyne team set a school record with 33 wins and played in the National Tournament. Michael Clontz and Israel Campbell were outstanding as pitchers while Will Combs and Craig Sizemore turned in record-breaking performances at the plate. (Courtesy of Lenoir-Rhyne College.)

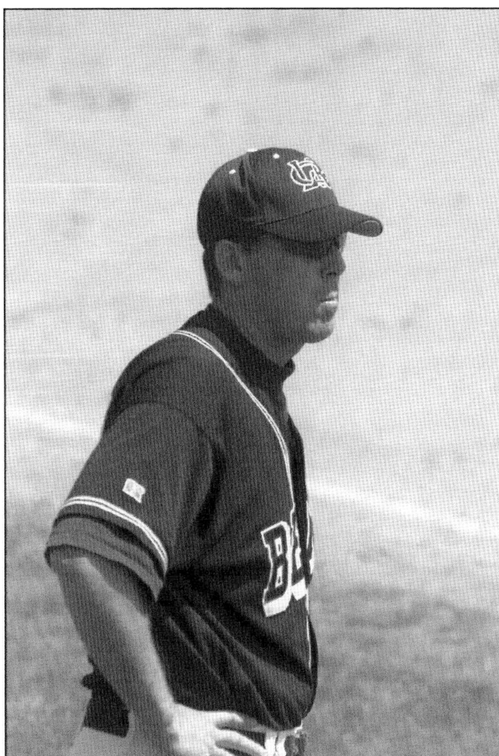

Coach Frank Pait, who became the head coach in 1997, began the 2004 season as the winningest coach in school history with 181 victories. His teams have won 30 or more games three times. (Courtesy of Lenoir-Rhyne College.)

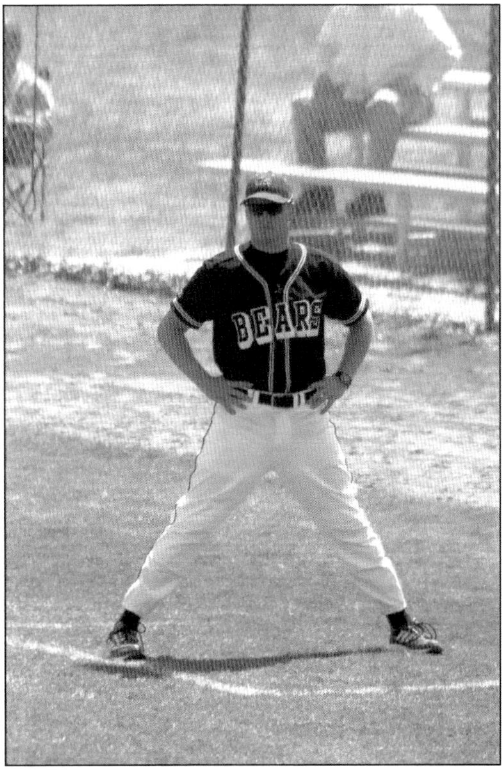

Former Bunker Hill High School and Catawba College star Israel Morrow works as the assistant coach.

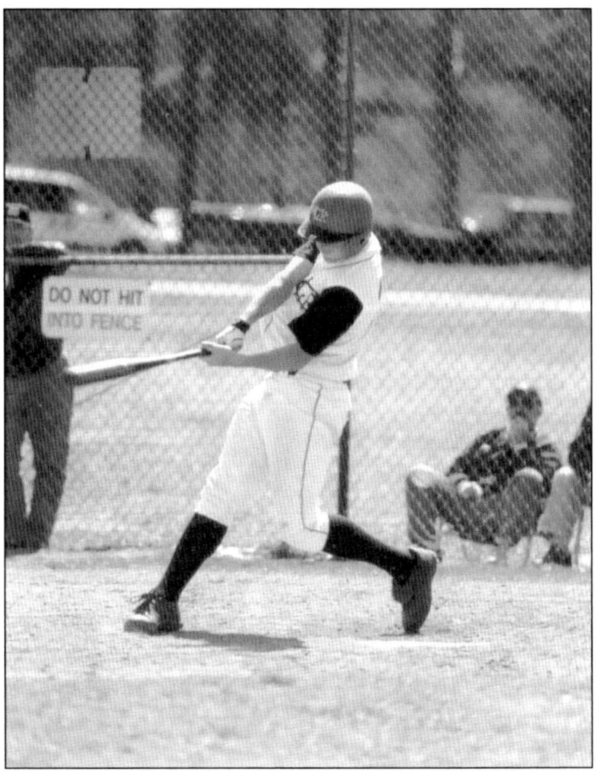

Will Combs, who helped elevate the Lenoir-Rhyne program in the late 1990s, is at or near the top of all the hitting records.

The following are pictures from the 2004 season. Matt Sigmon, a solid-hitting first baseman from Newton-Conover High School, holds the runner at first.

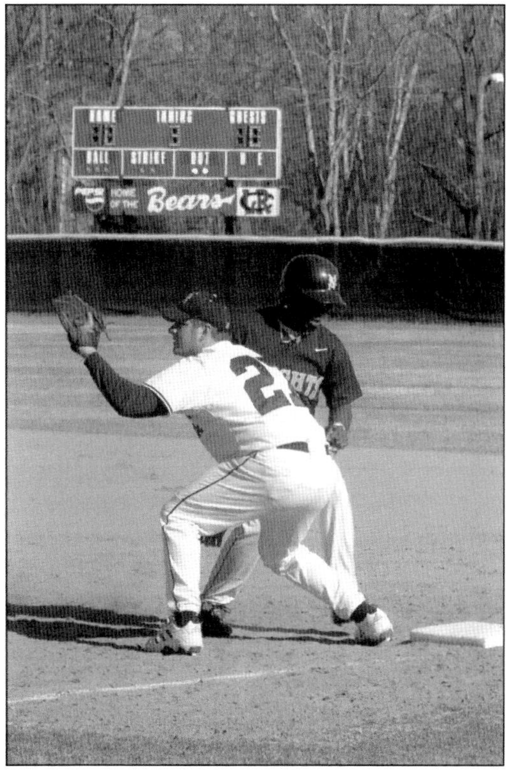

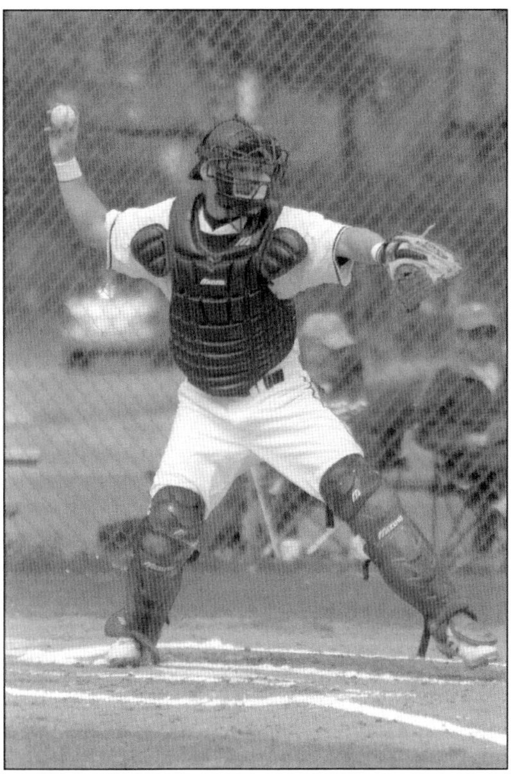

Brian Tester of Watauga County shared catching duties for the 2004 team along with John Verdinek.

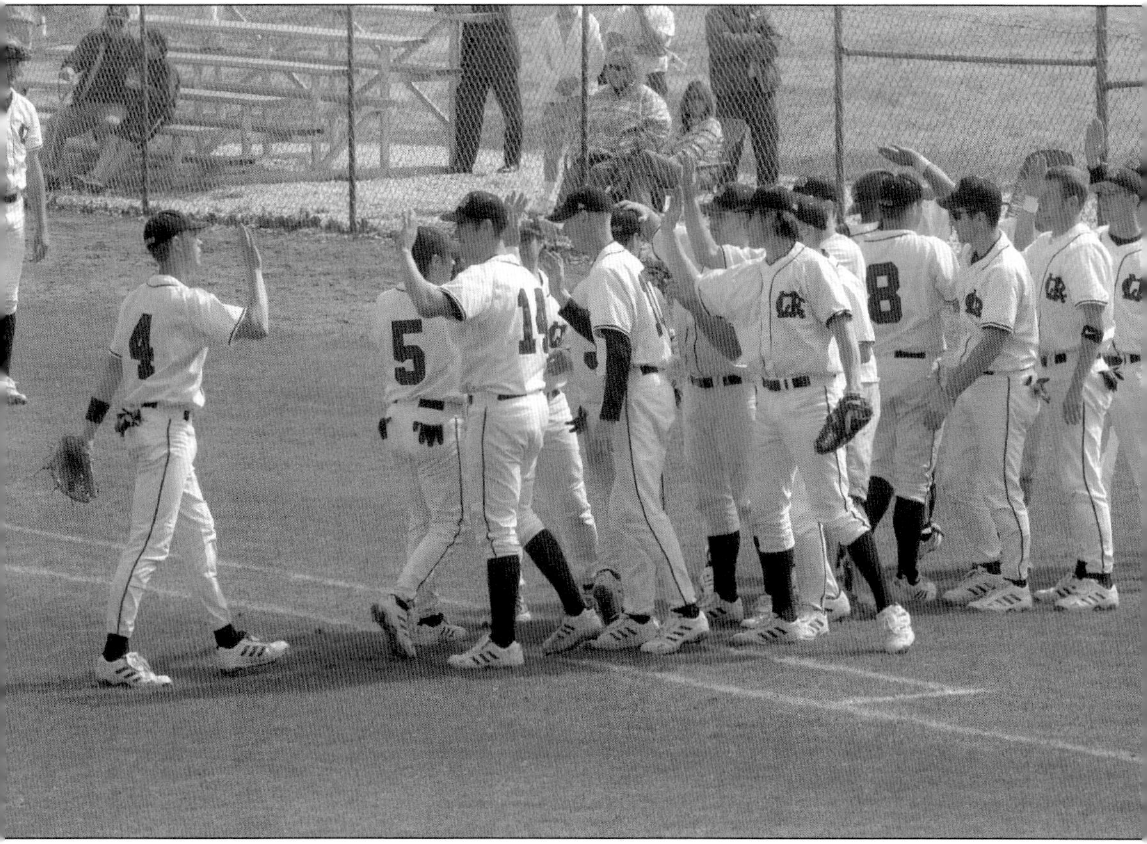

Another sweet victory—and the story goes on.

FIVE

Spinners

I would go straight from work to the ball field, never even stop by the house to eat. There is no better life a man could have had than baseball.
—Harold Lail

It is difficult to tell exactly when organized baseball games began between mill teams in Catawba County. In his book *Brookford Memories*, Dyke Little notes that baseball began as soon as the mill opened in 1898. In the historical account *The Catawbans*, Gary Freeze says, "Baseball was played [in Newton] as early as 1883, when nines from the town and the college played one another. Blacks played ball as well although never with whites. . . . The Newton team got its first uniforms in 1899, blood red except for white stripes sewn around the stockings."

The semi-professional competition between mill teams has borne many names over the years: mill ball, textile league ball, sandlot ball, and industrial league ball. In Catawba County, this form of recreational entertainment began to flourish in the 1920s. Teams represented the towns of Maiden, Brookford, Longview, Conover, and Newton, and the communities of Highland and West Hickory (a separate town until the 1930s). Teams from the nearby towns of Granite Falls and Taylorsville also participated. Many of the players who played for the Class D minor-league teams also played for these semi-professional teams. In the post–World War II era, the play has been described as often at the same level as that of the local professional teams.

Locally, the most enduring record of play belongs to the Hickory Spinners, who represented the Shuford family's Longview textile plant and played from 1925 until 1955 in a ballpark that rivaled many minor-league facilities. For many years, this team was managed by Fred Dale, who was also a plant superintendent and later the mayor of Longview. In the second half of the 1950s, large scale semi-professional baseball gave way to fast-pitch softball, the emergence of television as an entertaining force, and a generally wider range of entertainment opportunities.

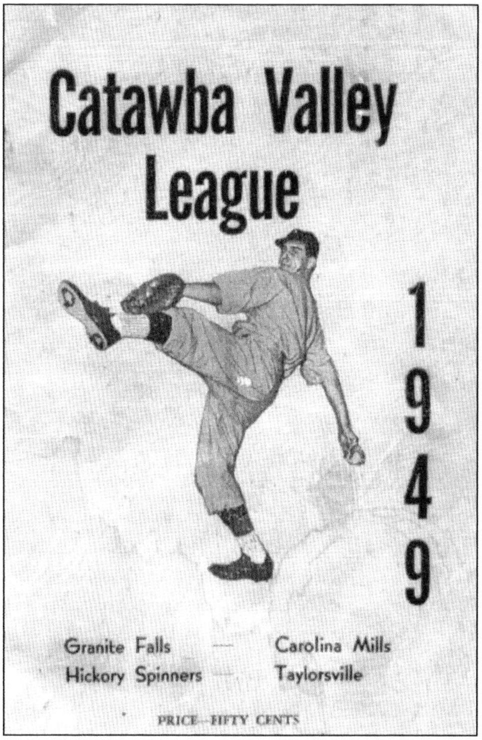

Note that only four teams are listed on the cover of the 1949 Catawba Valley League Program. (Courtesy of Harold Lail.)

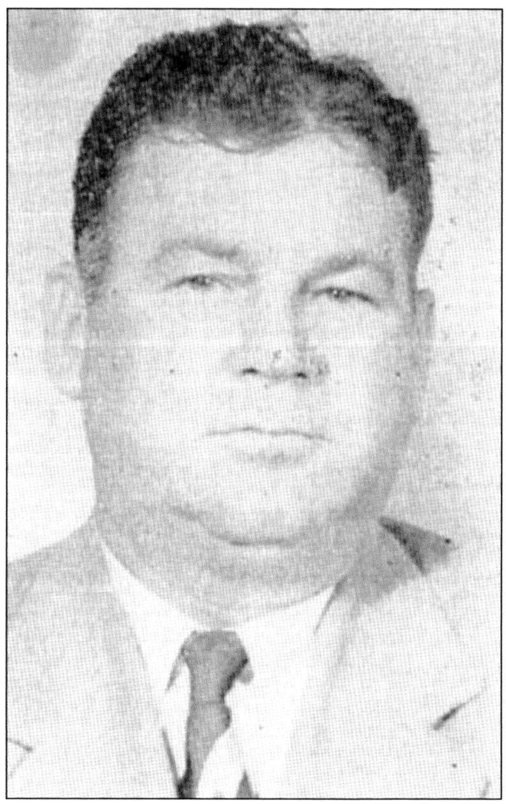

Advertisement pages in the program featured league executives, managers, teams, and players. Pictured here is league president T.R. Clark. (Courtesy of Harold Lail.)

Pete Fox is pictured at right. The caption notes that he "is a real hustler, exceptionally fast on the bases, and is respected by all of his players." (Courtesy of Harold Lail.)

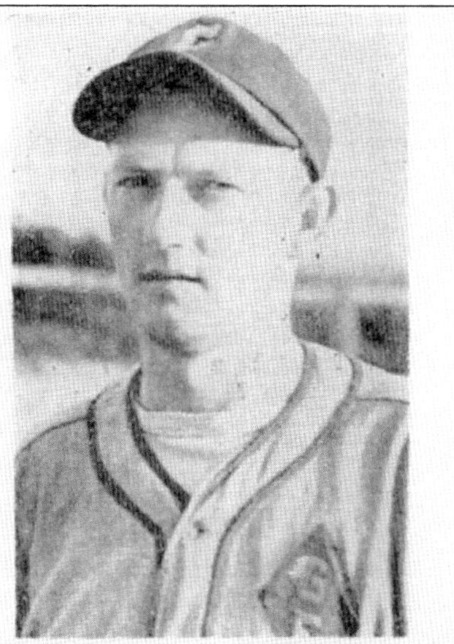

PETE FOX
Age 30, Ht. 5 ft. 10 in., Wt. 157
Throws right, Bats right Bat. Ave. .357

Pete Fox is one of the steadiest players in the league. He is the manager of the local team, and is very popular. For the last three years he has lead the team in hitting and two of those years he hit over the coveted .400 mark. This is Pete's first year as manager, but he has been playing second base for the local team for four years. Pete is a real hustler, is exceptionally fast on the bases, and is respected by all of his players.

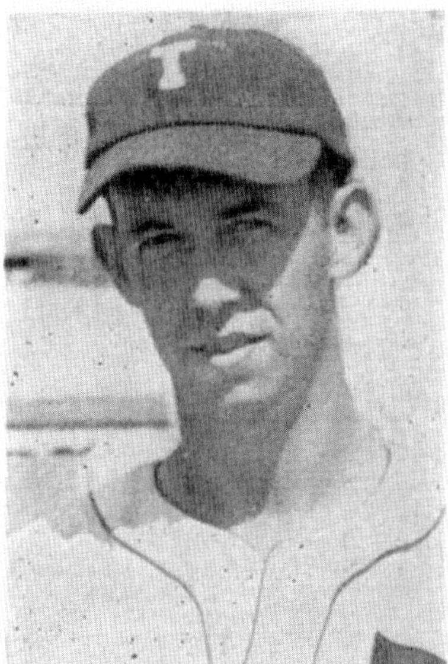

HOWELL ICENHOUR (Manager, 1-Base)
Age 25, Ht. 6 ft. 2 in., Wt. 185
Hometown: Taylorsville, N. C.
Throws right, Bats left Bat. Ave. .345

This is his first year as player-manager and 2nd year at 1st base. At present his boys are well on top in the standings. He is leading the league in home runs with 17 and the only player in league history to hit one over the right field fence at Granite Falls.

Howell Icenhour of Taylorsville is pictured at left in his first year as player-manager. (Courtesy of Harold Lail.)

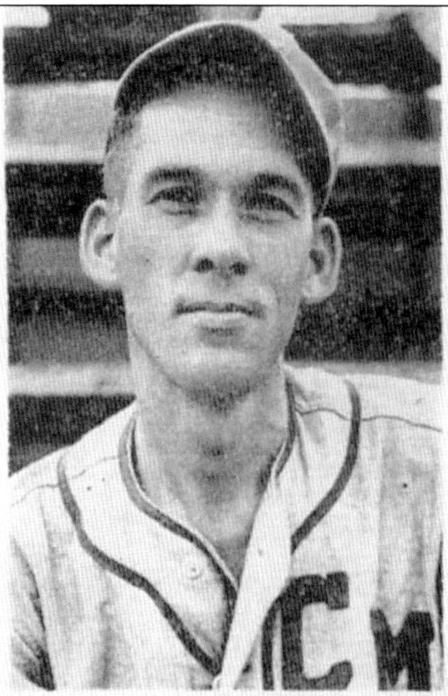

MGR. FRANK SIGMON
Age 35, Ht. 5 ft. 11 in., Wt. 172; Hometown: Maiden
Throws right, Bats right
Frank, Carolina manager for seven years, his most successful year was the '48 season, when his boys rated 4th place in State Tournament in Asheboro.

Frank Sigmon is pictured at left. He was the Carolina manager for seven years. (Courtesy of Harold Lail.)

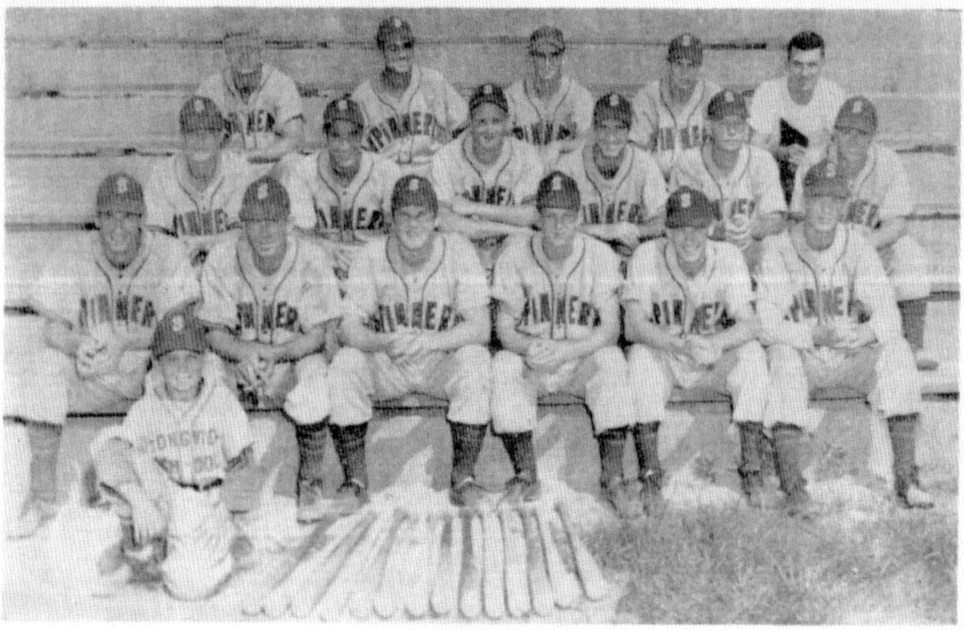

HICKORY SPINNERS
Front row, left to right—Gene Miller, Virgil Stamey, Gene Frye, Joe Shook, Odell Moose, Glen Ray Yoder; 2nd row—June Miller, Charlie Bollinger, Dick Bumgarner, Hal Lail, Henry Baker, Ralph Dale; 3rd row—Harry Dowda, Fred Dale, Sr., Fred "Sonny" Dale, Jr., Paul Jones, Sam Duncan (Scorekeeper).

The Hickory Spinners team is pictured here. (Courtesy of Harold Lail.)

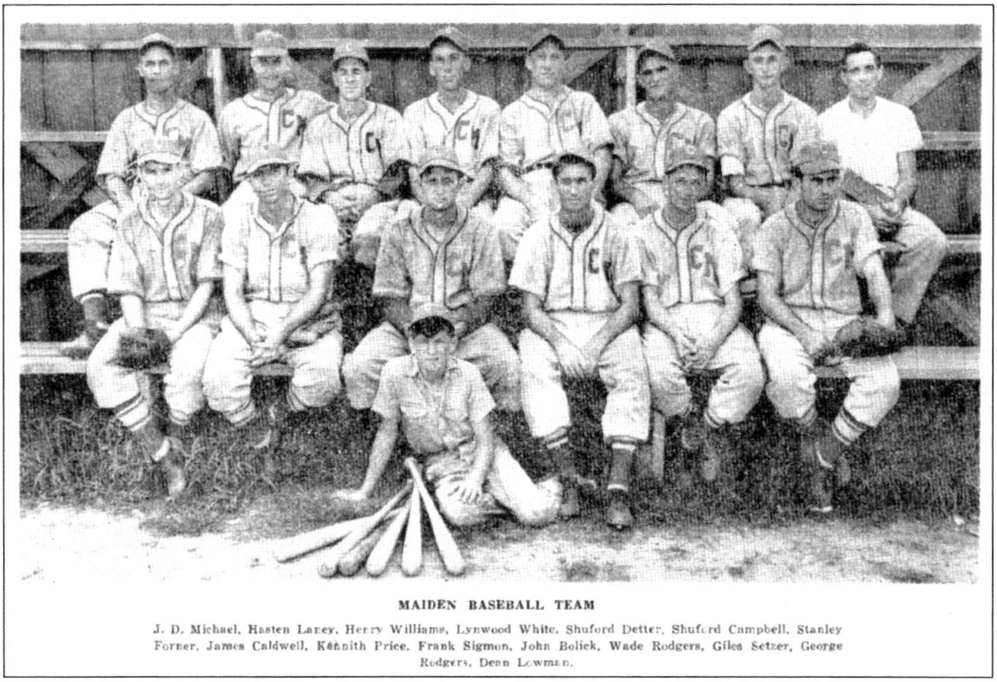

Carolina Mills of Maiden fielded many fine teams during the first half of the century. This team featured former legion and Lenoir-Rhyne star Giles Setzer. (Courtesy of Harold Lail.)

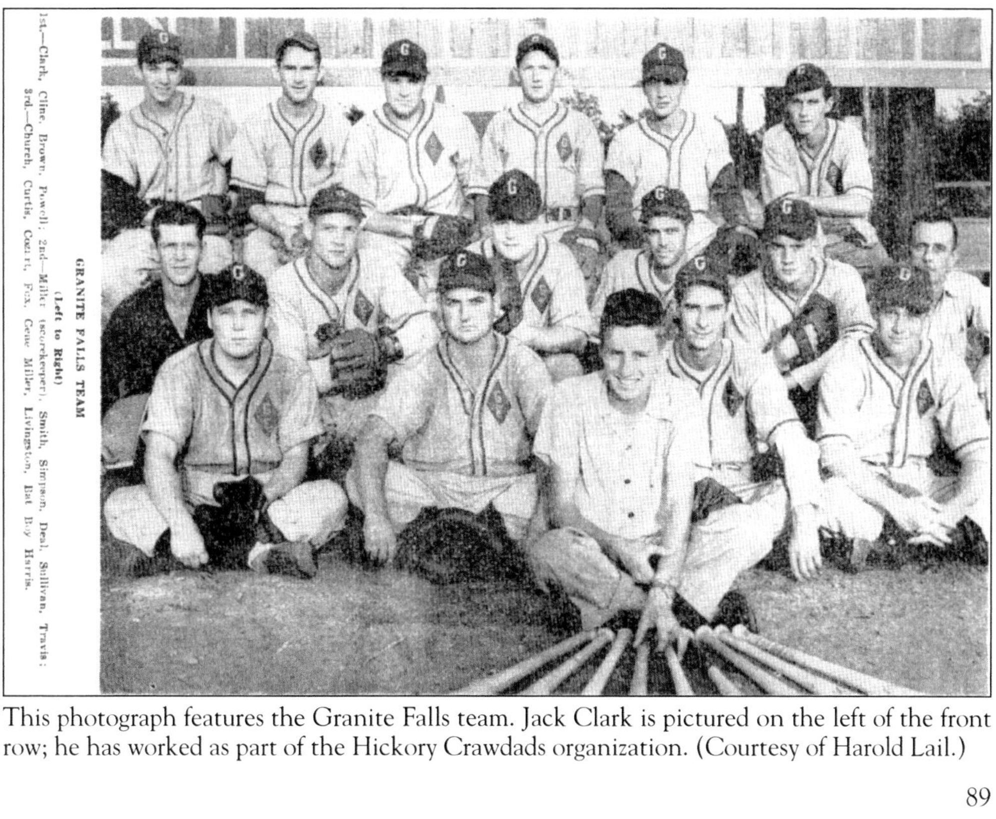

This photograph features the Granite Falls team. Jack Clark is pictured on the left of the front row; he has worked as part of the Hickory Crawdads organization. (Courtesy of Harold Lail.)

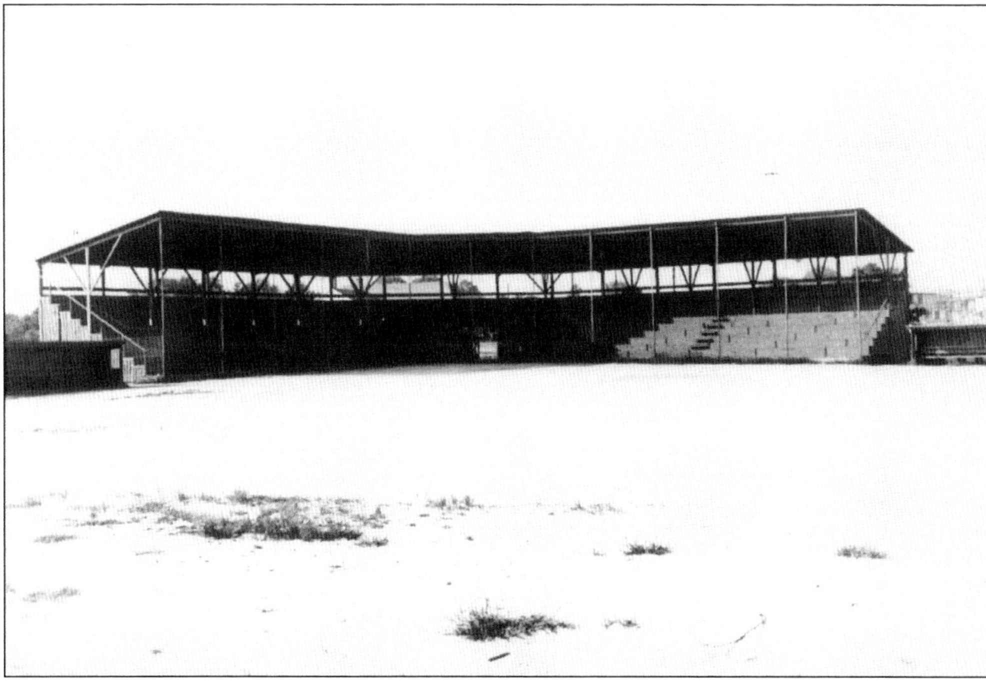

The Hickory Spinners ballpark was home to the Shuford Mills Hickory Spinners from 1925 until 1955. (Courtesy of Junior Young.)

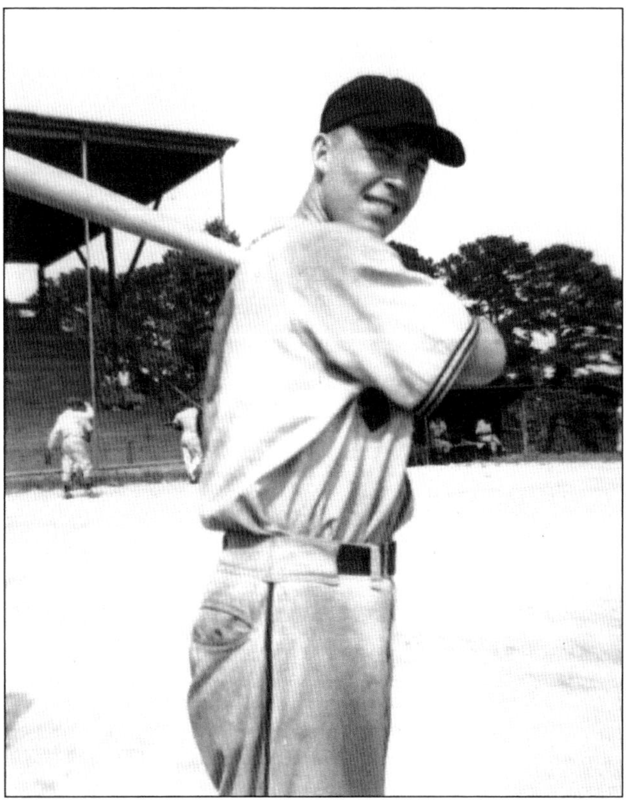

Gwen Miller, a key player for several championship Spinners clubs, is pictured at left. (Courtesy of Junior Young.)

John "Junior" Young, a solid hitting shortstop and pitcher, was one of the youngest players on the 1950s teams. (Courtesy of Junior Young.)

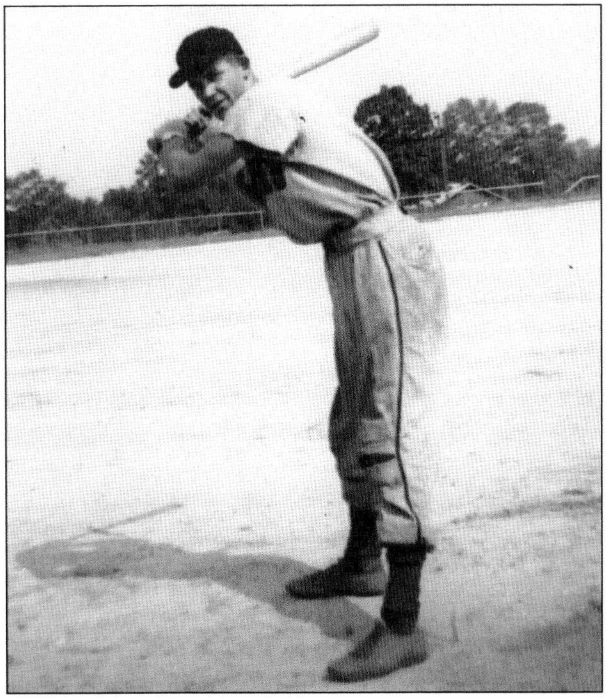

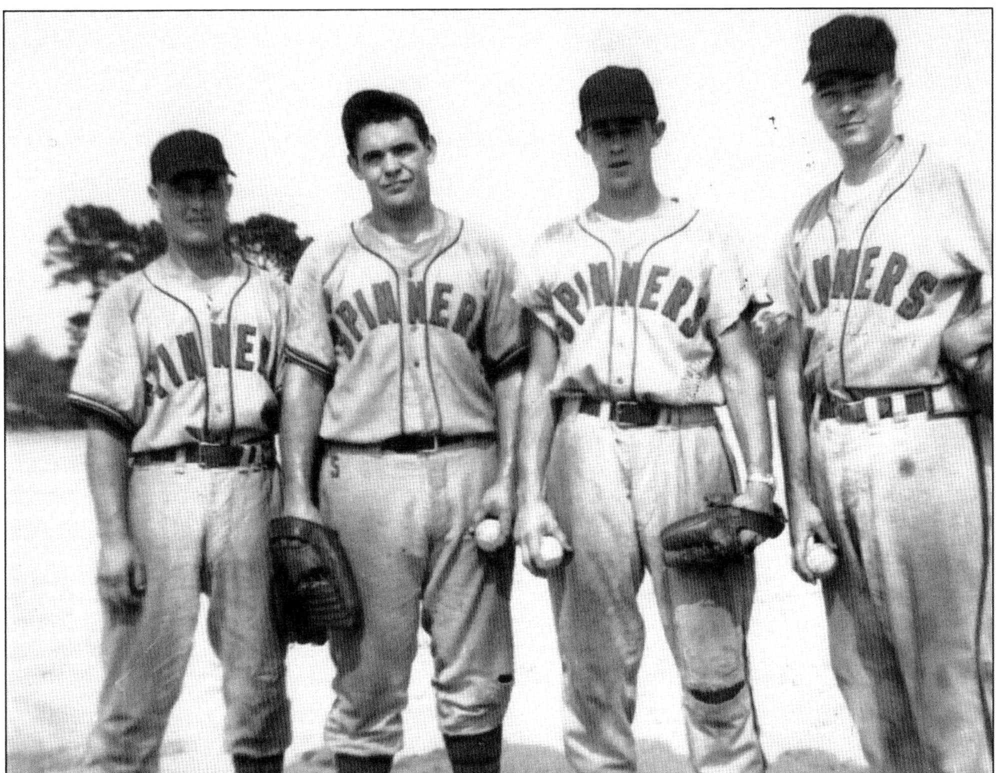

From left to right, Gwen Miller, Murl Whitener, Junior Young, and Murphy Lee Abernathy pose for a photograph before a game at Spinner Park. (Courtesy of Junior Young.)

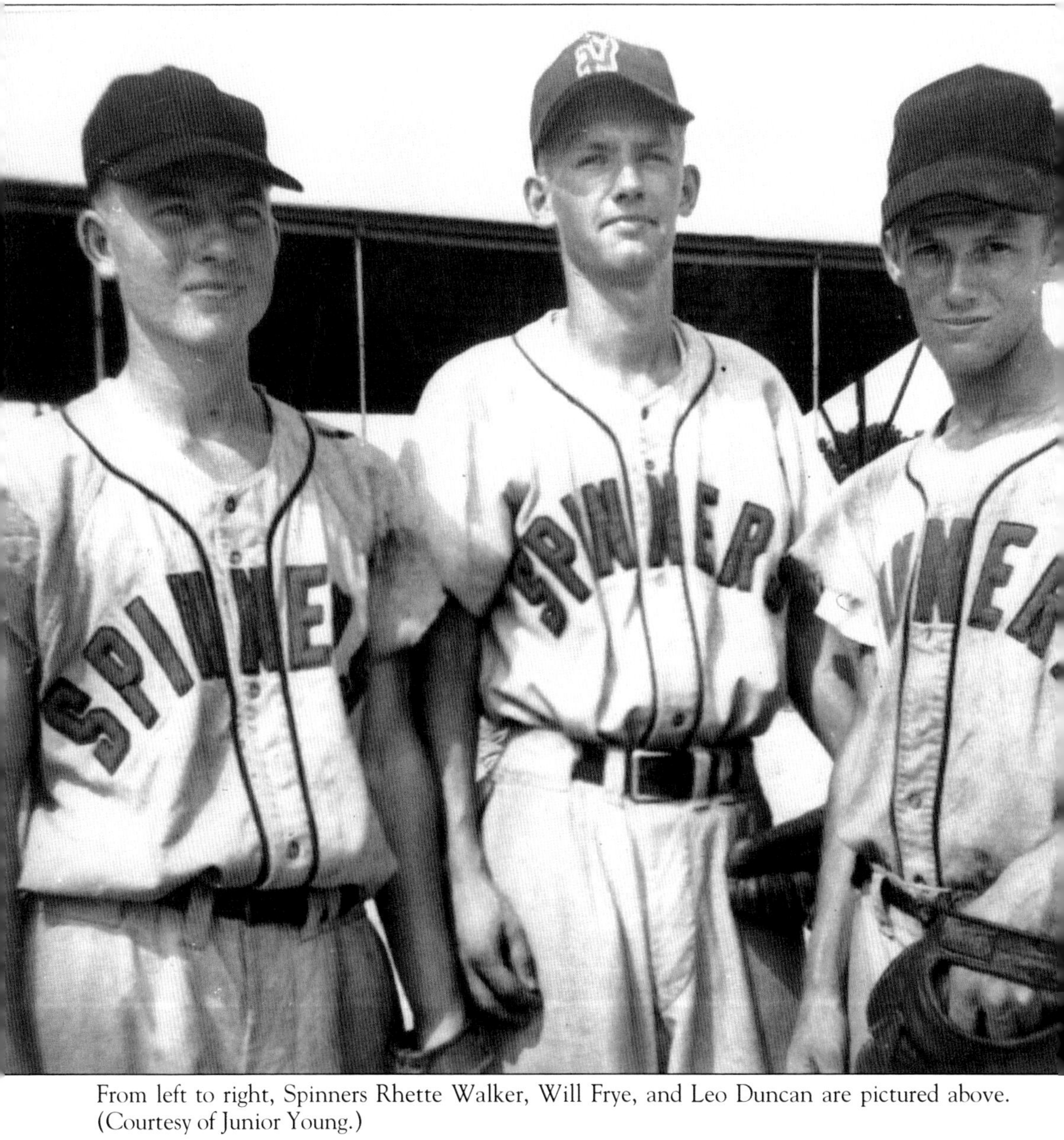

From left to right, Spinners Rhette Walker, Will Frye, and Leo Duncan are pictured above. (Courtesy of Junior Young.)

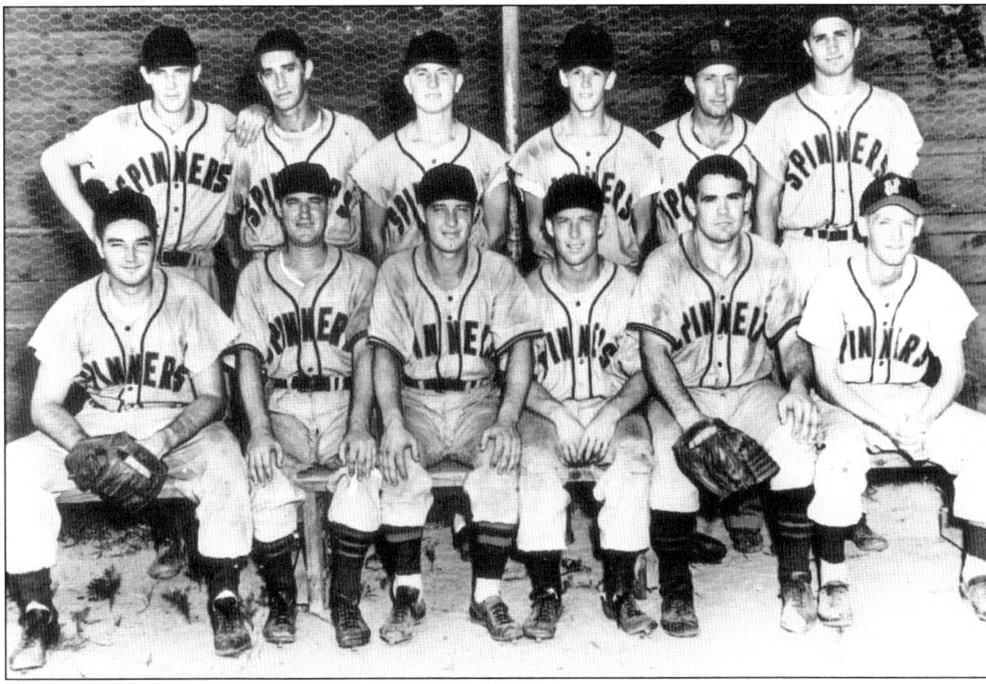

The Spinner team pictured won the League Championship with a 29-7 record. June Miller led the team with a .417 batting average, and Junior Young posted a 10-0 pitching record. The following team members are pictured from left to right: (front row) Murphy Lee Abernathy, Paul "Jiggs" Martin, June Miller, Gwen Miller, Murl Whitener, and Dick Beam; (back row) John Edward "Junior" Young, Leonard Wilkie, Rhette Walker, Leo Duncan, J.E. Frye, and Bob Lefevers. Gene and Will Frye are not pictured. (Courtesy of Junior Young.)

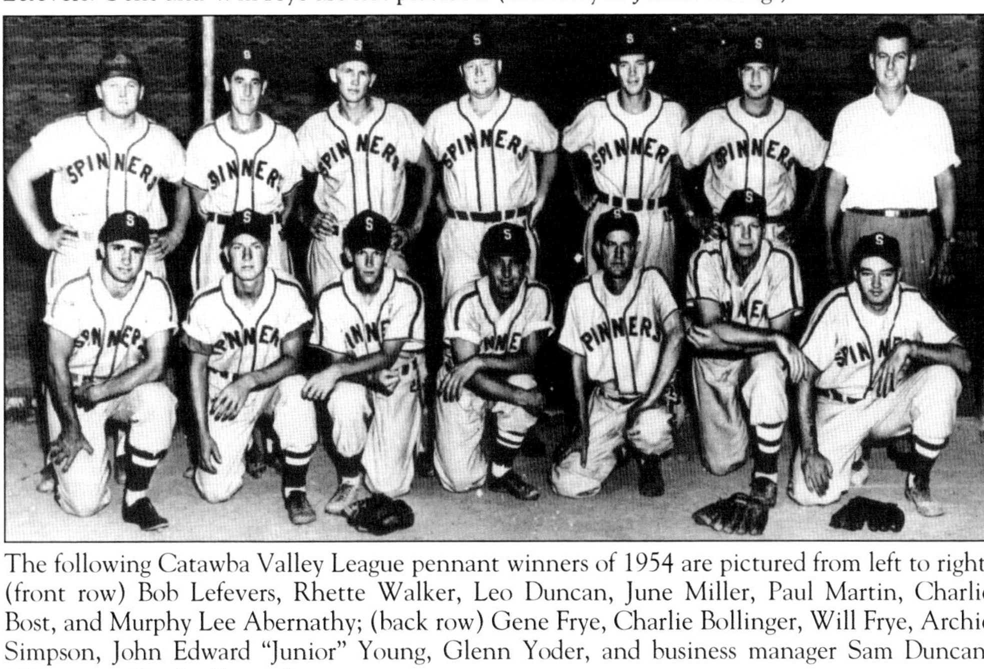

The following Catawba Valley League pennant winners of 1954 are pictured from left to right: (front row) Bob Lefevers, Rhette Walker, Leo Duncan, June Miller, Paul Martin, Charlie Bost, and Murphy Lee Abernathy; (back row) Gene Frye, Charlie Bollinger, Will Frye, Archie Simpson, John Edward "Junior" Young, Glenn Yoder, and business manager Sam Duncan. (Courtesy of Junior Young.)

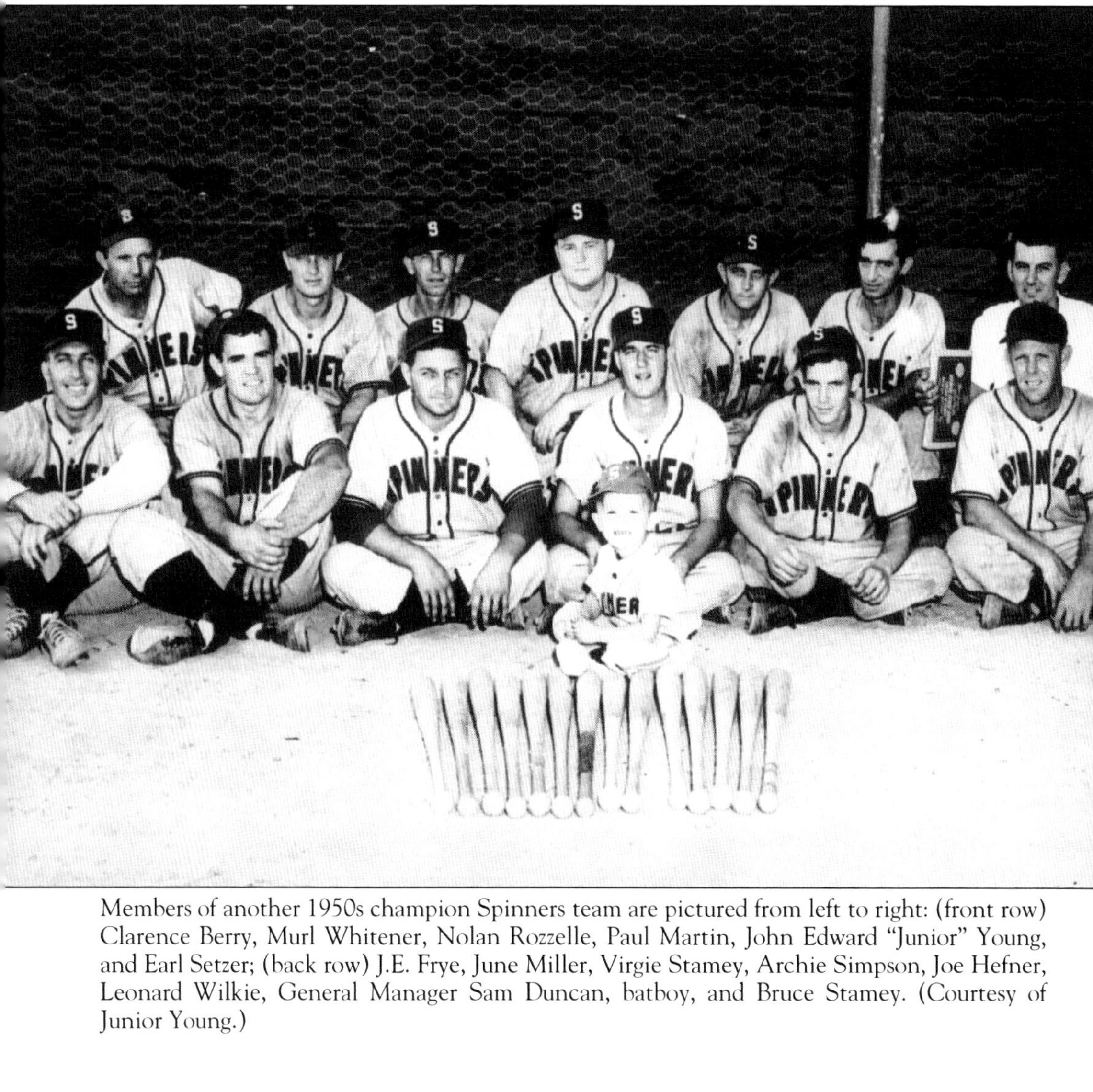

Members of another 1950s champion Spinners team are pictured from left to right: (front row) Clarence Berry, Murl Whitener, Nolan Rozzelle, Paul Martin, John Edward "Junior" Young, and Earl Setzer; (back row) J.E. Frye, June Miller, Virgie Stamey, Archie Simpson, Joe Hefner, Leonard Wilkie, General Manager Sam Duncan, batboy, and Bruce Stamey. (Courtesy of Junior Young.)

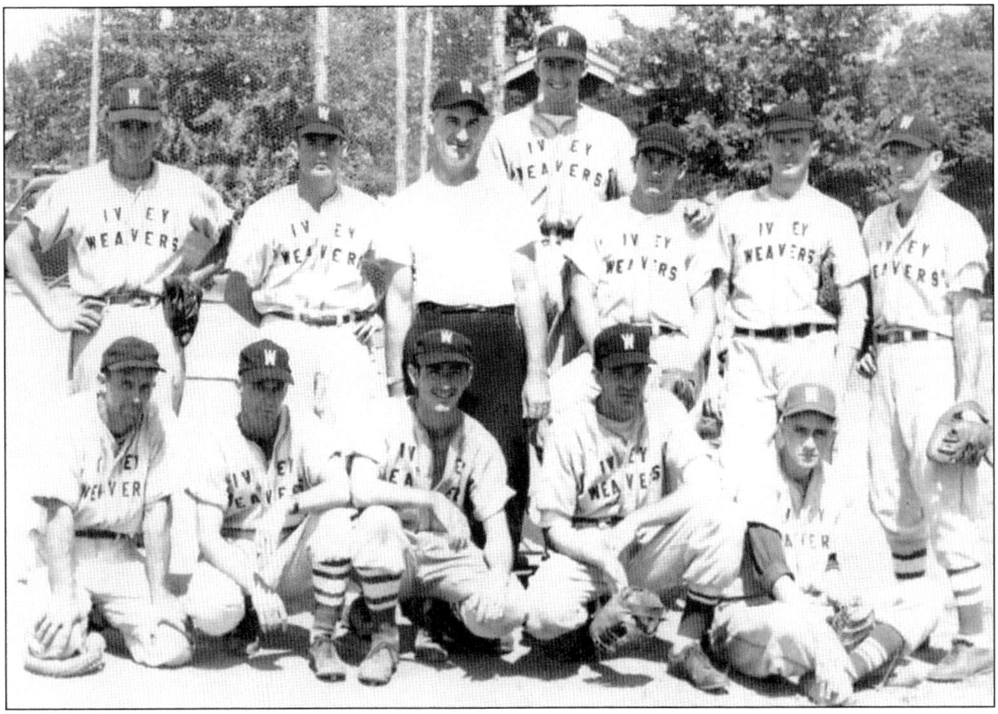

The Ivey Weavers was a team that represented a mill in West Hickory. They are pictured here at their ballpark, which is now a recreation department softball field. (Courtesy of Harold Lail.)

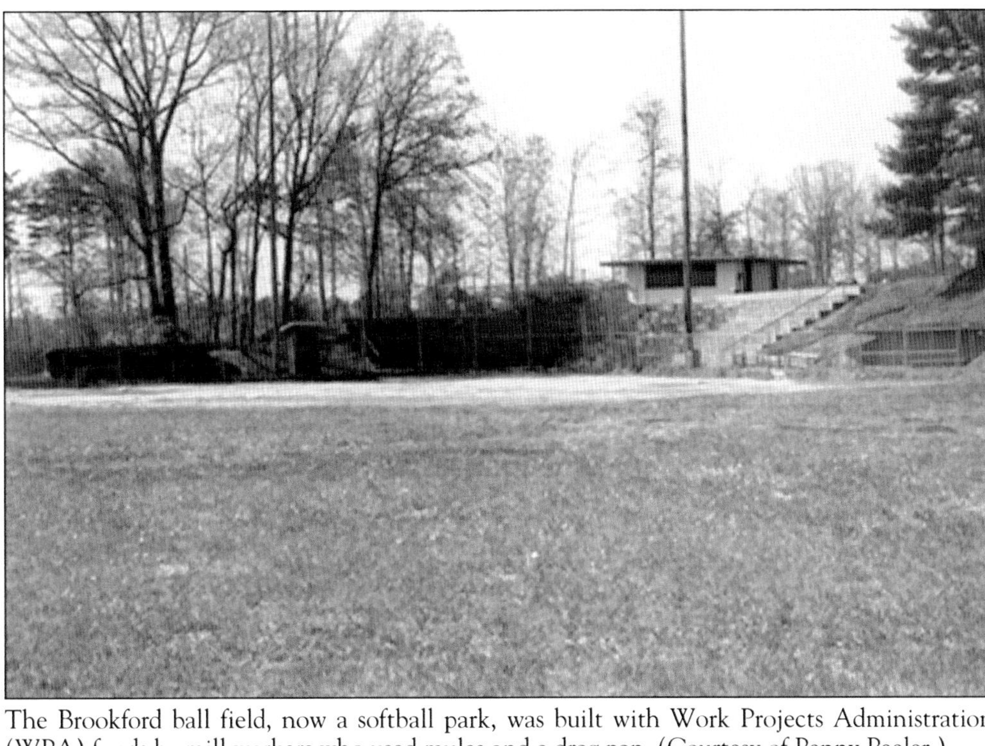

The Brookford ball field, now a softball park, was built with Work Projects Administration (WPA) funds by mill workers who used mules and a drag pan. (Courtesy of Penny Peeler.)

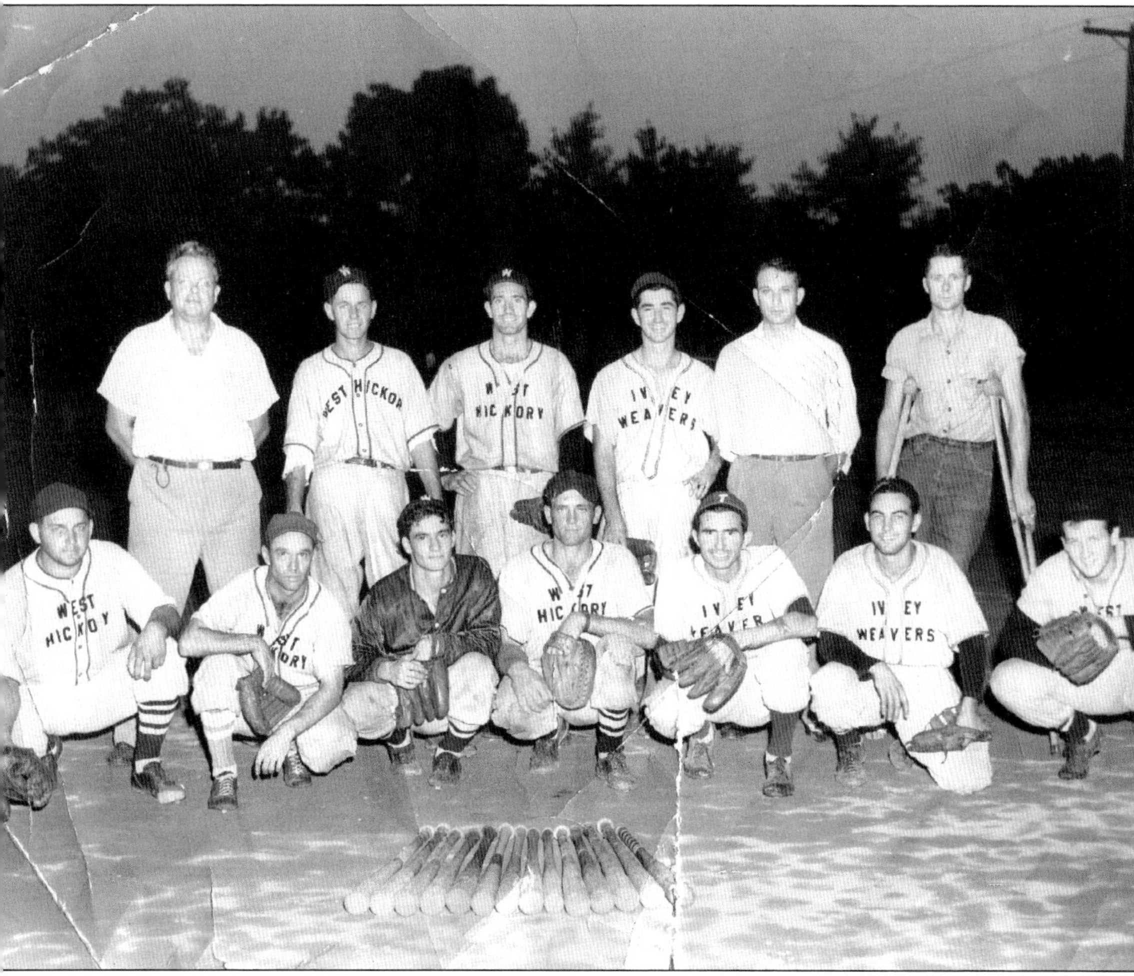

Note the variation in uniforms on this fine Ivey Weavers team. The following players are pictured from left to right: (front row) Nolan Rozzelle, Buddy Giles, Hom Isaac, Howard Rowe, Pat Patterson, and Gary Teague; (back row) Ellis Cochran, Joel Rozzelle, Harold Lail, Howard Wright, ? Reep, and Bill Reep.

Six

Tweener Years

The ball was dirty with deep brown scuffs across the wide crescent sections, like a badly scarred face. The field was sandy, red clay packed hard and salted with bits of mica and broken glass.
—Tim Peeler

Although the area was without professional baseball for 31 years, the game did not go away. One of the fine stories from the post–World War II era was Troy Washam's 1948 American Legion team, a national semi-finalist. The program carried its success and popularity forward into the second half of the century.

One of the biggest stories from this era was the three-time State Champion St. Stephens High School baseball teams of 1971 to 1973. Catawba County Sports Hall of Famer Harry Frye coached the Double-A Indians during their unprecedented run.

The local recreation department, under the leadership of Ace Parker and then Danny Thompson, developed a strong multi-level program of play that, coupled with C.O. Miller's efforts at the Hickory Foundation Center, provided local youth countless opportunities to play baseball. Other community programs began around the county in areas such as Sherrill's Ford, Mountain View, and St. Stephens.

Also included in this chapter are some area players and families who succeeded locally or nationally. This includes Catawba County native and current resident Bryan Harvey, arguably the most successful baseball player in the history of the county.

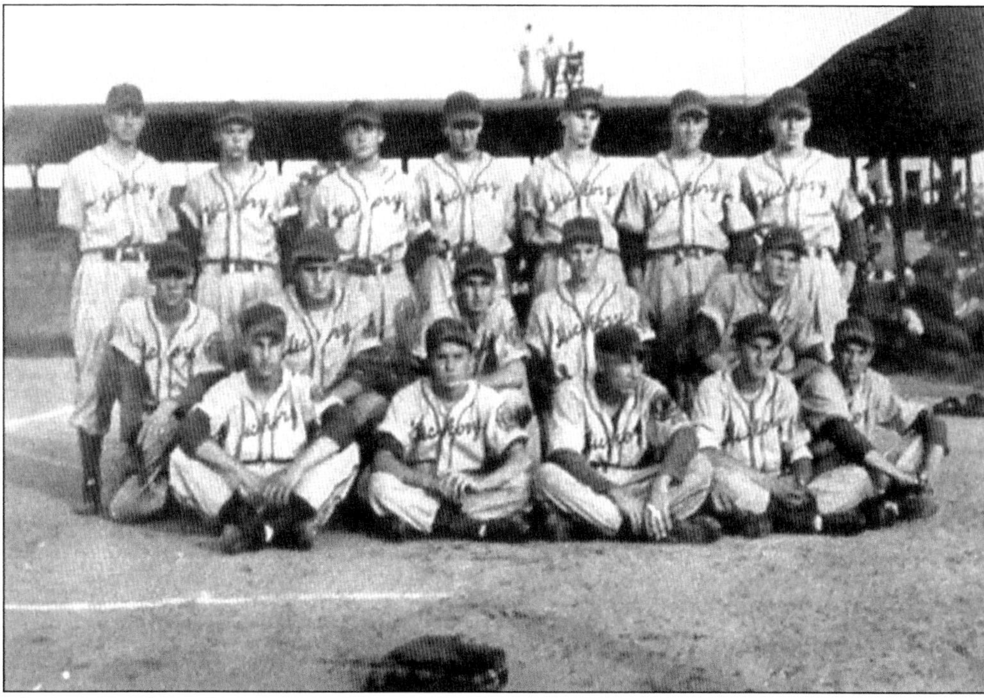

The 1948 Hickory American Legion team won the State and Southeast Regional titles before losing in the semi-finals. The following players are pictured from left to right: (front row) Ted Hefner, Wayne Davis, Jack Powell, Giles Setzer, and Bob Hendrix; (middle row) Reginald Munday, Charles Shook, Fred Dale Jr., Joe Shook, and Gene Frye; (back row) Coach Troy Washam, Charles Camp, Jim Mitchell, Dean Baker, John Coulter, Richard Bumgarner, and Joe Bill Church. (Courtesy of American Legion Post 48.)

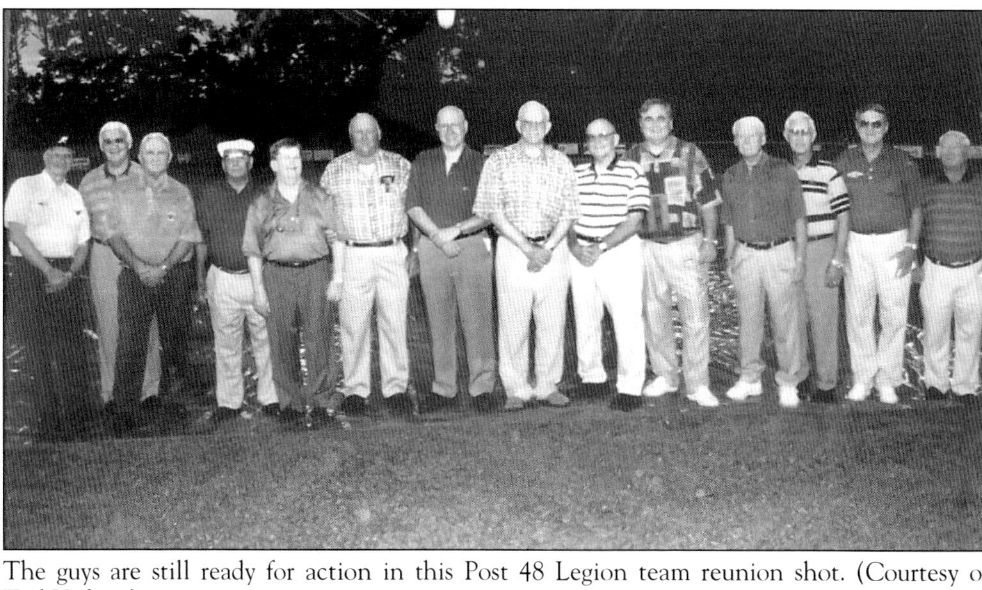

The guys are still ready for action in this Post 48 Legion team reunion shot. (Courtesy of Ted Hefner.)

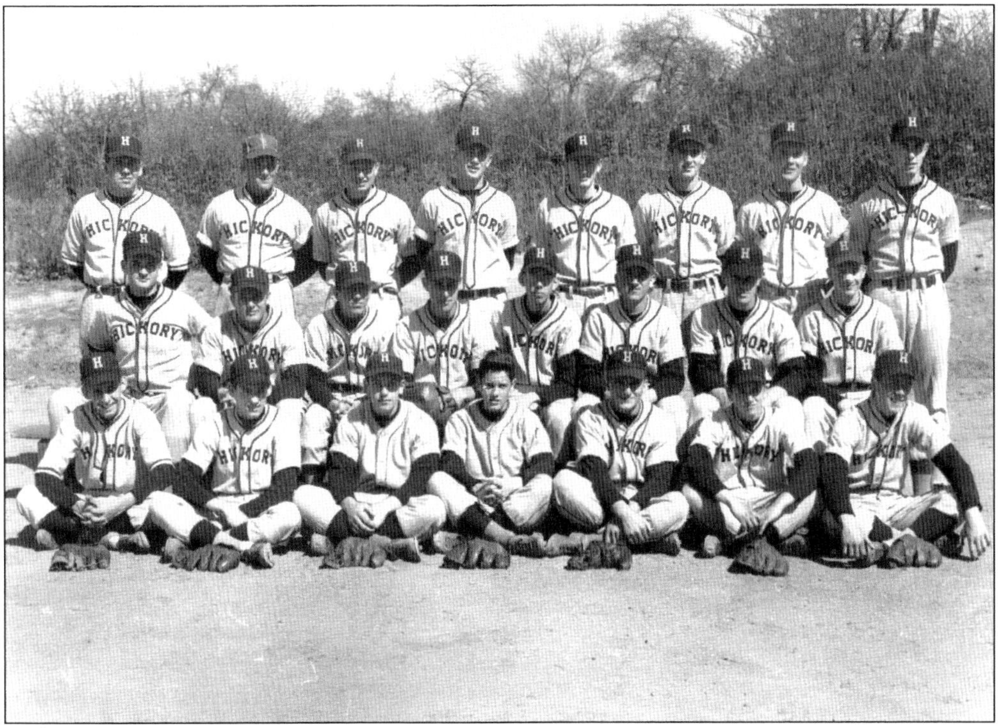

The 1948 Western Conference Class A Champion Hickory High Tornadoes were coached by Frank Barger, the legendary football coach for whom the current football stadium is named. Some of these young men also took the field for the 1948 Hickory American Legion State and Regional Champions. (Courtesy of Ted Hefner.)

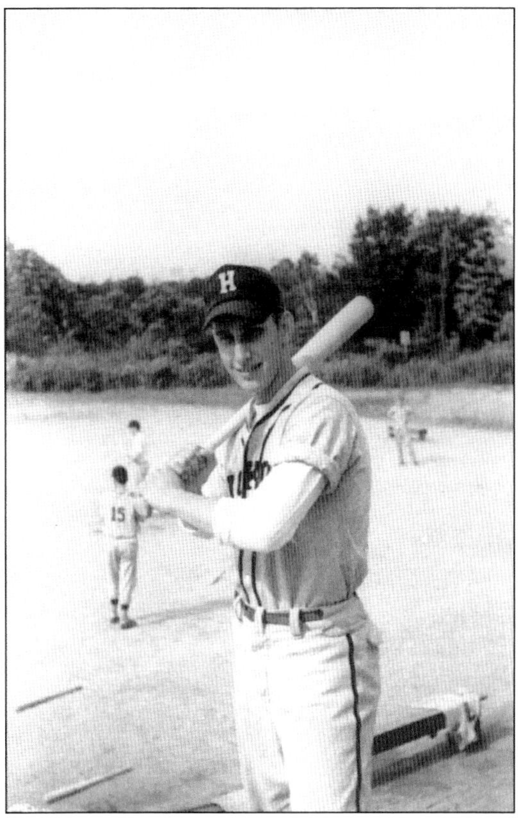

This is a family affair: Ted Hefner is pictured as a Hickory High School player. (Courtesy of Ted Hefner.)

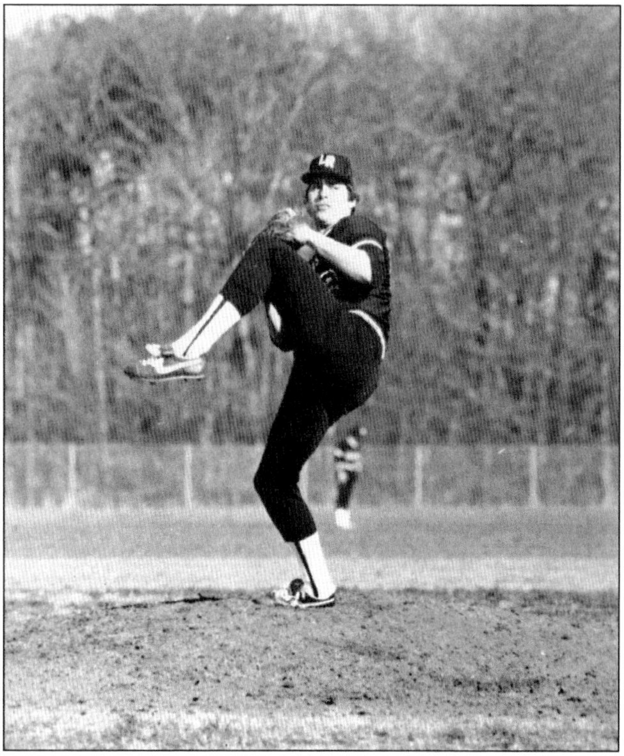

Ted's sons are pictured here: Dave, warming up between innings for the 1979 Lenoir-Rhyne team, and Gregg, an assistant coach on the same team. Gregg had an outstanding college career at Gardner-Webb College. (Courtesy of Lenoir-Rhyne College.)

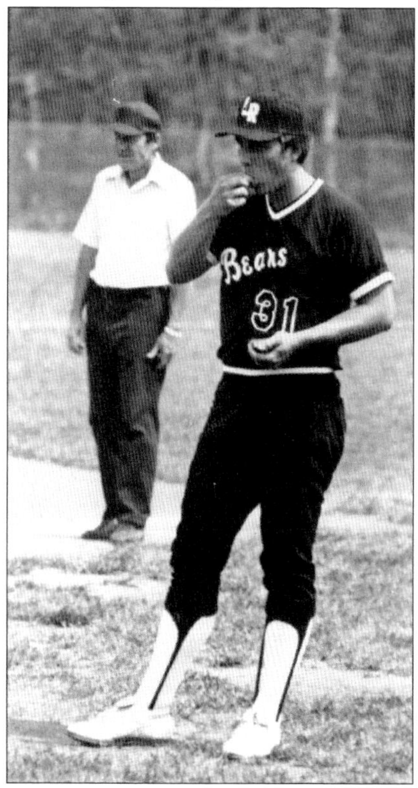

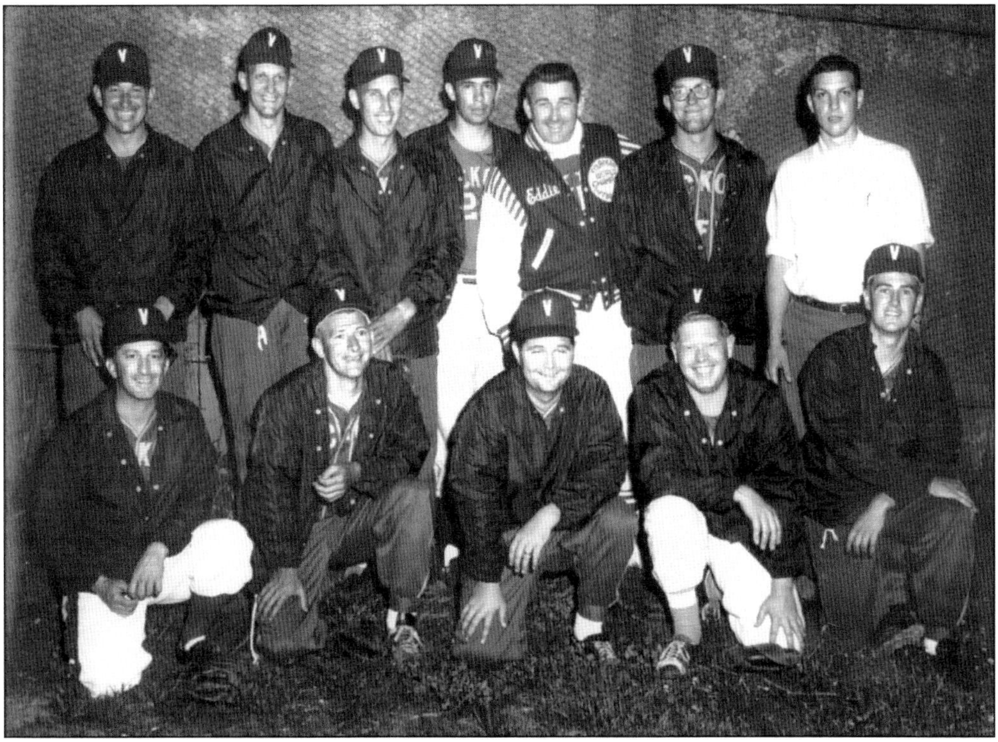

As the days of semi-professional and minor league baseball waned, the sport of fast pitch softball began to take hold in the area. Pictured here are the Veterans of Foreign Wars (VFW) team and Eddie Feigner, the King of "The King and His Court," a softball touring team. (Courtesy of Ted Hefner.)

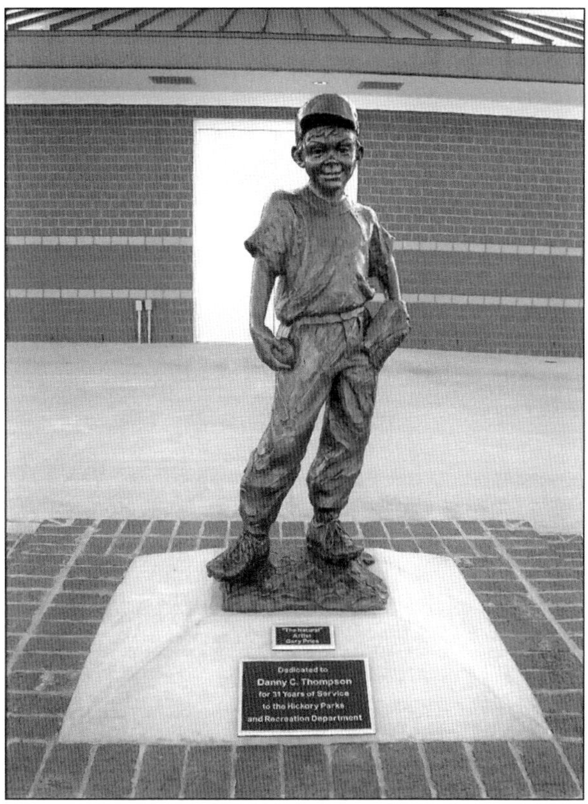

Danny Thompson oversaw many years of growth in the programs offered by the Hickory Recreation Department. This statue titled *The Natural* by Gary Price stands in Thompson's honor at the new Stanford Park Recreation Facility. (Courtesy of Brian McLawhorn.)

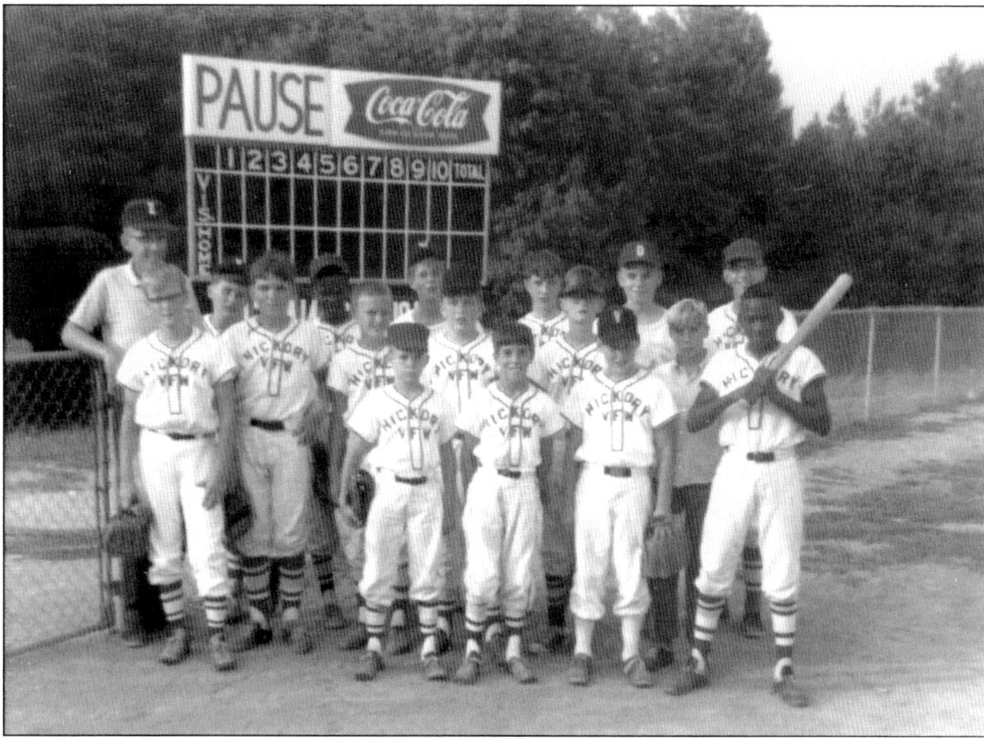

Hickory's first integrated Little League All-Star team won a double-elimination tournament in 1968 at the Howard's Furniture Field in Denver, North Carolina. Future Hickory High sports stars include Tim Coffey, Eddie Gillam, Gregg Hefner, Mike Hester, Marty Houston, Dana Reed, and Timbo Robinson. (Courtesy of J.L. Peeler.)

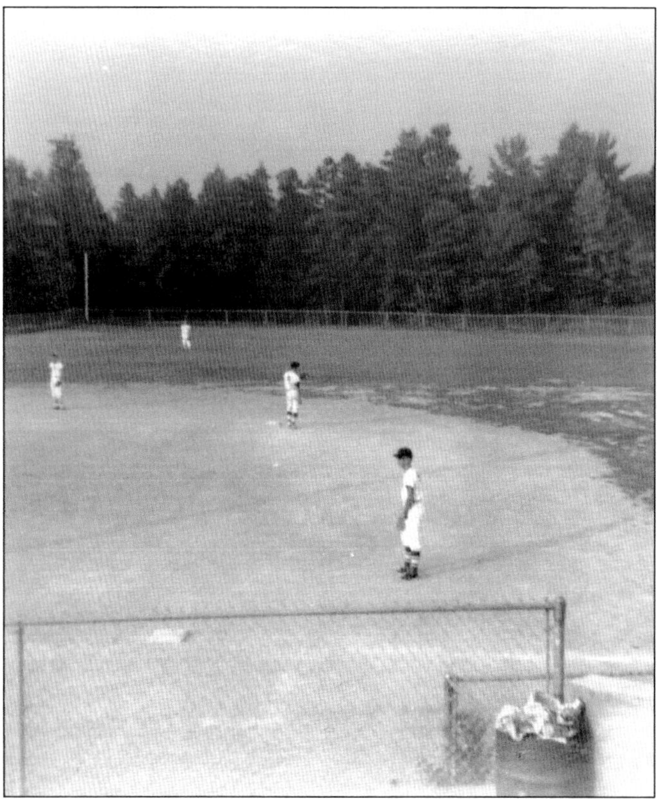

This is a picture of the 1968 team on the Howard's Field; first baseman Paul Peeler is in the foreground. (Courtesy of J.L. Peeler.)

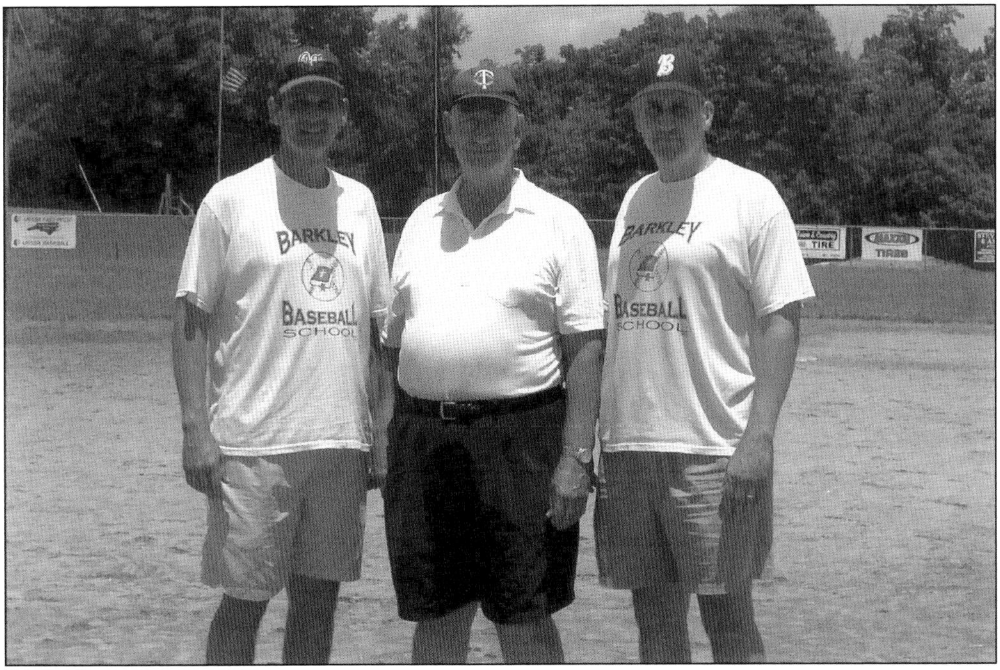

Jeff, Bill, and Matt Barkley of the Barkley Baseball School are pictured above. Matt pitched for The Citadel and in the minors, Jeff pitched for The Citadel and earned a stint with the Cleveland Indians, and their father, Bill, pitched at the Triple-A level before retiring to raise his family. (Courtesy of Brian McLawhorn.)

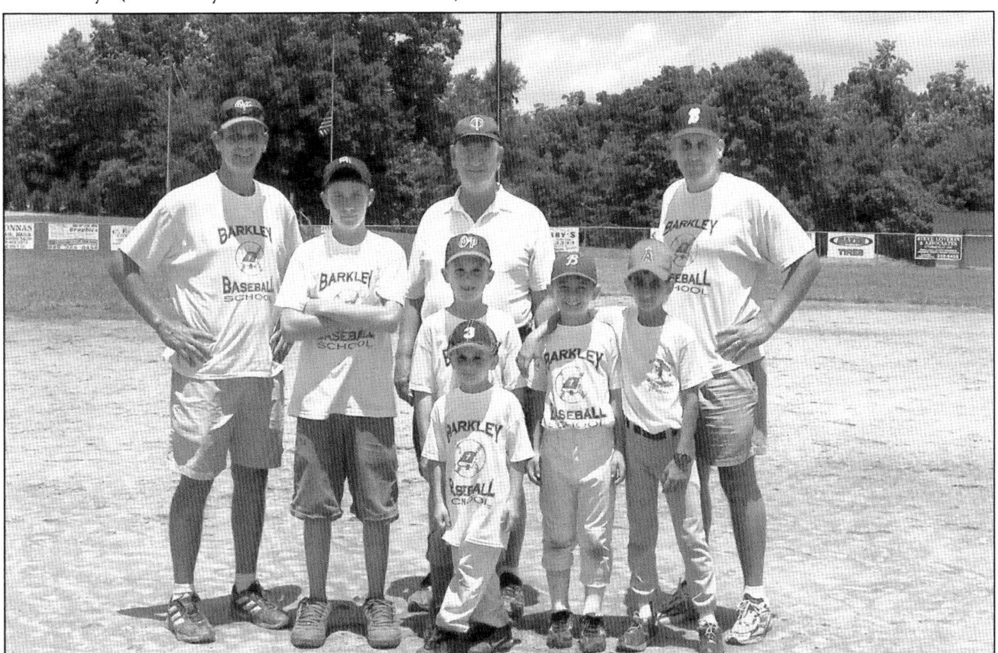

Jeff Jr., Nathan, Daniel, Nick, and Gabriel Barkley are pictured along with their fathers and grandfather. The Barkley Baseball School, which emphasizes game fundamentals and Christian morals, has just completed a successful 16th year. (Courtesy of Brian McLawhorn.)

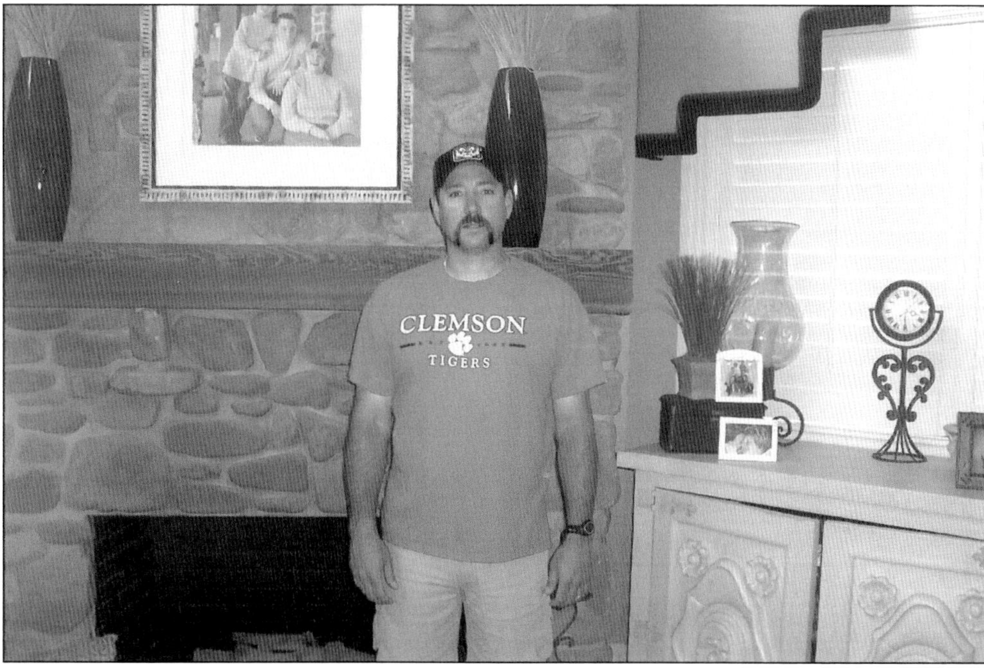

Bryan Harvey pitched for nine seasons with the California Angels and the Florida Marlins. He was in two All-Star games and was named Rookie Pitcher of the Year for the American League in 1988 by *Sporting News*. His save totals of 46 and 45 in 1991 and 1993 still rank him in the top 20 all-time in that category, and his lifetime ERA of 2.49 is outstanding. (Courtesy of Brian McLawhorn.)

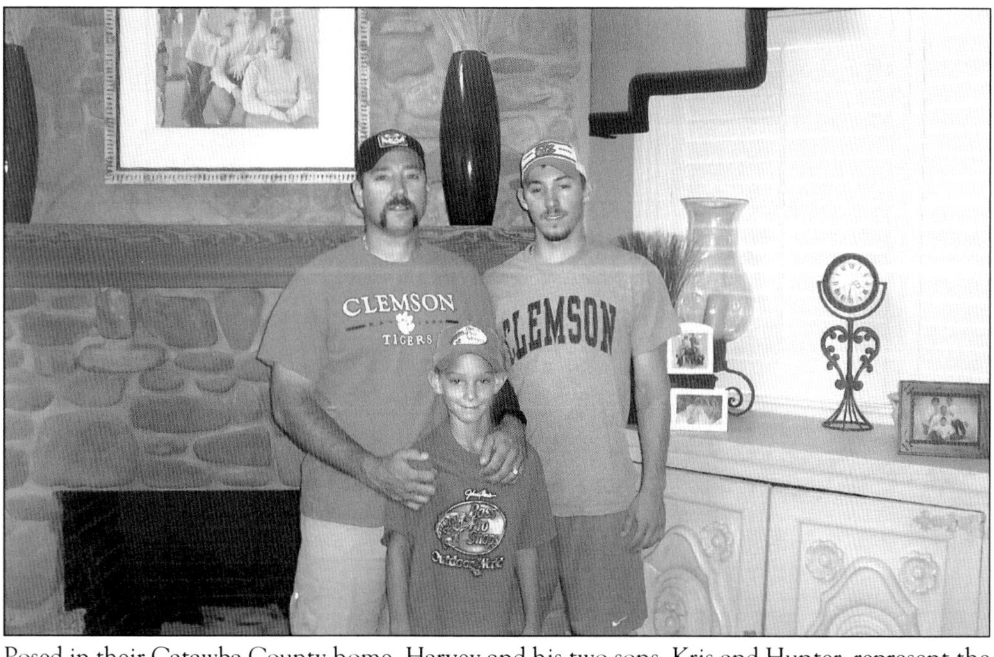

Posed in their Catawba County home, Harvey and his two sons, Kris and Hunter, represent the past, present, and future of the game. Kris, a rising junior at Clemson, is a top hitter and pitcher for the Tigers. Hunter is just getting started. (Courtesy of Brian McLawhorn.)

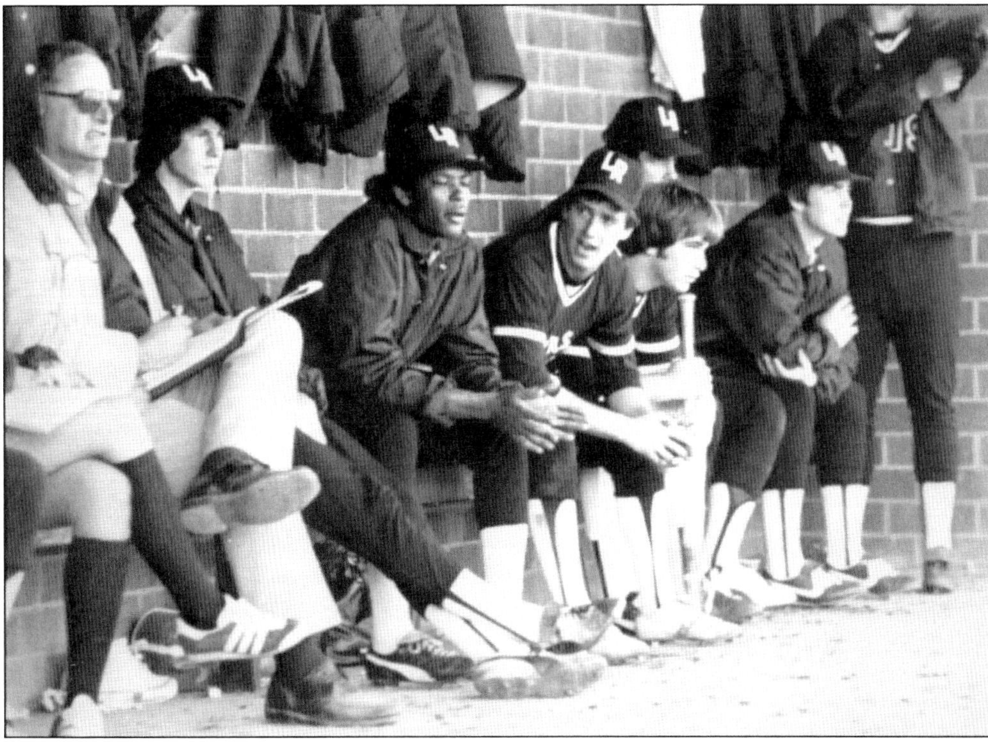

Dan Richards (left) covered local sports for the *Hickory Daily Record* for many years. (Courtesy of Lenoir-Rhyne College.)

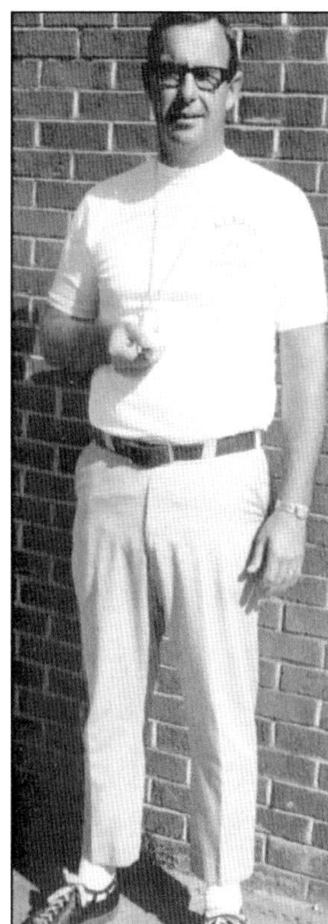

Harry Frye entered the Catawba County Sports Hall of Fame in 2002. His St. Stephens High School baseball teams won three consecutive State Championships from 1971 to 1973. (Courtesy of St. Stephens High School.)

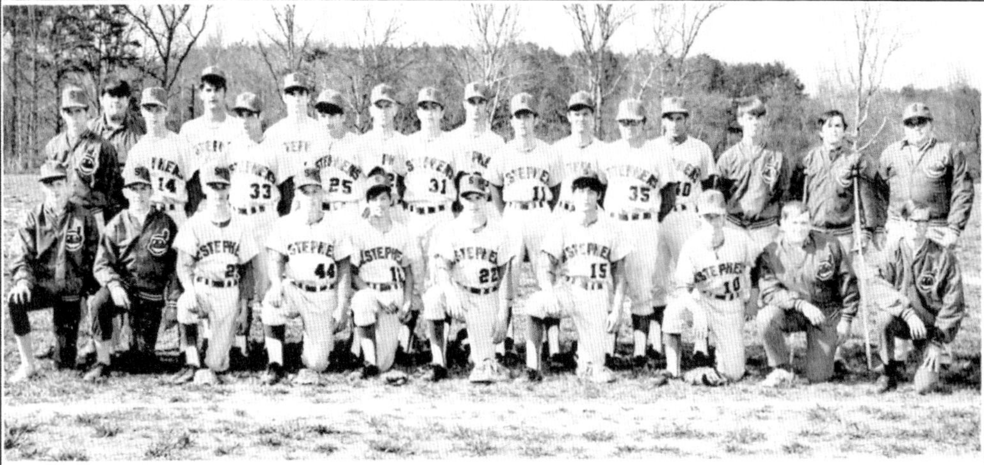

First Row: R. Hefner, L. Harris, mgrs.; R. Barnette, K. Sipe, R. Allebach, M. Queen, S. Bridges, D. Bolick, S. Weaver, mgr.; D. Green, scorekeeper. **Second Row:** T. Gilbert, C. Bumgarner, L. Justice, T. Mitchell, D. Guest, S. Simpson, M. Beck. **Third Row:** J. Johnson, scorekeeper; L. Eckard, D. Stallings, D. Clontz, R. Huffman, M. Bortz, A. Dunton, G. Miller, B. Good, scorekeeper; L. Sullivan, trainer.

The first of the three championship teams, the 1971 team, was led by David Clontz and Donnie Stallings. (Courtesy of St. Stephens High School.)

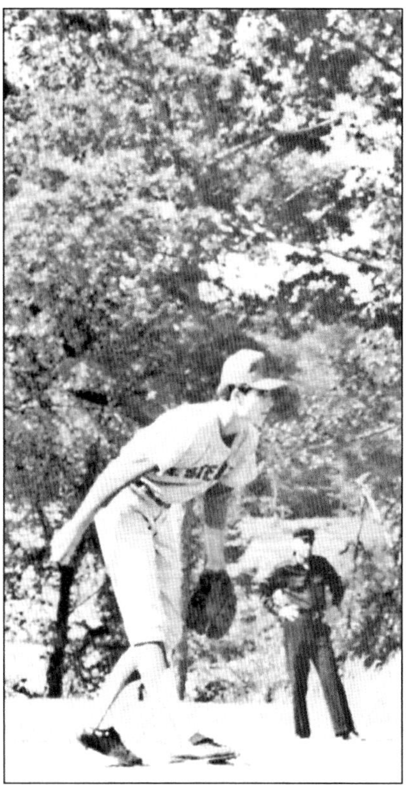

Donnie Stallings was the top hurler for both the 1971 and 1972 teams. He also starred for Troy Washam's Hickory American League team. (Courtesy of St. Stephens High School.)

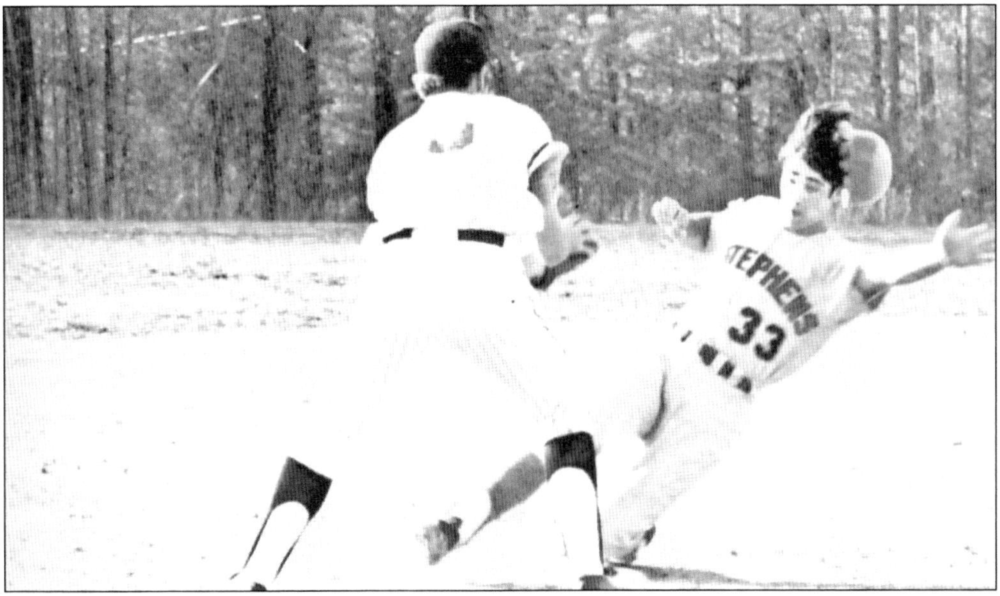

Larry Justice makes a hard slide during a 1971 game. Justice, who was also a top-notch football player, was an integral part of three championship teams. (Courtesy of St. Stephens High School.)

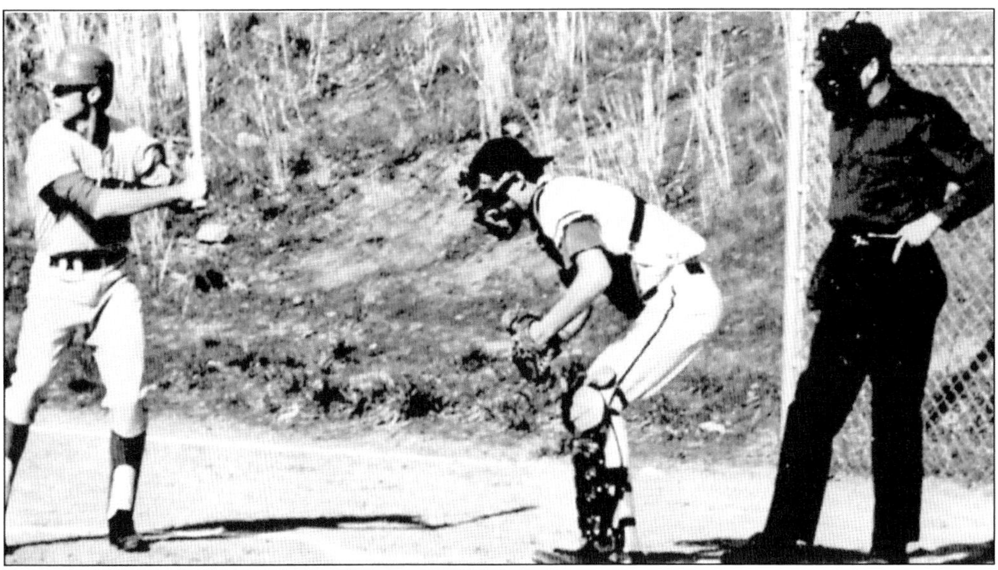

Rusty Huffman was a leading hitter for the 1971 squad. (Courtesy of St. Stephens High School.)

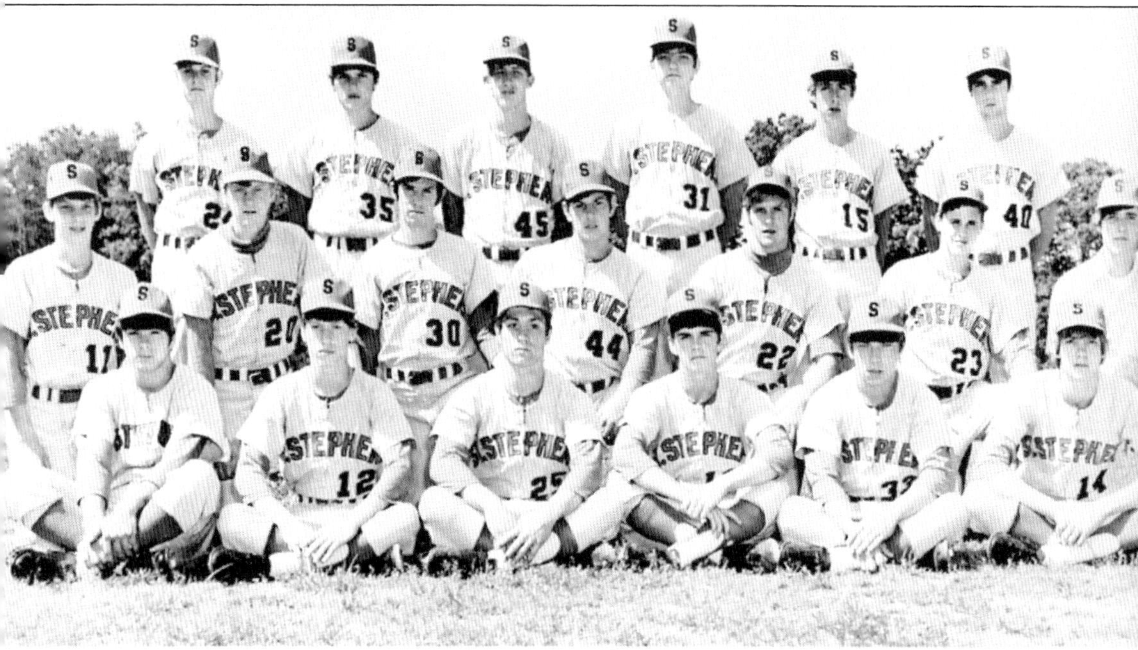

st **Row:** *M. Cockerham, E. Kent, E. Lane, L. Miller, J. Kale, C. Bumgarner.* **Second Row:** *K. Niewulis, D. Wilson, D.*
e, B. Thornburg, D. Eggers, D. Starr, mgr. **Third Row:** *R. Barnette, M. Queen, B. Lawing, K. Niewulis, R. Sullins, L. Just*

The 1973 St. Stephens team only lost two games all season and won many games by huge margins. (Courtesy of St. Stephens High School.)

SEVEN

Crawdads

It was the enthusiasm of the people here that made me realize this could be a success.
—Don Beaver

In 1993, professional baseball found its way back into Catawba County. This time it came in the form of the new minor-league Class A Hickory Crawdads. The Crawdads would become the newest member of the Chicago White Sox organization.

During the early stages of bringing a team to Hickory, many community leaders—like former mayor George Murphy, Dean Proctor, and Phil Yount, just to name a few—worked to convince current majority owner Don Beaver that baseball should return to Hickory. After these community members made their case for the new team, Don Beaver joined up with his brother Luther, Charles Young, Don Murphy, and Paul Fleetwood to create the Crawdads ownership group. Once these men put together a staff and got things rolling, baseball was ready to start.

The first Crawdads team struggled, as expected for a new ball club, finishing with a 52-88 record in 1993. Despite the tough start, fans continued to support the newest member of the community as 283,727 people passed through the gates at L.P. Frans Stadium. The team had flashes of success when young players like Magglio Ordonez, Chris Tremie, and Mike Bertotti began to break out of their shells. This success was a sign of good things to come for the Crawdads.

The Crawdads' 86-54 record in their second season was nearly a complete flip-flop from what it was in the inaugural season. The 1994 Crawdads team saw eight of its members make it to the South Atlantic League All-Star game.

The team took a slide the next two seasons finishing with records of 49-89 and 55-85. The 'Dads bounced back with a solid 76-64 record the following season, but they would go on to have their third losing season in four years during the 1997 campaign, ending up with a 56-84 mark. The 1998 season would be the last for the partnership between the Crawdads and the parent Chicago White Sox. The final season with the Sox ended on a tough note as the team finished with a 56-84 record.

The following season was the start of a new era for the team as the Pittsburgh Pirates took over as the Crawdads major-league affiliate. In their first year as part of the Pirates organization, the Crawdads managed to reach the .500 mark, concluding the season with an overall record of 70-70. The team improved in their second season with the Pirates, posting a record of 75-67. With the departure of many top players from the 2000 season, the team was forced to replace many of their top position players with young talent. The result of this was a 67-73 season in 2001, leaving the team with its only losing season to date as part of the Pirates minor-league system.

The last two seasons, 2002 and 2003, have gone in the record books as being two of the best seasons for the Crawdads. The team finished at the top of the league both seasons with records of 83-56 and 82-54, respectively.

As players begin to make their way through the system, the Crawdads will continue to be the place where the Pirates break in their new talent. Although this brings a sense of uncertainty from year to year, one thing is for sure, the Crawdads staff and players will always provide an exciting form of entertainment to people in the Unifour (Catawba, Alexander, Caldwell, and Burke Counties).

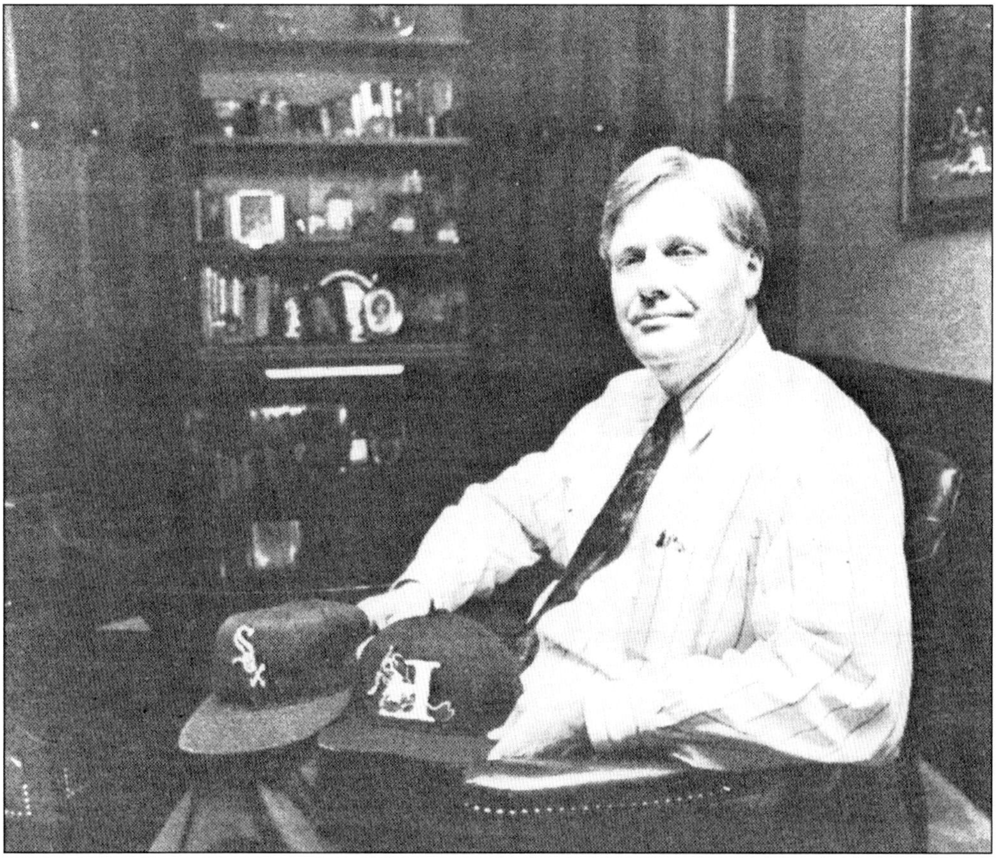

Principal owner of the Crawdads Don Beaver was recently inducted into the South Atlantic League Hall of Fame. (Courtesy of *Hickory Daily Record*.)

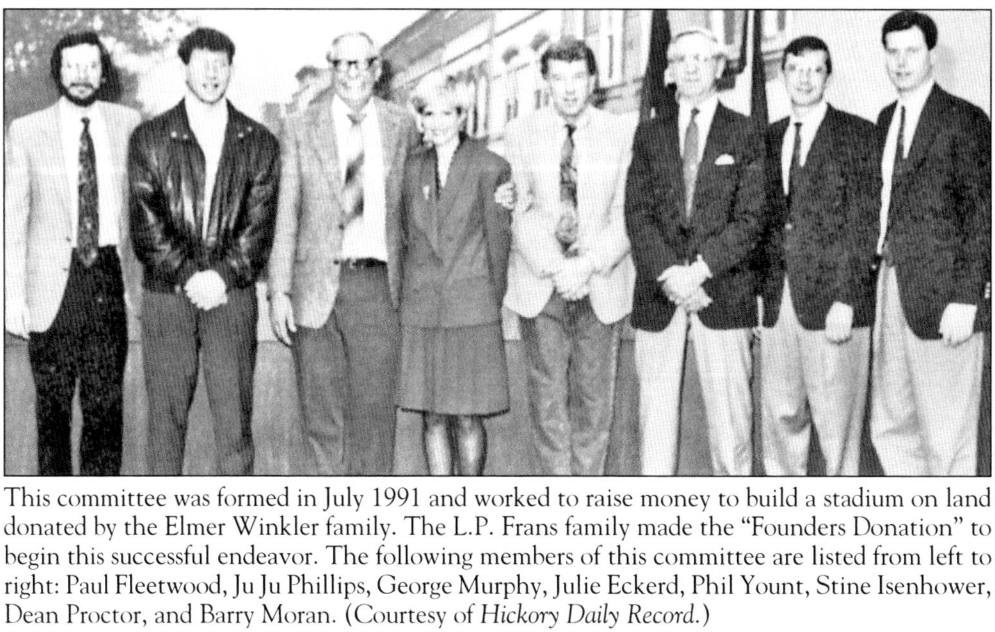

This committee was formed in July 1991 and worked to raise money to build a stadium on land donated by the Elmer Winkler family. The L.P. Frans family made the "Founders Donation" to begin this successful endeavor. The following members of this committee are listed from left to right: Paul Fleetwood, Ju Ju Phillips, George Murphy, Julie Eckerd, Phil Yount, Stine Isenhower, Dean Proctor, and Barry Moran. (Courtesy of *Hickory Daily Record*.)

Magglio Ordonez is the most famous former Crawdad. The White Sox outfielder began this season with a .307 career average and 178 home runs. He played in the 1994 South Atlantic League All-Star game in Hickory and has been an All-Star for the Sox. (Courtesy of Jim McLean.)

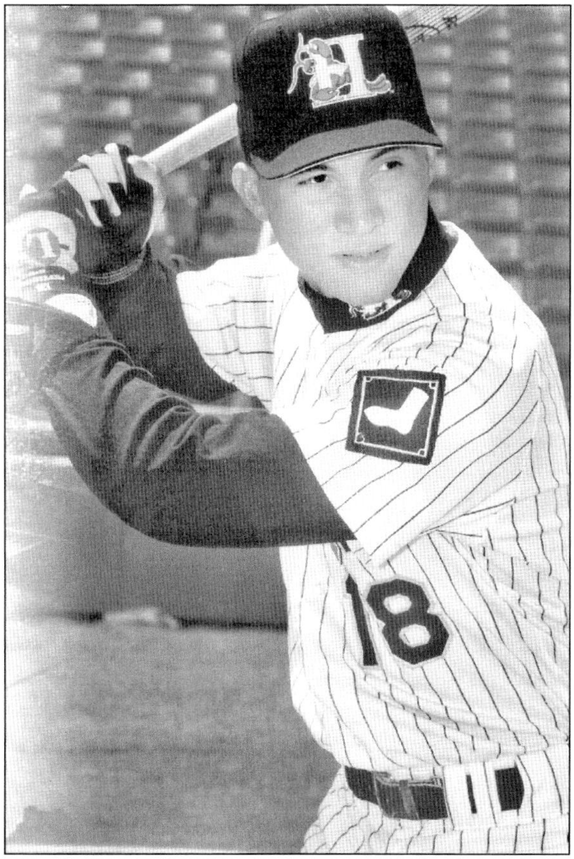

This is an overhead view of the L.P. Frans Stadium from right center field. (Courtesy of Jim McLean.)

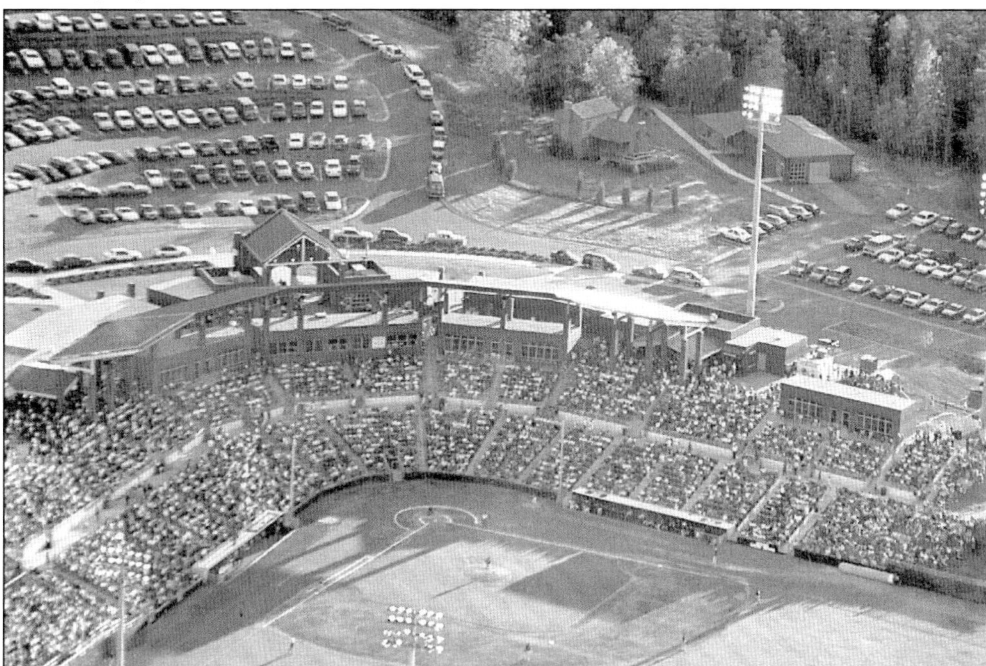

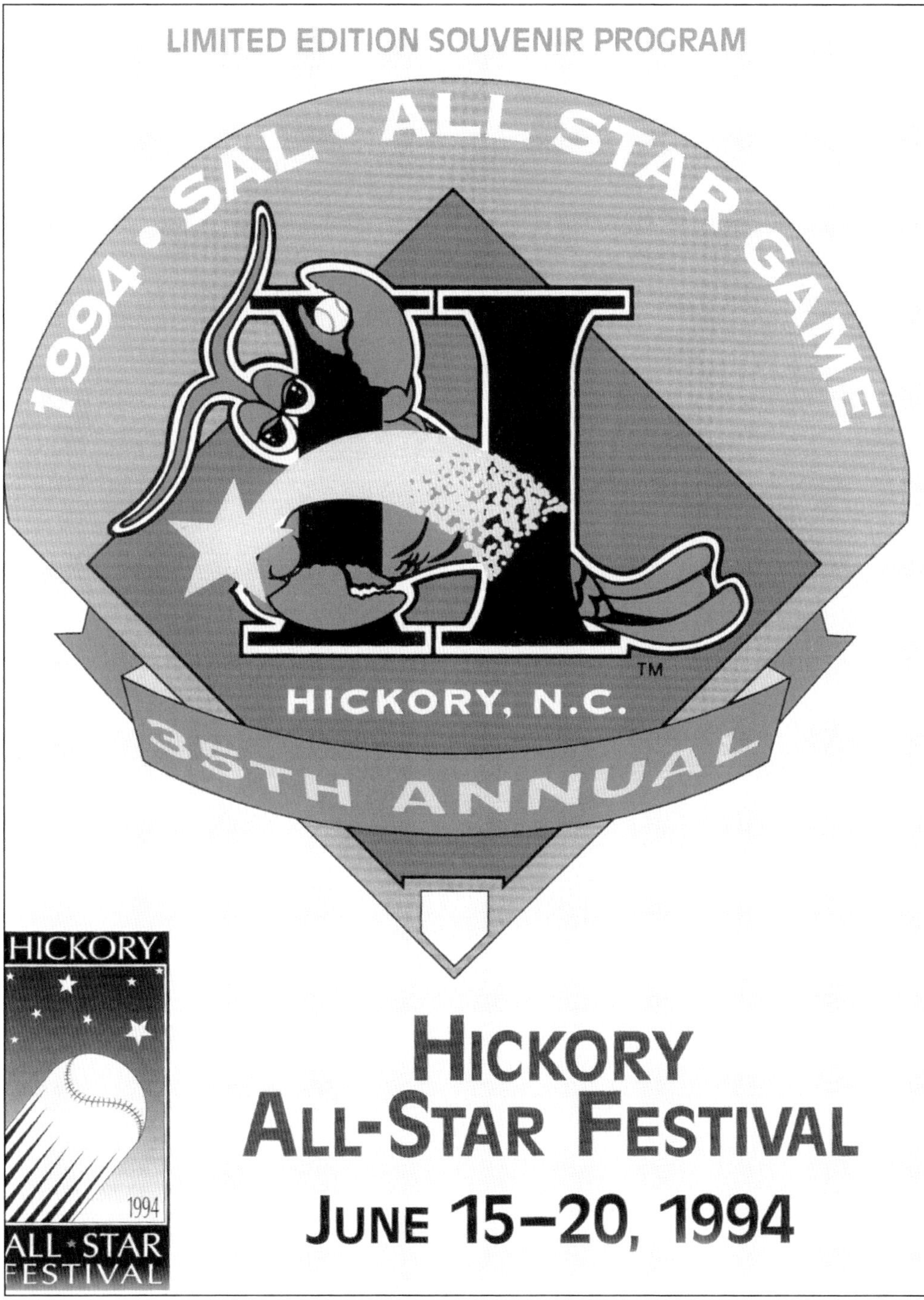

During their second season, the Crawdads hosted the South Atlantic League All-Star game. The game featured current big leaguers Magglio Ordonez, Jermaine Dye, Richie Sexson, and Shannon Stewart. (Courtesy of Hickory Crawdads.)

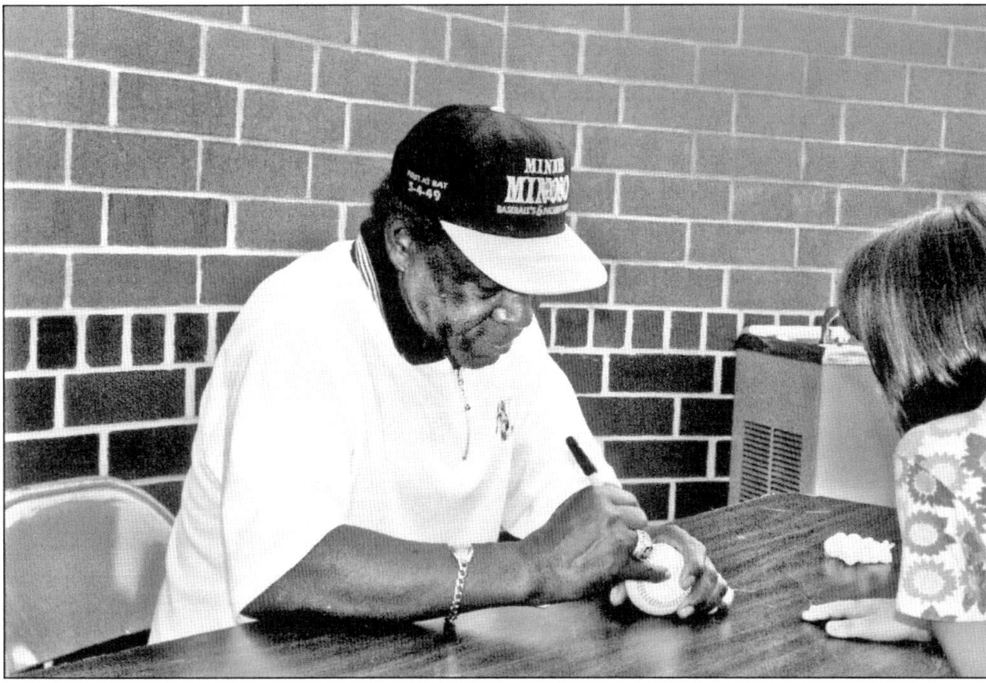

Minnie Minoso signs autographs on the concourse during the 1994 All-Star game in Hickory. (Courtesy of Hickory Crawdads.)

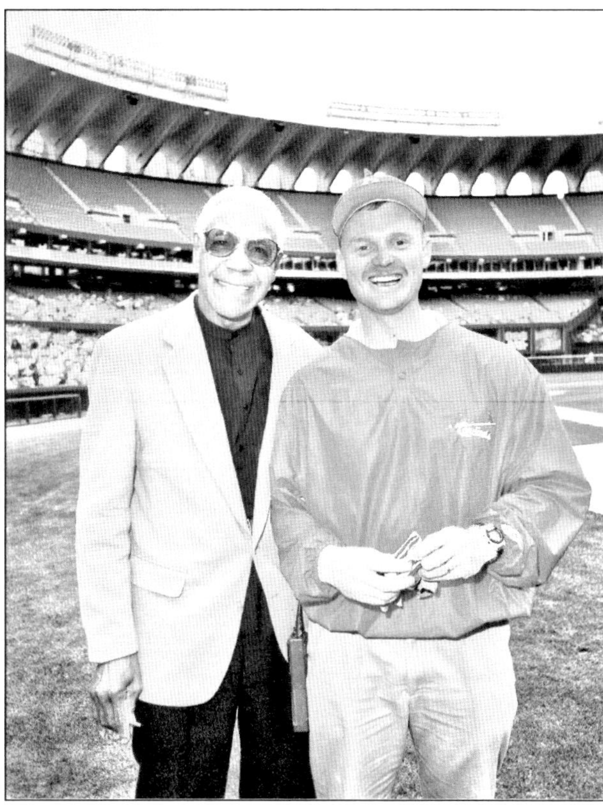

Steve Peeler, grounds manager for the first Crawdads teams, advanced quickly up the ladder. Here he poses with legendary Negro Leaguer Buck O'Neil in Busch Stadium, St. Louis. (Courtesy of Steve Peeler.)

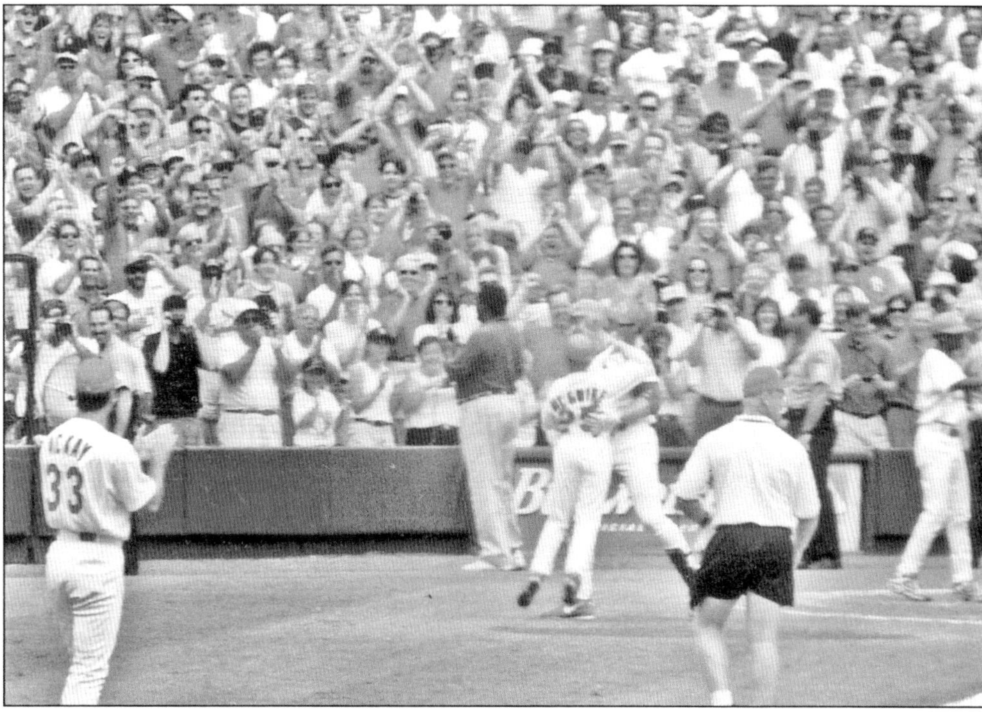

Mark McGwire grabs his son after hitting home run number 61 in 1998. Steve Peeler, a Catawba Valley Community College graduate, crosses the field toward the celebration. (Courtesy of Steve Peeler.)

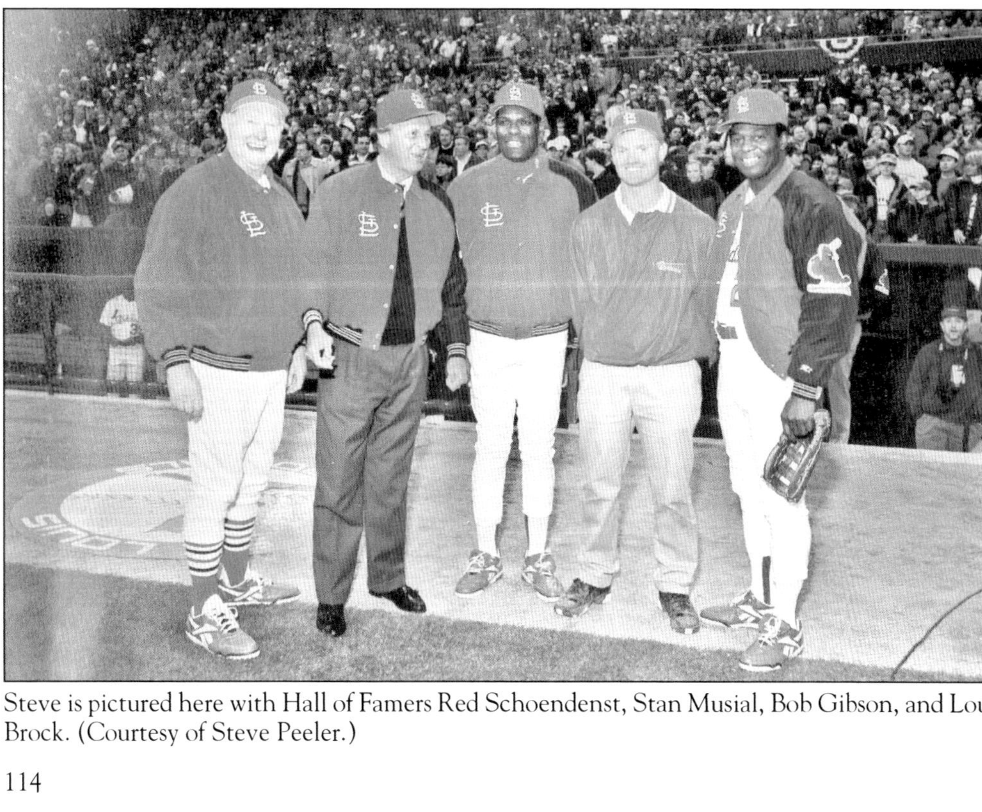

Steve is pictured here with Hall of Famers Red Schoendenst, Stan Musial, Bob Gibson, and Lou Brock. (Courtesy of Steve Peeler.)

Carlos Lee watches a home run sail out of L.P. Frans Stadium. (Courtesy of Jim McLean.)

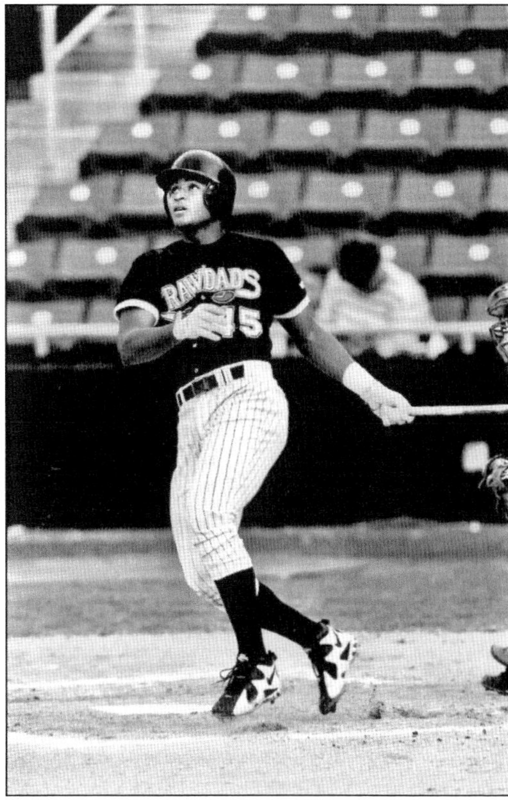

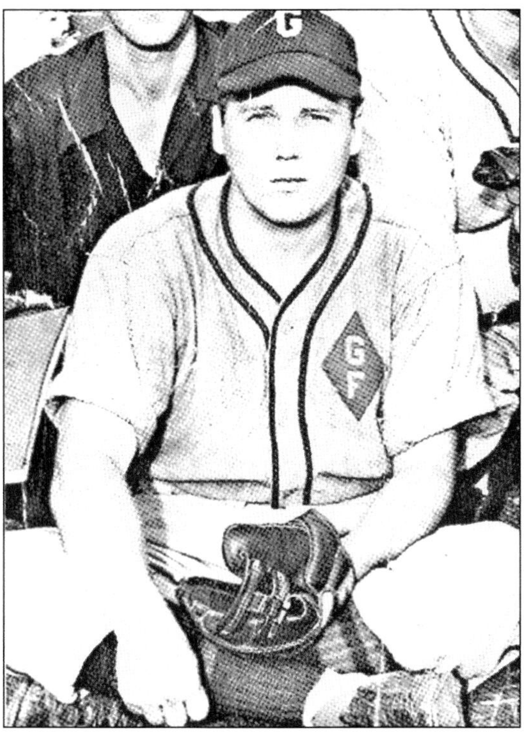

Jack Clark worked in concessions at the L.P. Frans Stadium. Here, he is seen in his ball-playing days at Granite Falls. (Courtesy of Hickory Crawdads.)

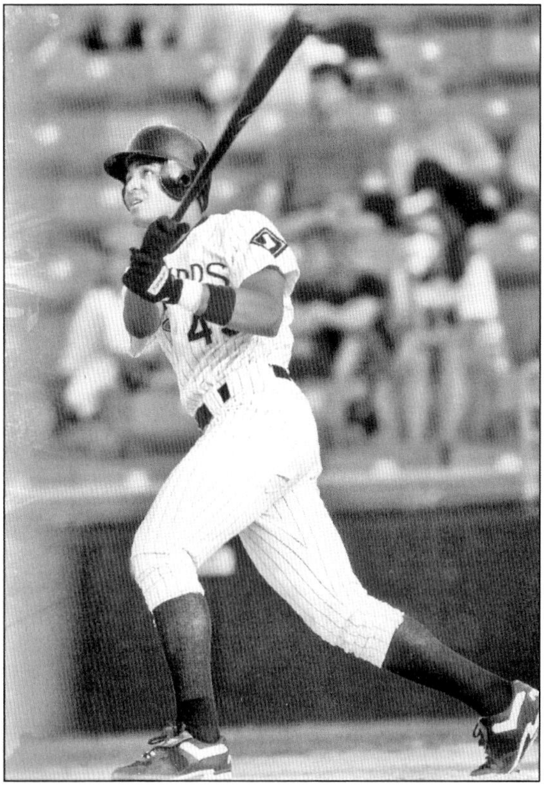

Carlos Lee spent two seasons with the Crawdads and was team MVP in 1996. He is now an outstanding left fielder for the Chicago White Sox, where he began the season with 121 career home runs. (Courtesy of Jim McLean.)

This is a picture of the gate to the L.P. Frans Stadium—nearly 3 million fans have passed this way since 1993. (Courtesy of Jim McLean.)

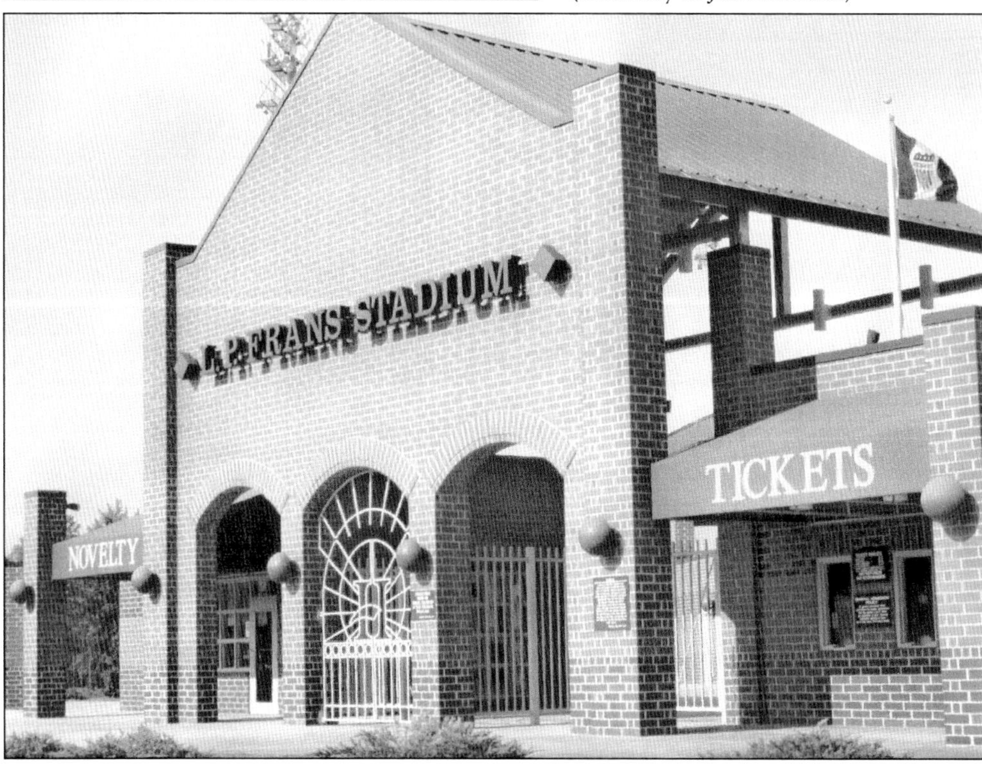

One of the most remarkable pitchers in baseball history, Jim Abbott once pitched a no-hitter for the New York Yankees. In 1998, he began a comeback with the Crawdads. (Courtesy of Jim McLean.)

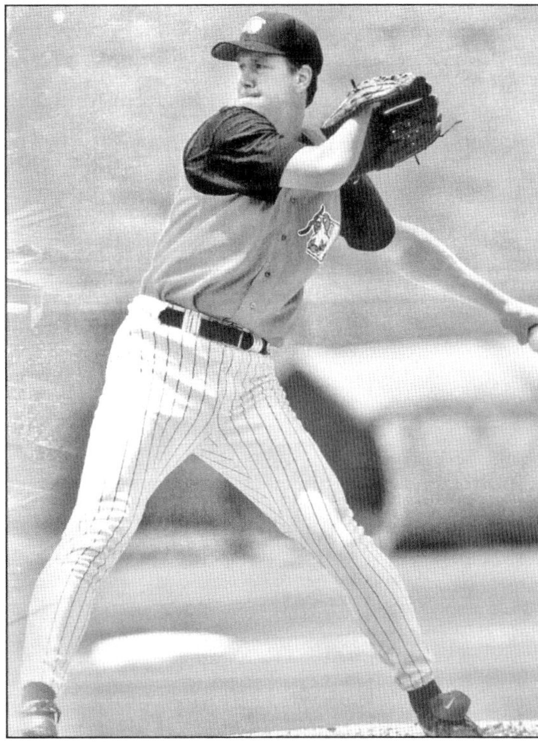

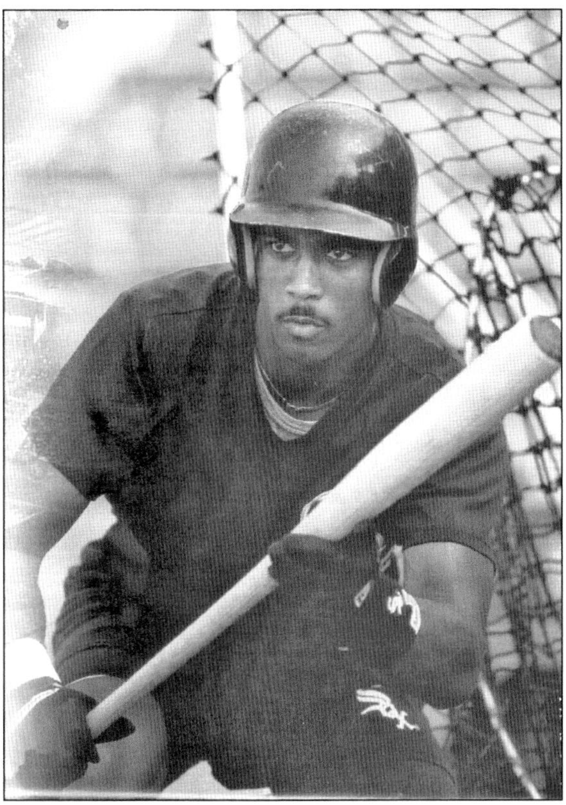

Harold Williams led the South Atlantic League with 104 RBIs in 1994. He was an All-Star that year and is remembered for hitting some of the longest home runs in team history. (Courtesy of Jim McLean.)

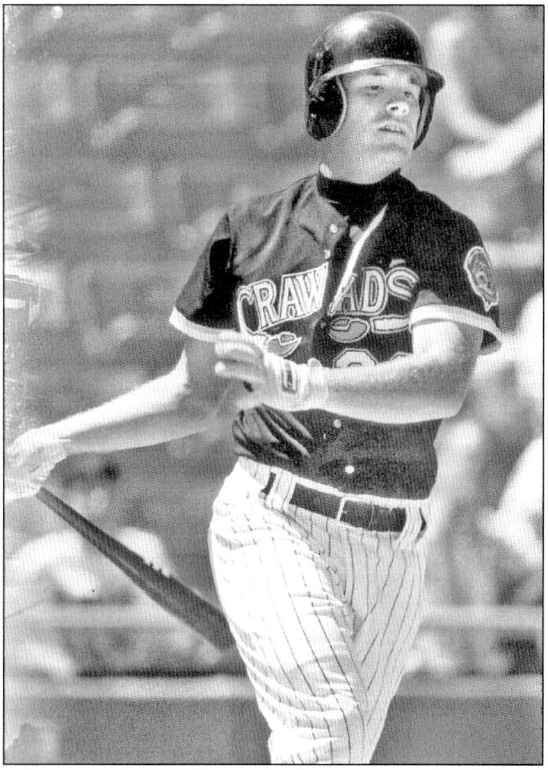

This Crawdads player with the "most famous" father played during the 1994 season. Pete Rose Jr., did not, however, enjoy his father's success on the field. (Courtesy of Jim McLean.)

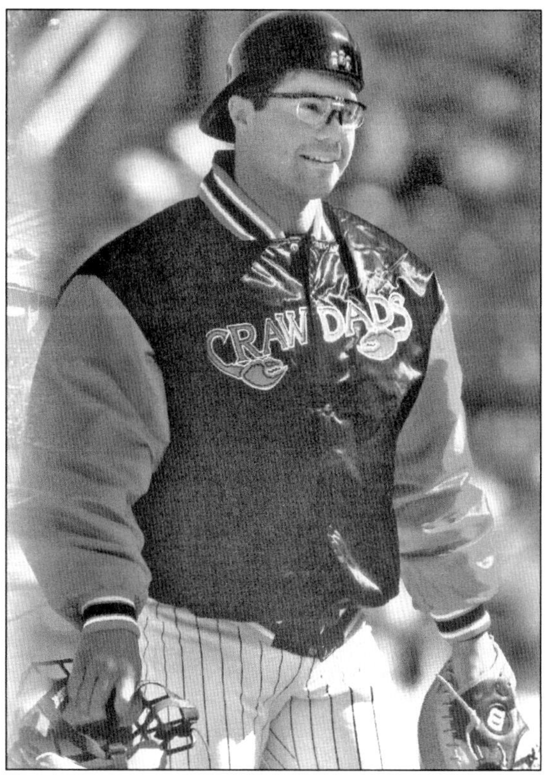

J.R. House was the co-MVP of the South Atlantic League in 2000. He led the team that year with a .348 average, 23 home runs, and 90 RBIs. This catcher is on the verge of breaking through to the parent Pirates team. (Courtesy of Jim McLean.)

Eddie Pearson got the first base hit in L.P. Frans Stadium on April 16, 1993. (Courtesy of Jim McLean.)

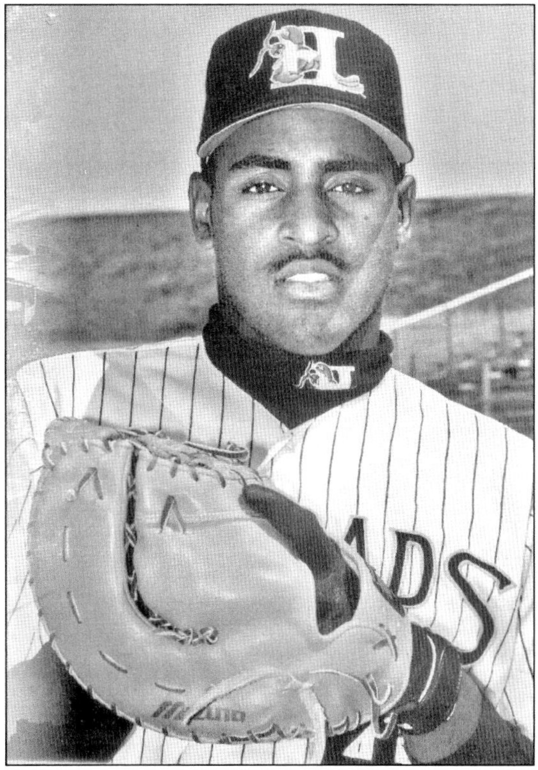

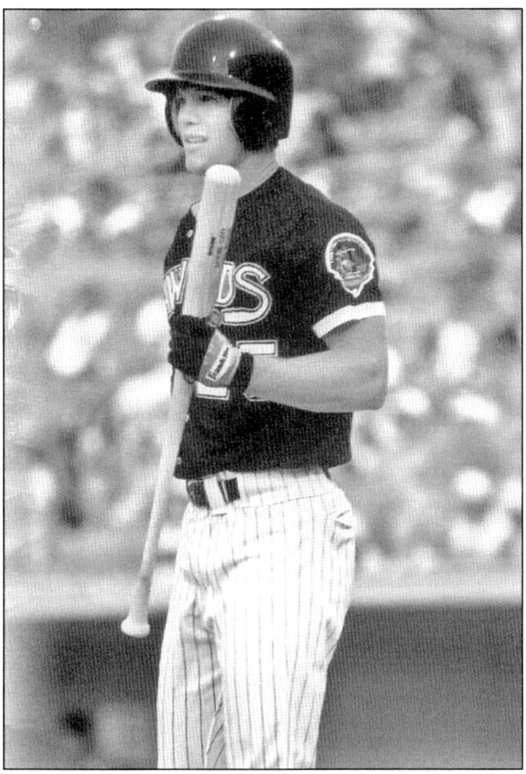

Jeff Abbott earned the highest batting average—.393—in team history in 1994. Jeff now plays for the Florida Marlins. (Courtesy of Jim McLean.)

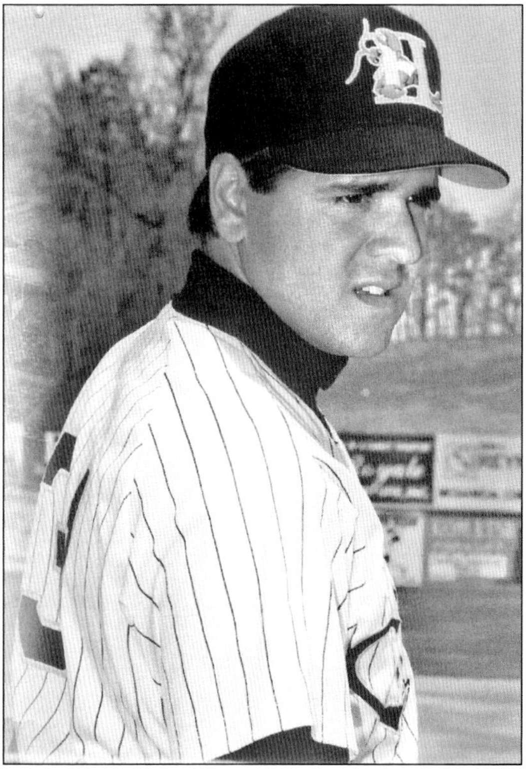

Mike Bertotti recorded 77 strikeouts in only 59 innings in his 1993 season with the Crawdads. He was the first team pitcher to make a major-league squad. (Courtesy of Jim McLean.)

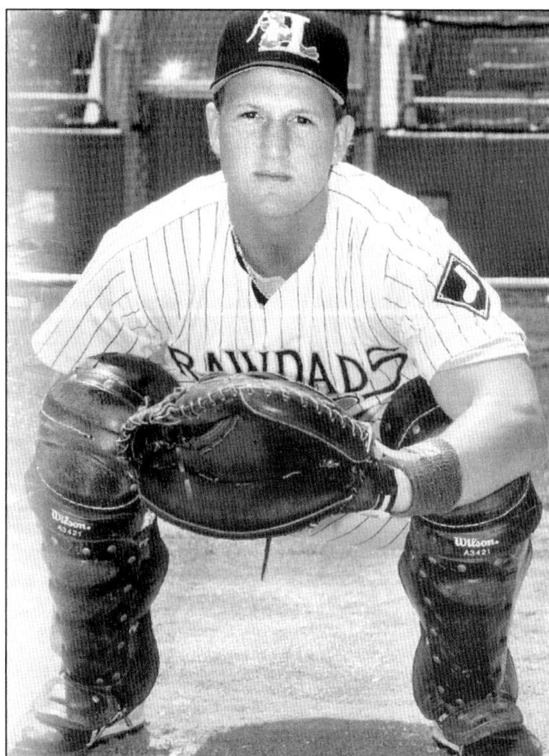

A catcher for the 1993 Crawdads, Chris Tremie was the first team member to make it to the majors. (Courtesy of Jim McLean.)

The 1994 and 1995 Crawdads second baseman, Steve Friedrich, represented the team in the 1995 All-Star game. (Courtesy of Jim McLean.)

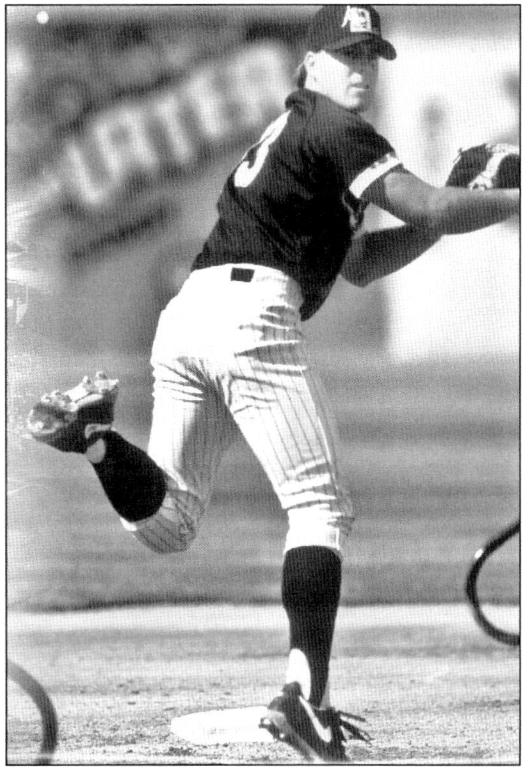

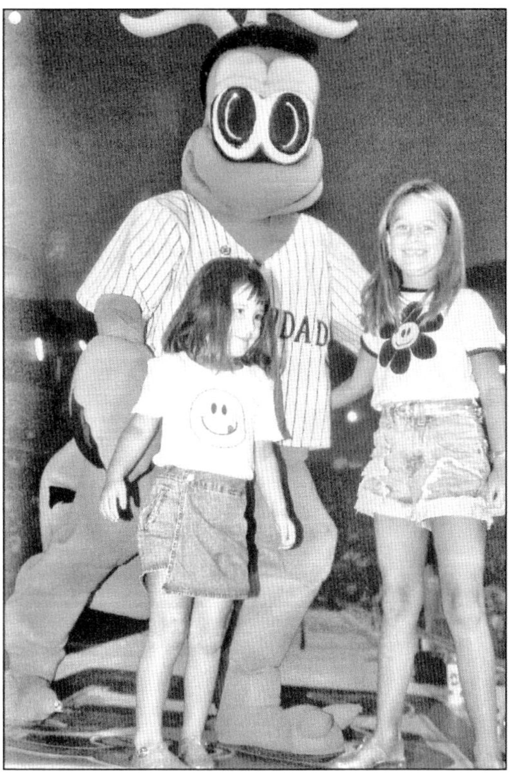

Whether he's speeding into the stadium on a four-wheeler or entertaining the youngsters, Conrad the Crawdad is quite a popular guy. (Courtesy of Jim McLean.)

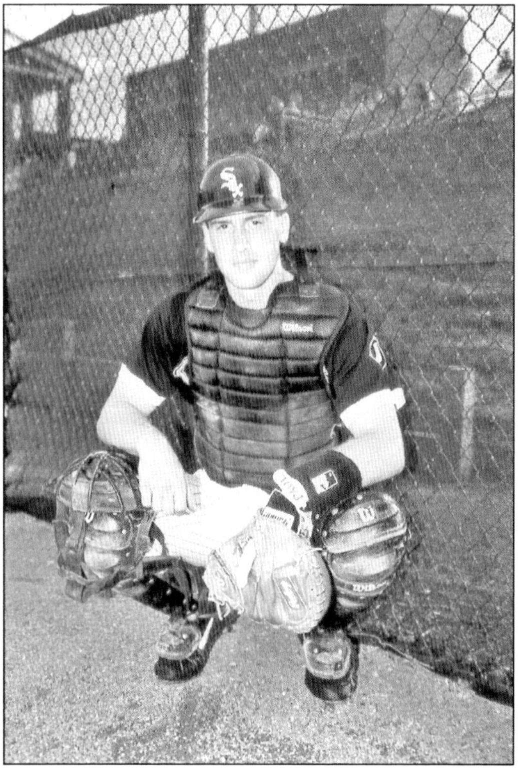

In 1996, catcher Josh Paul finished near the top of the South Atlantic League in hitting, posting a .327 average. He currently plays for the Anaheim Angels. (Courtesy of Jim McLean.)

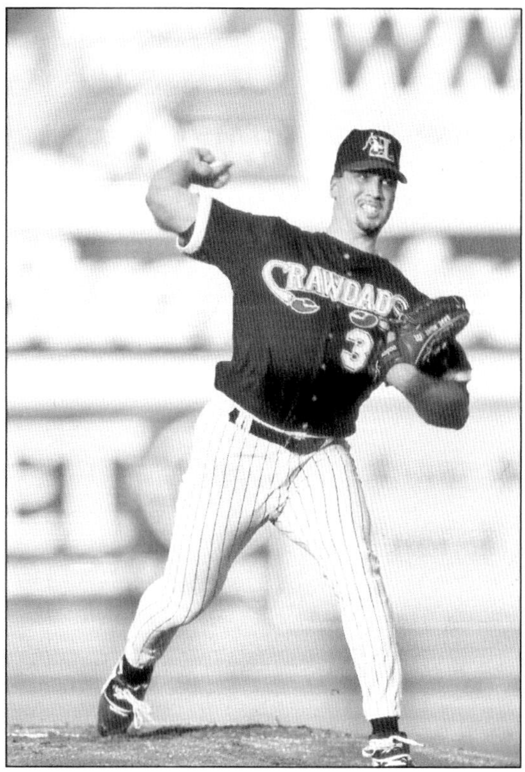

Jason Bere, one of Major League Baseball's top pitchers in 1993, was sent to the Crawdads in 1996 to rehabilitate an injury. During Bere's stay in Hickory, he posted an ERA of 2.25. (Courtesy of Jim McLean.)

Jovanny Sosa became one of the fan favorites during the 1999 and 2000 seasons, hitting for a combined 40 home runs over the course of the two years. (Courtesy of Jim McLean.)

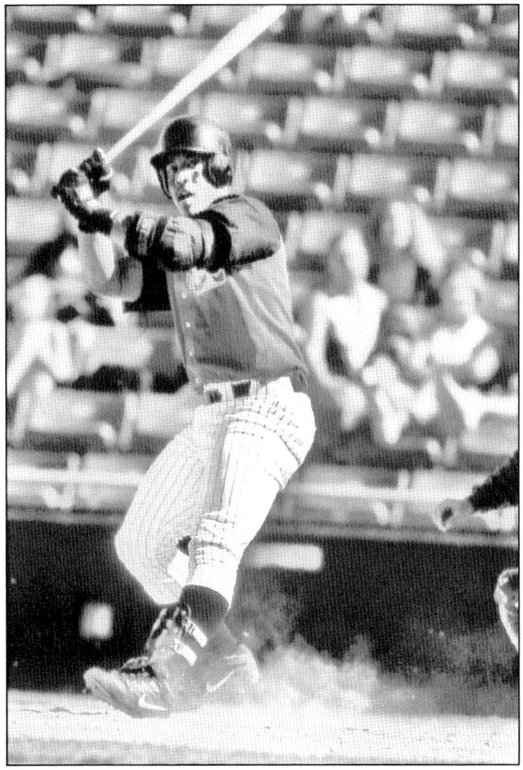

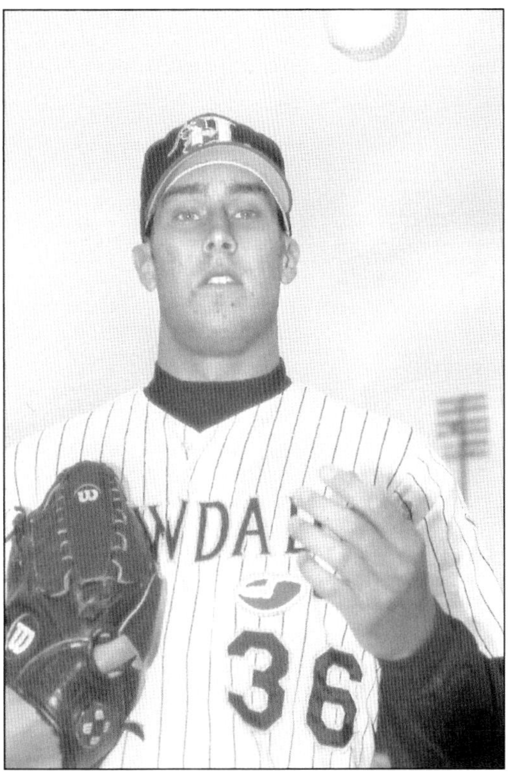

In 2000, Dave Williams had one of the best seasons for a Crawdad pitcher as he led the South Atlantic League with 193 strikeouts. (Courtesy of Jim McLean.)

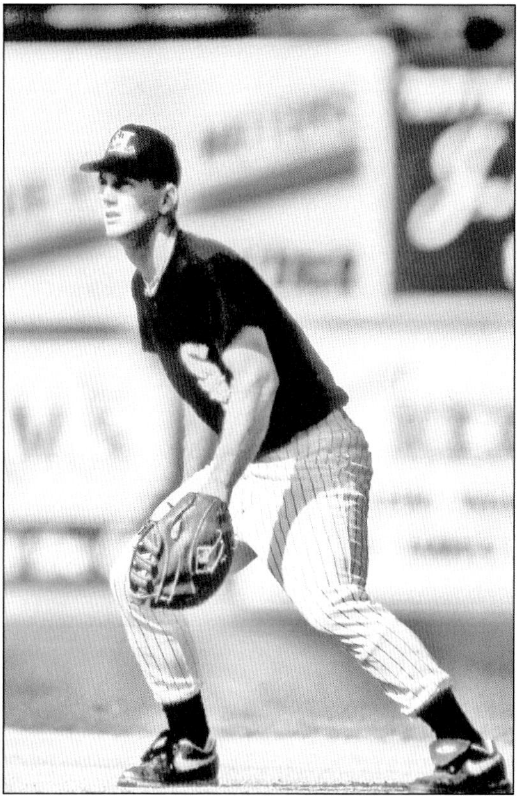

Third baseman Chris Mader was an early fan favorite for the 1993 and 1994 Crawdad teams. He was honored during those seasons by having a sandwich named after him. The "Mader Sandwich" quickly became a hit at L.P. Frans Stadium. (Courtesy of Jim McLean.)

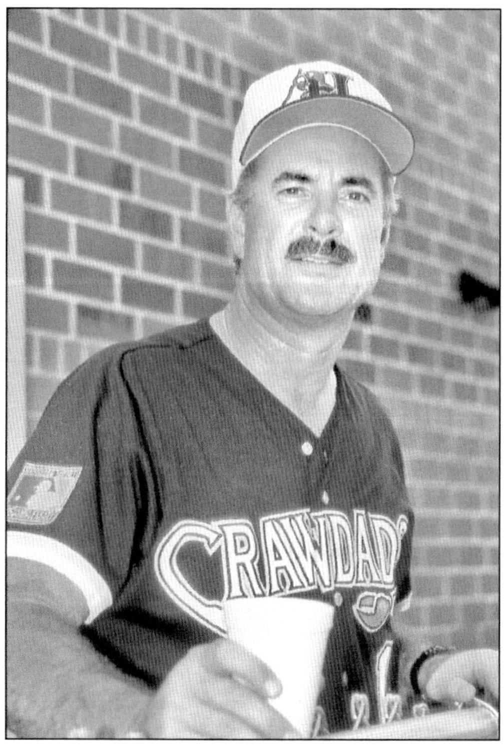

Fred Kendall, the Crawdads first manager, had his best season at the helm in 1994 when his team finished with a record of 86-54. His hard work earned him a spot as a manager in the 1994 South Atlantic League All-Star game. (Courtesy of Jim McLean.)

Joe Crede spent the 1997 season as the Crawdads top third baseman. Although a mediocre hitter during his time in Hickory, Crede has quickly earned respect for his clutch hitting with the Chicago White Sox. (Courtesy of Jim McLean.)

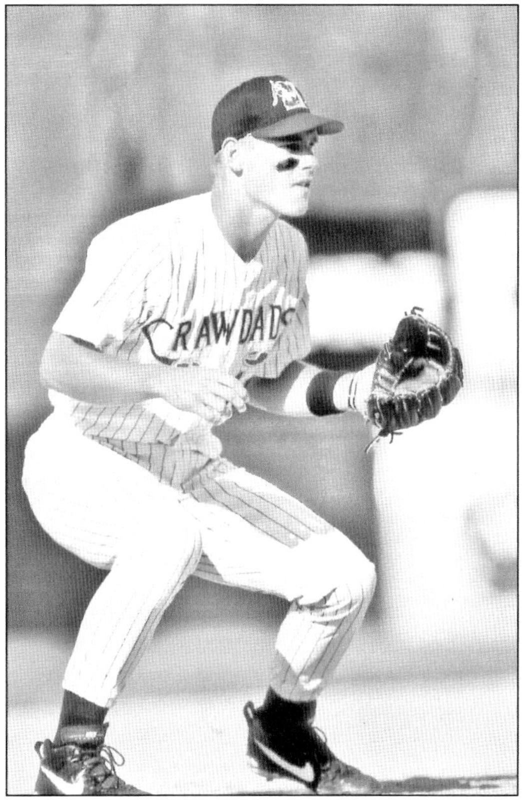

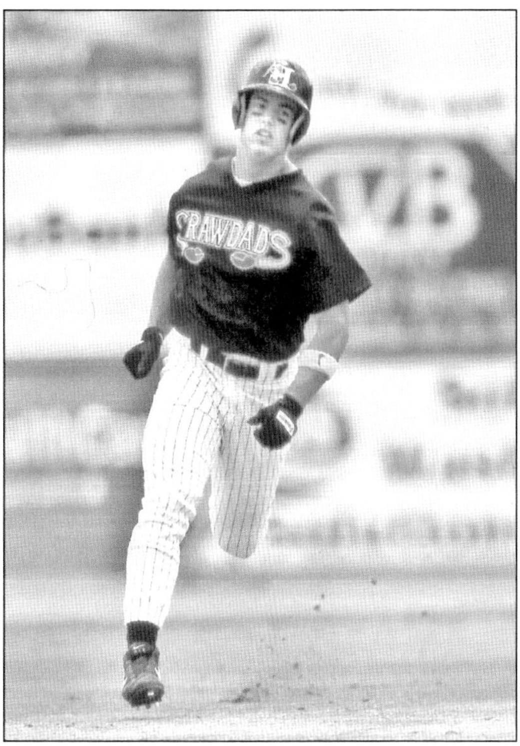

In 1998, Aaron Rowand led the team with a .344 average. After only 60 games in a Crawdads uniform, Rowand began making his way up the ranks. He is now an up-and-coming center fielder for the Chicago White Sox. (Courtesy of Jim McLean.)

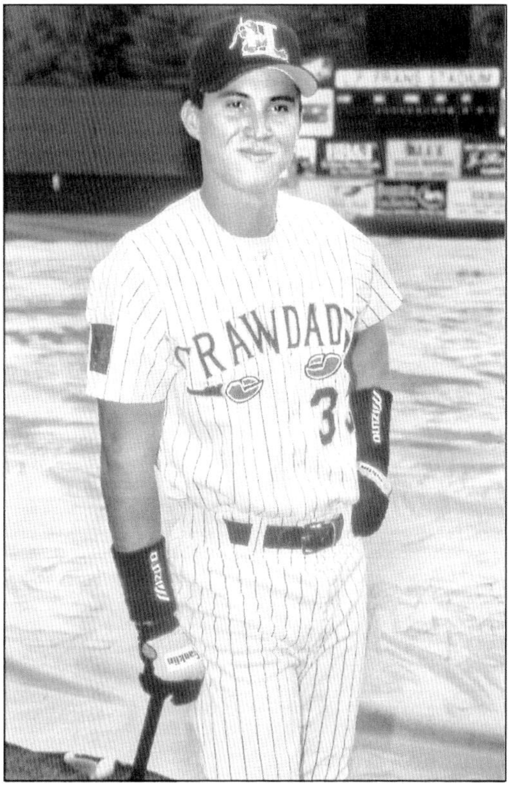

Magglio Ordonez relaxes before a game in 1993. (Courtesy of Jim McLean.)

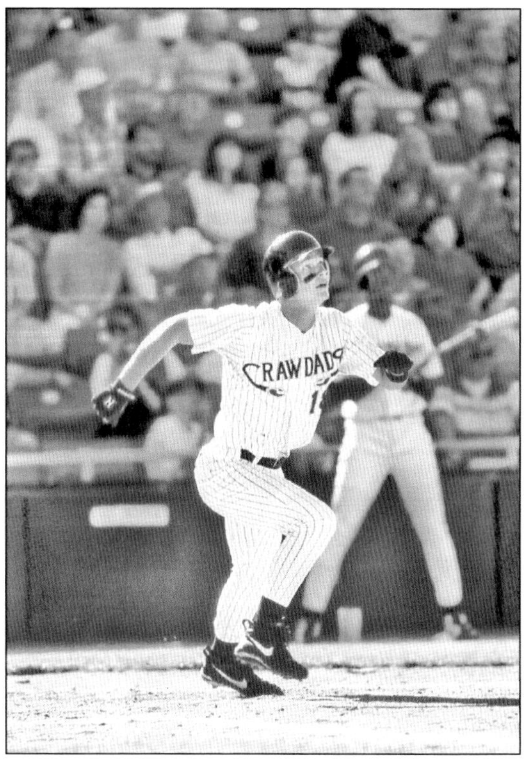

Joe Crede heads to first base as he watches the ball fly out of the park for a home run. (Courtesy of Jim McLean.)

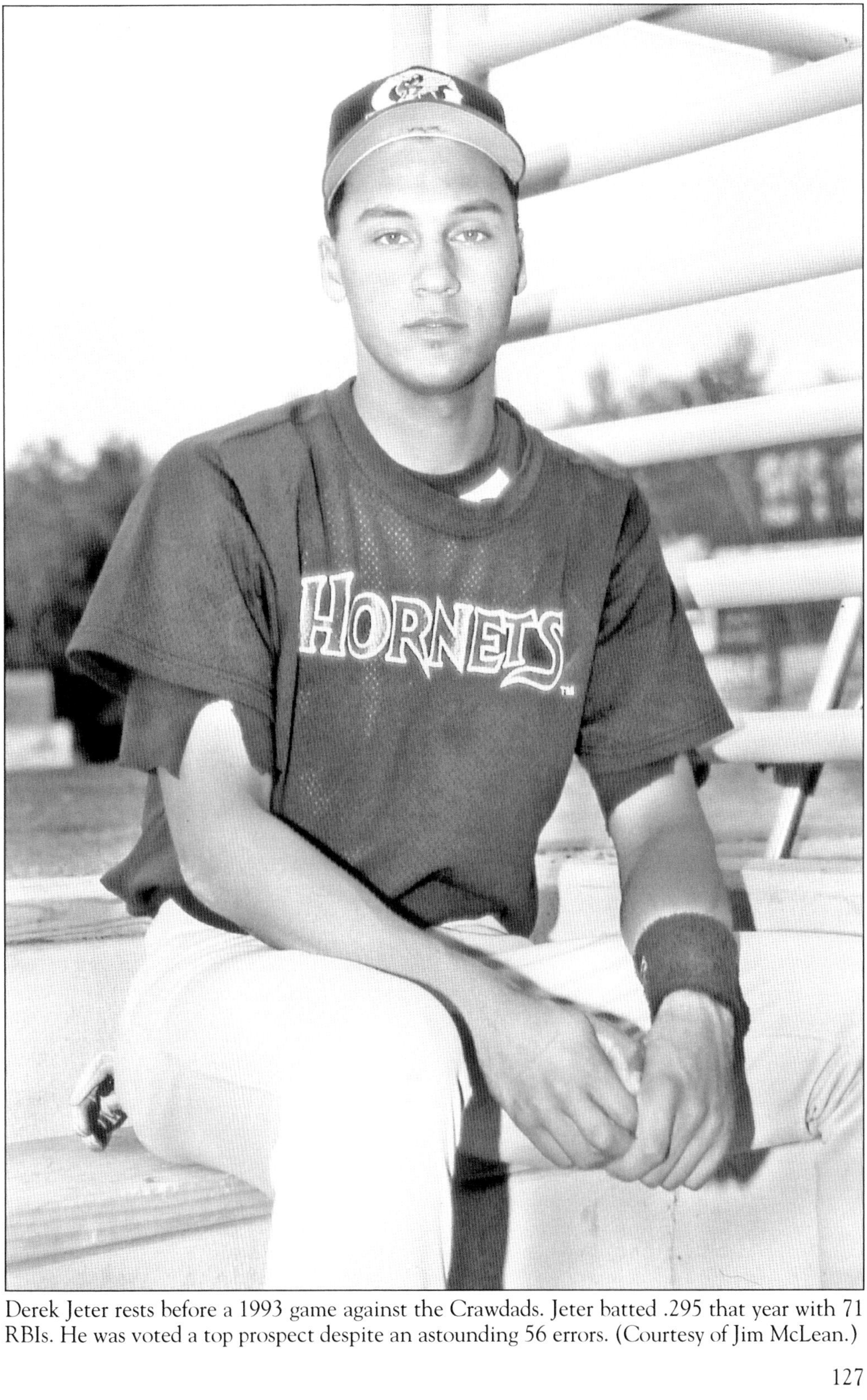

Derek Jeter rests before a 1993 game against the Crawdads. Jeter batted .295 that year with 71 RBIs. He was voted a top prospect despite an astounding 56 errors. (Courtesy of Jim McLean.)

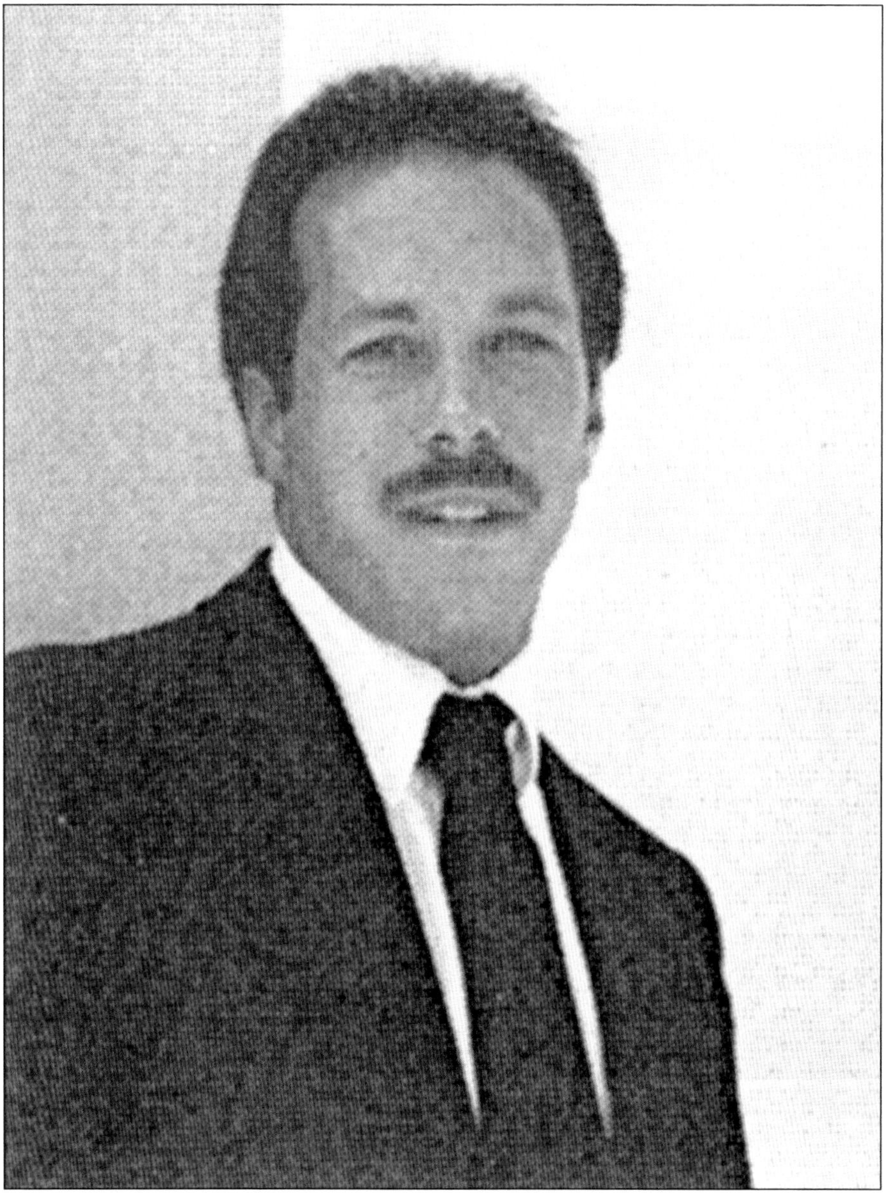

This book is in Memory of Tim Coffey (1957–2003), who knew how to play the game.